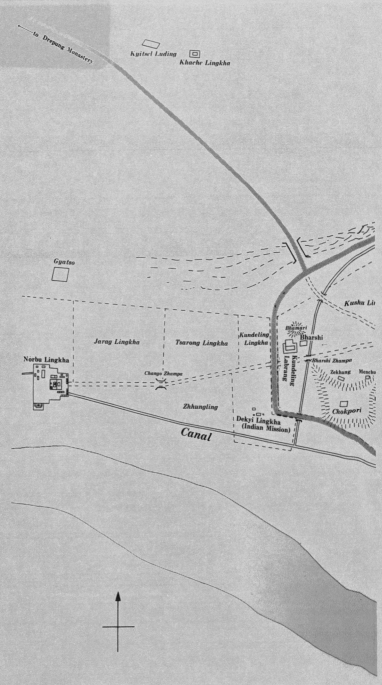

to Drepung Monastery

Kyitsel Luding
Khache Lingkha

Gyatso

Kushu Li

Bhamari
Bharshi

Jarag Lingkha   Tsarong Lingkha   Kundeling
Lingkha

Bharshi Zhampa

Kundeling
Labrang

Zekhang   Menchu

Norbu Lingkha

Chango Zhampa

Chokpori

Zhhungling

Dekyi Lingkha
(Indian Mission)

Canal

SKETCH MAP OF LHASA

Drawn by Zasak J. Taring from his memory, 1959

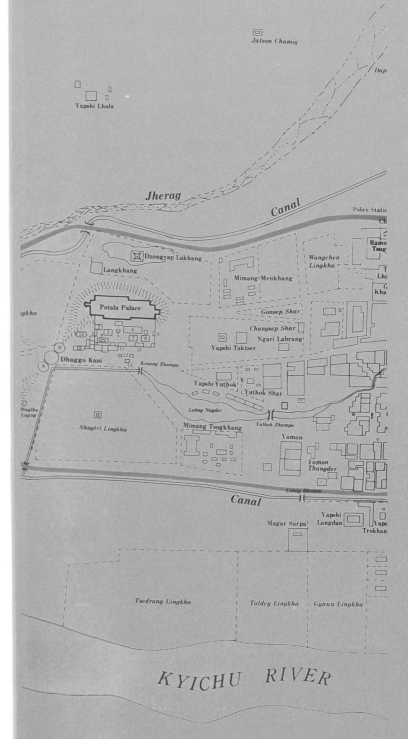

Jatson Chumig

Yapshi Lhalu

Jherag Canal

Police Station

Dzongyap Lukhang

Langkhang

Wangchen
Lingkha

Ramo
Tsug

Mimang Menkhang

Lha

Kha

Potala Palace

Gonsep Shar

Changsep Shar

Ngari Labrang

Yapshi Taktser

Dhaggo Kani

Kesang Zhampa

Yapshi Yuthok

Yuthok Shar

Lubug Nagder

Dhagtha
Lugug

Yuthok Zhampa

Shugtri Lingkha

Mimang Tsogkhang

Yamon

Yamon
Thangder

Canal

Yapshi
Langdun

Yaps

Magar Sarpa

Trokhan

Tsedrung Lingkha

Taldey Lingkha

Gyawu Lingkha

KYICHU RIVER

Map continued on back endpaper

Daughter of Tibet

Rinchen Dolma Taring

Wisdom Publications London

First published in 1970 by
John Murray, London.

This edition published in 1986 by
Wisdom Publications
23 Dering Street
London W1, England

British Library Cataloguing in Publication Data
Taring, Rinchen Dolma
    Daughter of Tibet.
    1. Taring, Rinchen Dolma   2. Tibet (China)
    —— Biography
    I. Title
    951'.5'0924   CT1828.T/

ISBN 0 86171 044 4

Set in Garamond 11 on 13 point by Setrite of
Hong Kong and printed and bound by
Eurasia Press of Singapore and Biddles of
Guildford, Surrey, on 85 gsm cream Graphic
Text paper supplied by Link Publishing
Papers of West Byfleet, Surrey.

To the children of Tibet
as a token of my love

Contents

Acknowledgements

EVER SINCE 1959, when I came into exile, I have wanted to write my story in order to give a picture of our life in Tibet and to show people that Tibet has always been an independent nation with its own unique language and rich historical background. It was not until ten years had passed that I was able to give my time to this plan because every moment has been taken up in helping to care for our refugee children at Mussoorie in India. Any money that this book earns for me will be given to the Tibetan Homes Foundation.

When I at last started to write, His Holiness the Dalai Lama blessed my work and allowed me to travel to England and Ireland, where I worked on the typescript, and I am deeply grateful to Him for his encouragement.

My family and friends also gave me strength to achieve my aim by their confidence in me and their unfailing help and I would like to thank them all – especially my husband, Jigme, who read my book with great care and helped me to recall our early life and all that I have written about him and our family.

Especially I would like to thank Mr. Hugh Richardson, who was in Tibet for many years and is an old friend of both the Taring and Tsarong families, for introducing me to my readers. And among the many others to whom I owe much gratitude I would like to mention Mrs. Joan Mary Jehu, for her hospitality in London and for lending me the treasured photographs taken by her father, Colonel Leslie Weir, when he was Political Officer in Sikkim; Miss Dervla Murphy with whom I stayed in Ireland and who gave me so much invaluable help with my typescript and Miss Jane Boulenger, who has given her advice and saw the book through to the printer; and my publisher, Mr. John Murray, for his wise advice and for bringing my book into being.

RINCHEN DOLMA TARING
HAPPY VALLEY
MUSOORIE, U.P.
INDIA
MARCH 15, 1969

ACKNOWLEDGEMENTS TO THE SECOND EDITION

For some years now, my book has been out of print. I am most grateful to my friend Mr. P.A. Skott of the Isle of Man for his efforts to find another publisher. I thank Mr. John Murray and Miss Dervla Murphy for very kindly surrendering the rights they held in the book. And I am delighted that Wisdom Publications is publishing this new edition, which has given me the opportunity to write an epilogue in which I bring up to date my life and the life of my family. I hope his new edition helps the people of the world see that Tibet has always been an independent country with its own history and rich culture.

RINCHEN DOLMA TARING
TARING HOUSE
5, SATYAN MOHALLA
RAJPUR
DEHRA DUN, U.P.
INDIA
AUGUST 1, 1986

Foreword to the First Edition by Hugh M. Richardson

MOST OF THAT handful of foreigners who were fortunate enough to visit Tibet will have affectionate memories of Jigme and Mary Taring, whether in the warm hospitality of the country house, near Gyantse, of Jigme's father or in their own delightful home in Lhasa. Wherever it might be they created a unique atmosphere, not just because they were happy and infinitely thoughtful hosts – many of our Tibetan friends shared those endearing qualities – but because at that time they and some of their younger relations were almost the only Tibetans who had lived in Western surroundings. They had learnt perfect English and spoke it beautifully and they had gained a good understanding of Western ways of living and thinking – very different in some manifestations from those of Tibet – so that they were able to act as a bridge between the two worlds and to give us a better insight into Tibetan life and thought.

I would not dare claim that Mary La (as from long habit I must call her) learnt from the West anything of her capability in practical affairs – Tibetan ladies are notoriously capable – but the experience may have helped her later to take her place in a wider world as the respected and beloved Mother of the Homes for Tibetan children in Mussoorie. The ease and skill with which her husband Jigme mastered the mechanical appliances of the outside world also demonstrated in a remarkable way the natural ability of the Tibetans. But whatever the Tarings acquired from outside – and what they took was chosen with good taste – they never

ceased to be sincere and devoted Tibetans. They saw the
weak points in the Western world as well as the good and
could poke quiet fun at foreign pretensions, always with
innate, good-natured, politeness.

Mary La has written that critics later said they were pro-
British. If the critics had known what they were talking
about they might have said that the Tarings made us pro-
Tibetan. Whatever I may have learnt about Tibet I owe
largely to them; and it is a particular honour to have been
asked to write this foreword. It is, also, a particular pleasure
to go on learning from Mary La's book which throws an
intimate light on Tibetan family life and customs and on
aspects of Tibetan domestic history in the past fifty years.

Mary La writes from the heart, without artifice but with
an enviable gift of expression and a delightful humour. Hers
is the unmistakable Tibetan voice, quiet, moderate, yet
determined. It reveals the deep kindness and sympathy for
want and distress, characteristic of all Tibetan women and,
also, the special influence and authority enjoyed, gently and
unostentatiously, by the ladies of the Lhasa nobility. In the
home they were equal partners and, although they never
made themselves noticed in public, it was common knowledge that behind the scenes they could and did exert a
power to soften harsh official measures.

The simple and warmly affectionate life of a great family was
not infrequently shot through by tragedy. Mary La experienced
more than her fair share in her young days; but one could not
live in Tibet without discovering the blend in Tibetan character,
at all levels, of a resilient endurance, a deep humanity and an
unaffected tolerance, infused throughout by unfailing faith in
and reliance on religion in every moment of existence.

Tibetan society was a small, closely-knit, world. Noble
children and those of their servants and farm workers were
brought up together and shared so much experience that a
close fellow feeling was a natural condition of their lives and
produced a protective consideration on one side, devoted
loyalty on the other, and genuine affection on both. Those

traits emerge without effort or emphasis from this book and make nonsense of Communist propaganda about Tibet as an oppressive and unpopular feudal rule. It was that closely-knit feeling of responsibility that made not only possible but virtually inevitable what I may call Mary La's second life – as Mother of the Tibetan Homes in Mussoorie.

The story of the transition period between the old life and the new and of the adjustments Tibetans had to make to the strange régime of the Communist conquerors is fascinating especially to one who knew the old Tibet. Mary La's travels in China during that period, although lightly sketched, provide a valuable description of the way in which the Tibetan mind adapted itself to changed external circumstances without losing its own internal fixed points. Then tragedy struck once more, worse than that of Mary La's early days for it was the tragedy of the whole Tibetan people. Separation from her husband and children and many kinsmen and friends are seen against the turmoil, bloodshed and terror of the rising at Lhasa in March 1959 when the Tibetan people took up arms, in desperation, against growing oppression.

Mary La's straightforward and moving account of the fears, dangers and privations of her escape across the Himalayas, following the flight of the Dalai Lama and many of his officials, tells of a time when suffering of mind and body tested character and endurance in many different ways.

Inevitably there are lasting regrets for all that was left behind, but her journey ended in reunion with her husband and in a second life in India. Through it her circle of friends and admirers has extended all over the world. Others know far more than I do of her devoted and successful care for Tibetan refugee children in the homes at Mussoorie where they learn to adapt themselves to a new world while keeping the best elements of the old – above all, their sturdy individuality and self-respect. I saw that work only as a tiny embryo in the early days of 1960 when the great exodus from Tibet was still in full flood; but even then it was an inspiration to see Mary and Jigme Taring, together again, harnessing their generous courage and ability to the service of the Dalai Lama and his people. The Homes in Mussoorie have become one of the most valuable centres in which a new generation is growing up to the advantage of Tibet and, I believe, to that of India too, for whose generous shelter and support in the holy land of their faith Tibetans in exile never forget to be grateful.

The Tibetan children could have no better parents than the Tarings.

The directness of this book, combined with calm unexcitability, verging on understatement, and the devout, warm, humanity mark it clearly as Mary La's. No one else could have written it. It is herself.

HUGH RICHARDSON

Foreword to the Second Edition by His Holiness the Dalai Lama

Rinchen Dolma Taring is one of the first Tibetan women to write her autobiography in English. Her account is vivid and through it she has endeavoured to inform the public of the life in Tibet before the invasion and of the tragic events that ensued, culminating in the Tibetan National Uprising on March 10, 1959.

I am happy to know that Wisdom Publications, London, is publishing the new edition of her autobiography, *Daughter of Tibet*, at this time when interest in Tibet is growing. I hope the republication of her autobiography will assist more people in gaining a deeper understanding of Tibetan society and the facts relating to the issue of Tibet.

THEKCHEN CHOELING
MCLEOD GANJ 176219
KANGRA DISTRICT
HIMACHAL PRADESH
June 1, 1985.

1 My Family Background

MY FATHER, TSARONG *Shap-pē* Wangchuk Gyalpo, was descended from the earliest and most celebrated Tibetan physician, Yuthok Yonten Gonpo, who wrote several classical medical works and lived during the reign of King Trisong Detsen (A.D. 755 – 797). Yonten Gonpo is said to have visited India to study Sanskrit medicine at Nalanda University. A block print biography, of a hundred and forty-nine leaves, existed in the Government Medical College in Lhasa and stated that he lived to be a hundred and twenty-five; it contained most interesting diagrams and drawings by Yonten Gonpo. It also mentioned that gods and demons presented him with an immense quantity of turquoise and other precious stones by heaping them on the roof of his house. Hence he was called Yuthok (*Yu* = turquoise: *Thok* = roof).

My mother, Yangchen Dolma, also belonged to a family called Yuthok, being descended from the tenth Dalai Lama, Tsultrim Gyatso, whose family took its name from living near a bridge in Lhasa that has a roof of turquoise tiles.

My parents had about a dozen children, ten of whom survived babyhood. Chime Dolkar, who was very beautiful, died of small-pox at the age of sixteen. Samdup Tsering, the eldest son, came next. Pema Dolkar also had smallpox badly and was heavily marked: one of her granddaughters is now married to Losang Samten, third brother of His Holiness the fourteenth Dalai Lama.

Norbu Yudon, who was slightly pock-marked, became a nun when she was very young but later left her monastery to marry Theji Delek Rabten, a senior official of the Panchen Lama.

Tseten Dolkar married twice and had nine children.

Kalsang Lhawang was badly pock-marked; he was recognised as an Incarnate Lama of Drepung Monastery when he was a small boy.

Tashi Dhondup died of smallpox at the age of eight.

The next sister was born with a hare-lip and died after a year.

I was the ninth surviving child, born in 1910 when my mother was thirty-eight, and last came Changchup Dolma, my junior by about two years. She and I were always together, as we were so much younger than the rest.

My father was a tall and handsome man; he painted beautifully and played many instruments, including the *damnyen, piwang* and *lingbu* (banjo, fiddle and flute). His favourite instrument was the Chinese *yangjin*, which has strings like a harp and is beaten with two bamboo sticks. Tsipon Lungshar, who for a time was Commander-in-Chief of the Army, was often invited to Tsarong House by my father because he played the fiddle so well. My brother Samdup Tsering played the flute in our family orchestra and my mother used to dance beautifully to their music. Tsarong House, our Lhasa home, overlooked the Barkor (the marketplace) and when the family was enjoying itself in the evenings passers-by used to stop to listen with great pleasure. One particular Tibetan Muslim – the son of a famous flute-player – often paused to shed tears, saying, 'He plays the flute just like my father.' But happiness is not permanent until you have the truth of the inner happiness, and constantly the happiness of my parents was disturbed.

Tsarong House, where all of us children were born, was a three-storied stone building. On the first floor, in the east wing, my mother had her own suite of rooms – a small prayer-room, a sitting-room, bed-room, dressing-room, lavatory and a hall that was her servants' sitting-room. From the dressing-room a secret staircase descended to the treasury-room. In the centre of the house – which faced south, like all Tibetan houses, to get the sun – was my father's private prayer-room where he used to receive visitors. On the western side there was another suite of rooms, the *Gonkhang* (Deities' house), another visitors' hall and a small hall from which a staircase led to the roof. The main staircase branched into two on the second floor, where there were guest rooms, servants' quarters, a food-kitchen and a tea-kitchen, store-rooms and a big hall called *Tsomchen* – containing a huge image of Tsongkhapa – where New Year ceremonies, wedding ceremonies and other important events took place. As Buddhists believe that the prayers of holy people are always answered, we had the custom of inviting monks from various monasteries to read prayers in this hall for the prosperity of the house.

My father's prayer-room had a big altar against the wall facing the windows. In the centre of this altar was an image of the Lord Buddha and during every minute of the day there was incense burning in front of it. On either side were book-cases filled with books on Buddhism and before the altar was a finely carved walnut table holding a hundred and eight silver cups of water offerings and several silver butterlamps. My father's two-foot-high seat stood against the wall facing the door and was draped with a lovely oblong of Tibetan carpet, which had a square satin centrepiece. An elaborately carved lacquered table stood in front of it, holding a silver spit-pot, a call-bell and a jade tea-cup with a silver stand and lid, all placed on little white cloth mats. A side table held my father's silver ink-pot and lacquered pen-case. Along the wall, under the window, was a seat about one foot high, three feet wide and eighteen feet long. It was made of matting, stuffed with musk-deer hair, and was covered with beautiful rugs and satin

sausage-shaped cushions to lean on. In front of it stood three
smaller lacquered tables, each always holding at least one cup
with a silver stand and lid, so that tea could be served
immediately to visitors. On the walls we had beautiful *thang-
kas* (temple banners on which monk artists painted religious
subjects). The stone floor – studded with special stones – was
always shining because it had to be wiped thoroughly every
day and it was carpeted in the centre.

Next to this room was a small hall where the room-servants
waited: the head servant had to be ready to come at once when
the call-bell rang.

Every morning at sunrise my father used to pray for about
an hour, before his breakfast was served. Then visitors would
call to discuss business or government affairs. The tea-cup
which my father used in his prayer-room had to be kept there
always; he had another special cup in Mother's sitting-room,
which was similarly furnished. He used to spend most of his
spare time in her rooms, when not busy with visitors, and
every day she helped him to put on his official robes before he
went to *Kashag* (Council) meetings.

A heavy, iron-studded, wooden double gate led from the
street into the main courtyard, which was paved with stone
slabs. Around the courtyard were stables for fifteen horses, the
grass-storage rooms, the syces' room and the *chang*-room
where our *chang*-girl made all the beer required by the family.
Tibetans always have square mounting-blocks outside their
homes. We had two on the street outside the main gate and one
in the courtyard, to which all members of the household and
important visitors might ride. When high lamas or very
important officials were expected, or when one of the family
was departing on or arriving from a long journey, the syce
spread a special satin carpet on the mounting-block.

Our country estate was near Sakya, in western Tibet, a
twelve days' journey on horseback from Lhasa. We take our
surnames from our estates and the Tsarong Estate had been
handed down from father to son for many generations, but the
family had never lived there and the estate was always

administered by stewards, appointed from among our retainers. Every year, at harvest time, a member of the family went to see the crops of barley, wheat and peas and to check the books; later the steward would come to Lhasa to settle the yearly account. We stored some surplus grain each year, for ourselves and our retainers, in case of famine. Twice a year grain and dairy produce for family use were brought to Tsarong House on mules and donkeys.

As Tsarong was only a middle-sized estate, we were never very rich, yet the name was famous because of our being descended from Yonten Gonpo, the eight-century physician, and from Kalsang Chodak, the eighteenth-century *Chi-Kyap Khempo* (Lord Chamberlain). Our family had been settled in Lhasa for hundreds of years because the men of every generation worked hard serving the government in many capacities. My grandfather, *Tsi-pon* Tsarong, was one of the strongest characters among the Tibetan nobility of his day. In 1886 he was sent by the government to the Sikkimese border to confirm the demarcation of our frontier, because at that time the British were being a little troublesome about it. He died just after being appointed *Shap-pē*, (Cabinet Minister) before he had time to celebrate his appointment.

Our house on the estate was a big three-storied building, with a huge courtyard. Some special rooms, including the prayer-room, were not used by the steward but were kept clean and ready for any of the family who came to stay.

The Tsarongs were patrons of the nearby Sakya Monastery and we greatly respected the Sakya Lama as a teacher. There is no religious rivalry between the four sects of Tibetan Buddhism. These sects are: Nyingmapa (meaning 'the old', which follows Padmasambhawa's teaching), Kagyupa (the sect of Marpa, the great translator and the teacher of Milarepa), Sakyapa (of the translator Sakya Panchen, known as the 'gracious teacher' of Tibet) and Gelugpa (the sect of Tsongkhapa, the reformer of Tibetan Buddhism), to which the Dalai Lama and most Tibetans belong. Tsongkhapa was born in the northeastern province of Amdo and one of his great disciples was Gedum

Drup, the first Dalai Lama, who built Tashi Lunpo Monastery, the seat of the Panchen Lama. Though the Gelugpa sect became the State religion the State had equal respect for the other three sects. Their teachings on the methods of reaching enlightenment are slightly different, but all four sects observe the fundamental teachings of the Lord Buddha about Cause and Effect and the impossibility of escaping from one's karma. Gelugpa monks do not marry or drink alcohol, and among the other sects many take the ordination of Gelugpas and observe the same rules. Among the Gelugpas, thousands study deeply the teachings of Nyingmapa, Sakyapa and Kagyupa. All Tibetans believe that the Dalai Lama is the reincarnation of Chenrezig, Lord of Compassion, the karma deity of the Land of Snow, and once we have found the true incarnation everybody, without one spot of doubt, has faith in him. The Dalai Lama himself studies the teachings of all sects and respects them equally and no disagreement in practice is debated. All the great scholars of the four sects contributed at different times in different ways to strengthen Tibetan Buddhism and each sect had images in the Jokhang, the main temple in Lhasa. Our ancient Bön religion exists still in Tibet, on a very small scale, and its spirits are considered to be defenders of Buddhism.

At Tsarong our medical temple – the chief symbol of our descent from the famous physician – stood on a hill, at a little distance from the house. It contained an image of Yonten Gonpo, who to this day is worshipped by all Tibetans. We were responsible for its upkeep and we kept our treasure there under seal; the main objects were the skull of Yonten Gonpo, his medical books, medicine bag, wooden drinking vessel and rosary. We also had very old curios that were never brought to Lhasa, such as religious objects that had belonged to the early Tibetan Kings and labelled gifts from various Dalai Lamas.

In Tibet all land belonged to the government. Estates were leased to noble families and monasteries, and sometimes to people who were not nobles and paid their tax direct to the government. The big monasteries were given land to meet their expenses, but there were some small monasteries which possessed no land and simply depended on charity. As long as the noble families had one layman in each generation to serve the government they held their estates for centuries. These officials received no salary because the estates were their sources of income, but some estates could not meet the family needs and therefore trade was greatly exercised among the nobility. The sizes of the estates varied, because many nobles had been given special land-rewards for patriotic work. There were also big land-owners who had joined two, three or more estates together by marriages. Since the family documents were always kept with care these estates could be separated if the people concerned did not get on well; to join or separate was not much trouble because the government did not restrict such dealings. In order to keep family ties bound well, polygamy and polyandry were common amongst both the nobility and the peasantry. We thought the government very kind to let us have estates and all Tibetan nobles did their best to serve their country.

Taxes were paid to the government in grain, butter, wool, meat, oil, paper, cheese and money. If a family was exempted from a tax by their local authority, because of crops failing or irrigation breaking down, they had to inform the *Tsikhang* (Financial Office) in Lhasa. Every year the *Tsikhang* held a contest to see which *Dzong* (District) had produced the best crops, and prizes were awarded to the *Dzongpon* (District Governor) who came first. There were about seventy *Dzongs*. (Tibet is a big country of some twelve million square acres, but it was sparsely populated. We never had a census but we always believed there were six or seven million Tibetans.) All estates were under the jurisdiction of their *Dzongpon*, who settled disputes and collected taxes, and in order to have a good administration each *Dzong* was governed jointly by a monk-official and a lay-official. If a *Dzongpon* exploited the people, a big group of men came to Lhasa to report him to the government, or sent a petition. The government then appointed special, good officials to investigate and stop the exploitation.

If the investigators were not impartial the people could also complain about them, and sometimes investigators were changed. In many cases such disputes were mediated by relatives or friends, because to go through all the formalities of government investigation took a number of years and then both parties got bored and suffered great losses, as the government often sealed up the barns of the disputing master and his retainers.

The Tibetan feudal system was established about a thousand years ago by the religious kings of Tibet. The thirteen points of the law laid down by King Songtsan Gampo include all necessary laws, and the principle was that the nobles should act as parents to their retainers. The theory was good but the practice varied. When members of the family were living on an estate they and their retainers usually created a nice feeling of belonging to each other, but when estates were leased, or left in the charge of a steward, exploitation was common. During the minority of the present Dalai Lama, while the two regents were disputing over their own power, many officials leased their *Dzongs* and the men who took the leases exploited the poor very much.

Retainers had to cultivate the fields of their master instead of having to pay rent, because he was leasing their land from the government and working hard as an official. They were paid and fed when they did this work and things were so organised that their own work and their master's work was done on different fixed days and even the water in the irrigation channels was shared equally. When there were government goods to be carried to Lhasa the retainers were obliged to take them and the goods were distributed for transport among all the estates of *Dzong*; the stewards saw to it that their retainers were not overloaded. Each estate also had to send recruits to the Army. These soldiers were paid by the government, but their special allowances had to be paid by the retainers, who gave them each a homespun outfit, a pair of boots and about £4 for the year they would be away.

Tibet had its own peculiar feudal system that no other country has ever experienced. It is interesting that the people were so contented, although the difference between their livelihood and their master's was so great. Lord Buddha taught the religion of deed and consequence and no matter how ignorant Tibetans may be an understanding of this doctrine is always with them.

It is said that one of Tibet's religious kings, Muni Tsanpo (A.D. 804), tried to equalise things by appointing ministers to redistribute land and property. After some time he asked how the reform was getting on and heard that the rich were becoming richer and the poor, poorer. He made two more attempts to reform things, but failed. This saddened him, and he consulted the great Indian sage Padmasambawa, who said that nobody can close the gap between rich and poor because everything 'is entirely dependent upon the actions of our previous lives and nothing can be done to alter the scheme of things'. Tibetans consider that the more wealth and luck one has, the better were one's deeds in previous lives. Yet people who do not know how to utilise their wealth properly are thought to be great sufferers and a contented poor person is considered luckier than a miserly rich one. Not to be satisfied with one's life is a big sin. The Tibetans believe in their karma and try their best to achieve a better life in their next incarnation. There can be sand in gold and one may find wicked people among us Tibetans, but most of the people were smiling, content, honest, and loyal. And this may be due to our religion.

The servants in the Lhasa houses were retainers who had been called from the estates and were well paid and fed. If retainers wished to make their children monks or nuns they got a document of permission from their masters without any difficulty and through being a monk the intelligent son of a retainer could become a government official of the highest rank. If a daughter or son married into a noble family they could be freed and become ennobled. There were also many free people who were not nobles. A large group of Tibetans called 'Indian Khampas' traded in India and sold their goods in Tibet and they and their children were absolutely free. The

Tibetan wives of the Nepalese and Muslim traders in Lhasa paid a small annual tax to the *Nyertsang Lekhung* (the Municipal Office) and were then free; their children had to pay no tax. The dancing groups were supposed to be under the *Nyertsang Lekhung* but their tax was only about ninepence per year. The beggars were also quite independent and some had home industries in tents at the same time as they were begging to get as much money as they could. A group of beggars called *Ragyapa* were very powerful. They had their own guild and were responsible for the difficult work of putting up and down the four huge prayerflag masts of the city of Lhasa. Their other responsibilities included such dirty work as disposing of all unclaimed dead bodies, providing the monks with human skulls and thighbones for special rites, putting out the eyes or chopping off the limbs of the few criminals who were punished in this manner and keeping other beggars away from parties if people did not want to be troubled by too many of them. Wherever anything was being celebrated, or even at houses where a death had occurred, they demanded big sums of money, shouting that they were entitled to it because of their great responsibilities and refusing to leave until they had been paid and given lots of chang. They always went home quite drunk and were satisfied with their gifts. The *Ragyapa* were well off and never begged like the other really poor beggars.

In Tibet we had no caste system, such as the Hindus have, because in the light of Buddhism all people are equal. Yet Buddhism also teaches that 'whosoever hurts or harms living creatures, and is destitute of sympathy for any living thing, let him be known as an outcast'. Therefore no Tibetan would marry a butcher or a blacksmith knowingly. In Tibet butchers wove belts and tweed at home, as their side-work, and they intermarried with blacksmiths. Most people ate meat, despite being Buddhists, because of the severity of our climate and the difficulty of growing enough grain; but no ordinary Tibetan would slaughter an animal for meat, so butchers were hired. However, we knew that even butchers could become holy people. Once a butcher felt terribly sad about slaughtering an animal and was so overcome by regret for his past deeds that he stabbed himself to death. The Lord Buddha then said that through his remorse he was enlightened immediately.

The men who disposed of dead bodies were also considered low because this job was done for common people by a poor group, in return for the clothes off the corpse and good pay. Noble bodies were disposed of by one's own people, like servants of friends. Yet the job itself was not looked down on because our religion teaches us not to feel dirty about such work.

The government and the people greatly respected all skilled workers and even the head of the blacksmiths' guild held the fifth rank title of *Letsanpa* and sat along with all other officials, eating the same food, in the halls of the Potala and Norbu Lingka palaces. We had *Letsanpas* of the goldsmiths', moulders', boot-makers', tailors', artists', carpenters' and masons' guilds. The influence of these men over their respective groups was tremendous and they sat above the junior officials of noble families. Each guild had its own very strict rules and the *Letsanpas* administered punishments when necessary and disciplined their men so that the government could organise them easily. They only went to law when they had very big disputes. All the members of these guilds were rich – even richer than some of the government officials because they earned a lot and had no public responsibilities. Yet no matter how rich they were noble parents would try their best not to have their children married to one of them, though the law did not prevent such marriages, which occasionally happened. The sons of skilled people could join the government service from the monk-official side and then could come right to the top, like the sons of peasants. If such a boy married – despite being a monk – after becoming an influential officer, nobody objected to his marrying anyone he chose.

There were nomads all over Tibet, belonging to monasteries, estates and special government offices like the Upper and Lower Treasuries. They led a happy life, always on their own in the green pastures, often shifting their camps. The richest families owned a few thousand sheep and eight or nine hundred yaks and it was beautiful to see the baby yaks playing on the green hills. Most of the high northern hills are bare, but make lovely grazing places; in southern Tibet the hills have trees and it is much warmer.

The nomads lived in tents made out of yaks' wool cloth, which is strong and waterproof; well-to-do families had big double tents, for extra protection from the cold, and these held about one hundred people. For fuel most nomads used small wild azalea bushes and yak-droppings, which is the most inflammable dung. Their main foods were *tsampa* (barley roasted whole and ground into flour), meat, butter and cheese. They had a number of cheese delicacies – cheese cakes and dried cheeses that could be hard, or soft and sweet. They strung the hard ones together and sold them in the towns, but their main trading products were butter and wool. The nomads' owners gave them animals and they paid taxes in one of two ways. Some paid about thirty pounds of butter annually per head of half the number of *dri* (female yak) in their herd (only half would be milk producing at a time), and even if they lost by death or gained by birth the tax was fixed according to the original number of *dri* in a herd. In these cases the wool and cheese belonged to the nomads. The second method was to pay the same amount of butter per head, but to account for deaths and births. Then the wool and cheese belonged to the nomads' owners, who were responsible for replacing the animals that died in epidemics. The owners regularly counted the animals, who had marks burnt into their horns with hot iron seals. The pasturelands were well demarcated, but occasionally there were disputes and the nomads came to Lhasa to have them settled by the government.

Yaks were a real gift for Tibet. We used them as both pack and riding animals and they gave the best milk and cheese. (The few without horns made the quietest riding animals and all yaks were wonderfully sure-footed on the roughest and steepest paths.) Their meat was delicious and if properly dried it kept well for a year or more; travellers found it very convenient because when beaten to a powder and flavoured with salt and red pepper it could be eaten with *tsampa* and no other dish was required. Yaks' horns were used to make bottles for water and ink and snuff-boxes which were sometimes ten inches long and looked magnificent when studded with coral, turquoise and amber. Yaks' hooves were eaten, their wool made strong cloth and the best kind of rope, and their ordinary tails were used as dusters while their white tails were valued as fly-whisks in India and even went as far as America to make Father Christmas beards. After motor-cars had come to Lhasa, one of my young cousins said to me, 'Aunty, we really ought to eat the donkeys in place of our precious yaks. These donkeys do not move an inch no matter how much we blow our horns – but the poor yaks are so sweet and humble that after just one blow they jump and kick and clear out of the way.'

The nomads sold butter, cheese, salt and borax and bought grain, which would not grow on their high pastures. They packed the butter in wet hides and it was so well compressed that it could be kept for a year or so; a load weighed eighty pounds, and a yak, or any big pack-animal, could carry two loads. Small pieces of butter, weighing from four to eight pounds, were packed in the stomachs of yaks or sheep and carried on the backs of sheep. When nomads came to the towns to pay their taxes they had special hosts, whose wives helped them to sell their produce. They could then buy cotton, tea, matches and soap for their own use. Some also bought housewares such as religious objects, and silver stands and lids for their wooden tea-cups. (Some also possessed jade china cups.) Many bought gold and silver to make ornaments to keep their wives happy and give themselves the satisfaction of feeling that they had a good investment. They were fond of coral and amber, which the women wore as necklaces or in their hair. They feared the heat and felt it very much when they came to Lhasa or Shigatse because they wore sheepskins, bordered with bright red, blue and green cloth, with the woolly side touching their flesh. They brought their babies in their *ambaks*, the pouch formed by the wrap-over fold of their gowns, or made baskets lined with sheepskin and put two babies on either side of a yak.

The dialect of the northern nomads is very difficult to understand; they talk eloquently and as fast and fluently as though reading from a book. They use many proverbs, attaching them to sentences most appropriately, and in the midst of their conversation they swear and say, '*Digpa Khur*' – meaning, 'I'll take the sin'. In the old days holy lamas used to request their disciples to undertake the hardship of visiting the nomads to give them blessings and preach and perform rites amongst them. Thousands of nomads are now in exile, as refugees from the Chinese, and it is very sad for them to have left their heavenly places. Life in Tibet was wonderfully happy for most people when I was a child.

2   The Conspiracy against my Father

IN 1642 HIS Holiness the fifth Dalai Lama became the head of the Tibetan government, as well as being our religious leader, and from that time until the Communist invasion of 1950, each Dalai Lama (or Regent) had a civil service with two branches to help him run the country. One branch was made up of one hundred and seventy-five specially trained monks (known as monk-officials) and the other of one hundred and seventy-five lay noblemen. The *Kashag* (Council) was the most important part of the Tibetan government. It usually had four members, three lay noblemen and a high-ranking monk who was respected as the senior member. These Councillors were known as *Shap-pēs*, which means Lotus-foot, and they shared responsibility for all decisions. They were not like Western cabinet ministers, each in charge of separate departments; instead, they gave their views on all government business to the Dalai Lama and also acted as a Court of Justice, though the Dalai Lama was the final judge. It was possible for four men to do all this because the government business was very simple.

Next to the Dalai Lama the highest religious official was the *Chi-Kyap Khempo* (Lord Chamberlain,) who headed His Holiness's personal household and was in charge of both his personal treasury and the official treasury of the Potala.

The *Yik-tsang* (Monastic Council) came below the *Chi-*

Kyap Khempo. Its four monk members supervised the thousands of monasteries all over Tibet and selected, trained and disciplined the young monk-officials.

Next came four lay *Tsi-pons*, who had the main responsibility of the government and trained young lay officials. There were also Political, Financial, Religious, Educational, Military, Municipal and Judical offices, each with one monk and one lay official sharing the work. All the officials worked from 9 a.m. till 5 p.m. six days a week. The offices were closed on whichever day of the week was inauspicious for the reigning Dalai Lama.

The *Tsongdu* (National Assembly) had about fifty members and was only called occasionally by the *Kashag* to discuss very important matters. The Abbots of the three great Lhasa monasteries — Ganden, Sera and Drepung — had much influence on its opinions because they represented about twenty thousand monks. Many of the higher officials also attended, but the *Shap-pēs* were not allowed to be present, though they received detailed reports after each meeting and conveyed them to the Dalai Lama. If something very critical was happening representatives of every class attended — nobles, traders, monks, craftsmen, farmers, boatmen, blacksmiths, nomads. The *Tsongdu* was responsible for selecting a Regent after the death of a Dalai Lama. It always strongly opposed Chinese attempts to rule Tibet.

My father was senior lay *Shap-pē* in the *Kashag* from 1903 – 12. Before that he was a *Dapon* (General) and in July 1903, he was sent to Khampa Dzong, near the Sikkimese border, to negotiate with Colonel Francis Younghusband's Trade Mission to Tibet. This mission had been sent to us by Lord Curzon, Viceroy of India, because of rumours that we were about to enter into a secret treaty with Russia. The British feared that if Russia got too much influence in Tibet she might cause trouble along India's northern border, so Lord Curzon wanted to make friends with us, and to have regular trading between Tibet and India and a British representative living in Lhasa. At the time the three powerful monasteries of Lhasa thought the

British were enemies of Buddhism. They therefore persuaded His Holiness the thirteenth Dalai Lama to instruct my father and a monk secretary-general of the *Yikt-sang* to go to Khampa Dzong – twenty miles inside Tibet, near the Sikkimese border – and request the British to hold talks only on the edge of Tibetan territory. The two representatives were also instructed to employ delaying tactics and as a result the British Mission was held up for about six months and became rather annoyed.

My father then went to his estate at Tsarong, four days' ride from Khampa Dzong, where he received a letter from the government appointing him a *Shap-pē* in place of Shatra *Shap-pē* who, with his three *Kashag* colleagues, had been imprisoned in Norbu Lingka – the Dalai Lama's summer palace – for saying that it was necessary to bring about a peaceful settlement with the British because Britain was so mighty.

When a letter of appointment was sent to a new *Shap-pē* it was regarded as a very important and auspicious document. My father received his with great courtesy from the special messenger, placed it on an altar and prostrated himself three times before opening it. He then went to Lhasa to celebrate his appointment publicly.

The position of *Shap-pē* was a difficult one. Apart from possessing the necessary administrative capabilities, each *Shap-pē* had a great number of expensive duties, such as throwing a big party for all the government officials every four years, providing twenty-four cavalrymen, with full armour and good horses, every year during the Great Prayer Festival, keeping seven official mounted servants and donating a big butter offering on the fifteenth day of the first month of each year. (These offerings of solid butter were about forty feet high and finely decorated by monk artists with coloured butter). Also, a *Shap-pē* had to celebrate his appointment by giving new dresses to the images of the chief deities in the Jokhang (Lhasa's most important temple). It took fifteen tailors a whole month to make these dresses of brocade, satin, silk and cotton, which cost about £800. Another expense was presenting a silver or gold wheel – The Wheel of Excellent Law – to the main image of the Lord Buddha in the Jokhang. The spokes of the wheel symbolise Pure Conduct, Justice is the uniformity of their length, Wisdom is their rim, Modesty and Thoughtfulness are the point at which the immovable axle of Truth is fixed. This wheel, if made with silver and gilded, cost about £150. The many brocade dresses required for taking part in the monthly government festivals and ceremonies were also expensive, but despite his responsibilities the salary of a *Shap-pē* was small. Sometimes when he came to power those who already had the necessary costumes would lend them to him, but the income from his estate had to cover most of the extra expenses and from the Tsarong Estate we only got about 3,060 *maunds* of grain, 20 *maunds* of butter and 50 *maunds* of wool per year. (One maund equals 80 pounds.)

In 1904 the British Trade Mission became a military expedition and forced its way to Lhasa, killing many hundreds of the badly-armed Tibetan soldiers who tried to stop it. Before it reached Lhasa His Holiness the thirteenth Dalai Lama fled to Mongolia and soon after was invited to Peking by the last Manchu Emperor.

My father was one of the four *Shap-pēs* who signed the 1904 Convention with Britain in the Potala Palace. This Convention – which forbade us to have any relations with any foreign power other than Britain – made it quite clear that Britain was dealing with us as an independent country, over which China had no control of any kind, and it arranged for British trade marts to be set up at Gyantse and Gartok, in western Tibet. (Since 1893 the British had had one trade mart at Yatung.) The Convention also demanded half a million pounds sterling as indemnity from Tibet; but the Secretary of State for India thought this very unfair, so it was later reduced to £166,000, to be paid in twenty-five annual instalments.

My father went to India in 1907 to pay the first instalment and while there learned how to use a camera and a sewing machine and brought some of each home with him. Such things had never before been seen in Tibet. He also brought boxes of 'No. 999' cigarettes and introduced Indian sweet tea. He was an excellent organiser, who took advantage of his Indian trip to modernise Tibet by bringing back to Lhasa a Muslim gun-smith and a skilled leather tanner. He then ran a government tannery and a gun factory near Lhasa, and soon a shoe factory was started, because we had lots of strong yaks' leather. He knew how to make many different kinds of knots and he taught my sisters this skill.

The Tibetan government did not know that in 1906 Britain and China had signed an agreement ratifying the 1904 Lhasa Convention. On 20 April 1908, this agreement was amended at Calcutta, in the presence of my father, who was representing our government. His enemies then claimed that he had signed what are known as the 'Tibet Trade Regulations, 1908' without consulting His Holiness, who at that time was in exile in China. But the Dalai Lama knew that my father was loyal to Tibet; when His Holiness had again to flee from Lhasa after the 1910 Chinese invasion, he appointed him one of the lay assistants to the Regent, Tri Rimpoche Tsemonling.

Only a few months after the Dalai Lama's return from six years of exile in Mongolia and China Chinese troops from Szechuan attacked Lhasa. They arrived on a New Year's Day, when I was a small baby, and killed people in the Barkor; my mother and my older sisters saw this shooting with their own eyes from the windows of our house. Then there was a rumour that the Chinese intended to capture the Dalai Lama and take him back to China as a hostage, so for the good of Tibet His Holiness decided to flee to India. The preparations for his journey were made by night and he left Lhasa on 13 February 1910. As soon as the Chinese discovered that he had fled their soldiers pursued him, with orders to bring him back alive or dead.

At this time His Holiness's favourite was Chensal Namgang, who later took the surname Tsarong when he was ennobled by marrying into our family, and who was then given the forenames Dasang Dadul and the title of *Dzasa* (similar to an English earldom) by His Holiness. Chensal Namgang was born in 1885 into a peasant family in Phenpo, north of Lhasa, where his father had a little farm and made arrows. He was serving the headmaster of the Potala monk-officials' school when he became the favourite of His Holiness because of his very clever ways and in 1903 he had accompanied the Dalai Lama into exile. During His Holiness's second flight to India it was Chensal Namgang who stopped the Chinese pursuers at Chaksam Ferry, two days' ride from Lhasa. Accompanied by his most faithful companions and by some brave soldiers – armed with thirty-four rifles – he stayed behind the Dalai Lama's party to defend it. Late one night he and his men arrived at Chaksam Monastery, on the river Tsangpo, captured the ferry-boats and had a little sleep. Then somebody slapped him hard on the face to awaken him and, looking out of the windows, he saw that the Chinese had arrived at the monastery, after crossing the river riding on huge logs. Already they had collected dry bushes and were beginning to set fire to the building, so Chensal Namgang quickly woke his men and led them behind the hill above the monastery. From the top they fired on the Chinese and by dawn most of the two hundred pursuers had been killed. Chensal Namgang then rode on towards India with a few companions, leaving the rest of his men in the villages around Chaksam.

His Holiness had requested all the village headmen on the route to India to assist Chensal Namgang and at Khangmar he was told that any British subjects he might meet would give him whatever help they could. At Phari he went straight to the British rest-house, where he got news from the headman that the Chinese had already arrived in the town to capture him. A British telegraph-line officer, who happened to be staying at the rest-house, suggested that if Chensal Namgang felt brave enough he could disguise himself in the officer's own uniform and dark glasses and, riding with a linesman, leave Phari in the morning just when the Chinese were also leaving to find him. Chensal Namgang accepted this plan and next morning rode down towards Chumbi Valley on the narrow track, shoulder to shoulder with the Chinese. Many years later he told me that near Yatung he was so afraid of being recognised that he left his pony with his servant and continued slowly on foot through the forest. In Yatung, Mr. David MacDonald, the British Trade Agent, hid him in his store-room and suggested his dressing up as one of the British post-runners while crossing Zelapla, the border pass. Next morning, when the bugle was blown to signal the departure of the post, Chensal Namgang joined the runners and got safely out of Tibet after a tough climb over a sixteen-thousand-foot snow-covered pass.

At Nakthang, servants and ponies, sent by His Holiness, met the Hero of Chaksam and brought him to join the Dalai Lama's party at Kalimpong. Later, Chensal Namgang accompanied His Holiness on pilgrimages to Buddhist sacred places. At Sarnath a British officer had found a pot of relics of the Lord Buddha and some were given to His Holiness and a few to Chensal Namgang who, on his return to Tibet, invited craftsmen to build three life-size golden images of the religious kings – Songtsan Gampo, Trisong Detsen, and Ngadak Triral – which were filled with prayers and these relics. The images were ornamented by my sister, Pema Dolkar, with pearls, coral, turquoise and amber. For many years they stood in the prayer-room of Tsarong House, which also contained wonderful copies of the Kagyur and Tenyur, bound with satin and labelled with brocade.

In 1910, when the Chinese occupied Lhasa, there was much fighting in the city and my mother, with her daughters and Rigzin Chodon, my eldest brother's wife, were given shelter in Tashi Khangsar, a college of Drepung Monastery to which women were admitted. (Drepung is a few miles outside Lhasa and was the biggest monastery in Tibet, with seven thousand seven hundred monks.) I have been told that we had to leave Lhasa in the night and because I cried the Chinese sentries woke and a few shots were fired.

We remained at Drepung for about two years, while the Chinese were in control of Lhasa, but my father and Samdup Tsering, my eldest brother, stayed on at Tsarong House, attending their offices everyday, Samdup Tsering was twenty-three in age – a brilliant young man who was already a *Kadon* (secretary to the *Kashag*). Rigzin Chodon was his second wife; his first wife died soon after their marriage because her father gave her powdered jewels to eat to make her more healthy. During those two years, my father was working so hard that when His Holiness asked him to come to India for discussions the Regent begged him not to go as their joint responsibility was very great and my father was a most skilful diplomat. His handling of the situation averted bloodshed and the destruction by the Chinese of temples, monasteries and the Potala Palace. But not everybody agreed with his policy of compromise and soon a terrible cloud of unhappiness came over our family.

In 1911 the Manchu Emperor was overthrown and in January 1912, His Holiness appointed Chensal Namgang to be Commander-in-Chief of the Tibetan Army and sent him back from Kalimpong to Lhasa to help drive away the Chinese – who were becoming much weaker because of the revolution in China.

At that time there was a lot of jealous friction among Tibetan officials. From Kalimpong, the Dalai Lama had ordered the formation of a secret War Department which was headed by the Secretary-General, Chamba Tendar, and *Tsi a pon* Trimon. Its purpose was to overthrow the Chinese military dictatorship by force and it was in direct communication with His Holiness but did not consult the *Kashag* as it was opposed to the *Shap-pēs'* cautious policy. Neither did it consult His Holiness about all matters, since Chamba Tendar and Trimon were both very ambitious men.

When Chensal Namgang returned to Lhasa he had to work with the War Department, which was then conspiring against the *Kashag*. My father was warned of this conspiracy by friends who advised him to join His Holiness in India, but he refused to run away and said, 'White blood will flow if ever my head is chopped off.'

A few months later a secret meeting of the *Tsongdu* was called by Chamba Tendar and *Tsi-pon* Trimon and it was decided to arrest all the officials who were considered pro-

Chinese, including the four *Shap-pēs*, three of whom had been appointed to the *Kashag* by the Chinese militaries marshal. My father was the only one appointed by His Holiness and ever since the Dalai Lama's flight in 1910 he had been giving all his best service to wipe out the Chinese.

On the twentieth-eight day of the third month of the Iron Pig Year (1912) my father went to Nechung Temple – just below Drepung Monastery – where the chief government deities were, with about one hundred monks in attendance on them. The State Oracle also resided there. Once a month the *Shap-pēs* used to go to Nechung in turns, to make offerings on behalf of the State to the deity who was the protector of religion, and on this date my nanny took me to the temple to meet my father. But I do not remember our meeting, as I was only two years old.

A couple of days later my father was arrested in the *Kashag* office at the Potala, dragged roughly down a long, steep flight of stone steps to the grounds of the Magistrate's building and murdered. His body was not even handed over to the family and for a long time my older sisters could not set their eyes on the front of the Potala. But to me the great palace became even more sacred, as I feel that our father's death was an important historic event and an honour to the family.

On the morning of that same day an official named Kyungram called at Tsarong House, saying that he wanted to ride with Samdup Tsering to the government offices. When Kyungram arrived my brother remarked to him, 'I had a bad dream last night.' But he only laughed and replied, 'Dreams are dreams.' One of the servants, Nyerpa Dorje, overheard this as he was handing Samdup Tsering his belt, boots and hat and told me about it many years afterwards. Kyungram and my brother then rode towards the Potala and when they reached the Yuthok Sampa – the turquoise-roofed bridge – a group of men from Kongpo, in southern Tibet, suddenly appeared, armed with daggers. Samdup Tsering had a pistol in his *ambak* but the appearance of these men was so unexpected that he could not defend himself and was at once stabbed to death. His servants were also overcome and arrested. Rigzin Chodon told me that he died in such a state of anger that for a long time he could not find his reincarnation and his mind remained with Gyalchen (one of the State Oracles) and often spoke through Gyalchen when the Oracle was in a trance.

The news of her husband's and son's death was brought to my mother at Drepung by the steward of my lama brother, and this man, being a Khampa, did not know how to break it to her gently. Rushing in breathlessly he said, 'Sawang Chenpo (His Excellency) has been killed today.' When my mother asked, 'What about my son?' he replied, 'Sey Kusho (the Prince) has also been killed.' She then fell unconscious, and had to be revived by the application of hot dough to her head and the burning of incense. She could not continue to feed my youngest sister, Changchup Dolma, who was then about four months old, so a wet nurse was hired. Everyone in the monastery did their best to help her, but poor Mother had been greatly shocked and remained sad and ill for the rest of her life.

It was rumoured that Chensal Namgang was among the conspirators, though he was a friend of Samdup Tsering and used to visit Tsarong House often to take lessons in photography from my father. Afterwards he told Rigzin Chodon that he knew of the plot but could do nothing because he had been threatened with arrest if he tried to help.

Two important secretaries, a treasurer and a monk-official were also killed; the three other Shap-pēs and my father's seven official servants were imprisoned. The servants needed bail but all our relatives were too frightened to help them. Then the Upper Tantric Monastery (Gyuto Dhatsang) gave their seal as security and the servants were released.

Few people know the truth about this plot of the War Department. Years later I was told that it may have been instigated by the Shap-pēs who were degraded when my father took office and later all became Shap-pēs again. Our family was often accused of liking foreigners very much, because we felt that it was necessary to be hospitable to all strangers; when I grew up it was said that we were too friendly with the British and the Americans. Samdup Tsering spoke Chinese fluently, but at that time there were many educated Tibetans who both spoke and wrote Chinese well. I believe the conspirators had him assassinated because they were afraid that he might take revenge against them. If Kalsang Lhawang, my younger brother, had not been an Incarnate Lama he would probably have been killed, too. All the Tibetans who knew the characters of my father and brother were very sorry about their cruel deaths.

A year later Mother brought us all back to Lhasa from Drepung. By then everyone was celebrating the end of His Holiness's exile, the chasing away of the Chinese and the declaration of Tibetan independence; it was very sad that my poor father did not have the pleasure of rejoicing after all his devoted service to his country. Yet the Dalai Lama remembered his loyalty and was most sympathetic towards my mother. During an audience he blessed her with his hands, though ladies are usually blessed with a silk tassel, and he allowed her to build a *mani* temple – called Tsarong Mani Lhakhang – near the main gate of Norbu Lingka. To pay for this my mother presented the Dalai Lama with some of our ornaments, but after many years His Holiness's private treasurer sent the Tsarong estate a big account, which was paid with great respect.

During his return journey from India, in 1913, the Dalai Lama waited for some time at Chokhor Yangtse, two days' ride from Lhasa, while his troops were completely wiping out the Chinese. His Holiness was accompanied by Tsawa Tritrul, a very learned Incarnate Lama who was one of his favourites. Tsawa Tritrul was the brother of Delek Rabten, my sister Norbu Yudon's husband; his sister, Rigzin Chodon, had been widowed the year before when Samdup Tsering was assassinated. At this time Chensal Namgang occasionally visited

Chokor Yangtse Monastery, to see His Holiness, and Rigzin Chodon also went there to visit her brother, to whom she was devoted.

Soon afterwards, Tsawa Tritrul wrote to my mother and the Tsarong servants, suggesting that they request His Holiness to let Chensal Namgang be married to Rigzin Chodon and take the Tsarong name. My brother, Kalsang Lhawang, was already a monk, and when a Tibetan family had no married son they could invite the bridegroom of their daughter – or daughters – to take the family name, as without one layman member to serve the government their estate might be claimed by relatives or the government might give it to a monastery or to any deserving cause. So Mother, supported by the servants of Tsarong House and our retainers on Tsarong Estate, accepted Tsawa Tritrul's suggestion. Thus Chensal Namgang came into our family and took the names Dasang Dadul Tsarong. From now on I will call him Tsarong.

In later years his enemies spread the rumour that Tsarong did not try to save the lives of my father and brother because he was plotting to take over their family. But we all trusted him and knew that he was not a schemer. He was then young, handsome, brave, honest, loyal and forthright – a strong personality already in a good position, and much liked by His Holiness. He had been given his own estate, Lhanga, as a reward for his valour at Chaksam Ferry, and though many ladies wished him to join their families fate brought him to our family through the influence of Tsawa Tritrul.

However, the Tsarong servants and retainers were not really satisfied, as Rigzin was not a Tsarong by blood. A few months after the marriage they requested my mother to arrange for Tsarong to take a second wife, by marrying one of her daughters, whichever he wished. (In Tibet the opinions of retainers counted for a lot. When they took an interest in important family affairs they held meetings to find out what the majority of their number wanted and sent a representative to convey their wishes to the family. Each estate had its own little school and most of the men could read and write.) Rigzin

Chodon was a charming, gentle lady and had no objection to this idea but her mother, the old lady of Delek Rabten, was very much against it because she thought it would damage her daughter's position. Despite this, Tsarong did take my eldest sister, Pema Dolkar, as his junior wife, and for many years she and Rigzin Chodon remained happily together at Tsarong House.

Rigzin Chodon had no children but she loved Pema Dolkar's children very dearly and they called her Ama Ayala, meaning step-mother. She was one of the finest people I have ever known, exceptionally kind and broadmined, well-read in religion, history and politics and remarkably good-looking. Being one year younger than Pema Dolkar she always paid her due respect since seniority, even by one year, was of great significance in Tibet. In ceremonies at Tsarong House, or when going out to official parties, she had to take the first seat as the senior *Lhacham* (Lady), but at home she was very sweet to Pema Dolkar and they dressed exactly the same, like twins, even to the colouring of their parasols. She was also devoted to my mother and took good care of Changchup Dolma and me, always remembering that we were the younger sisters of her first husband. Tsarong quite often lost his temper in his young days and then she would give him much valuable advice. At the age of about thirty-seven Rigzin Chodon became a nun and returned to her brother's remote estate, Lhuling, which was two weeks' ride from Lhasa.

At the time of Tsarong's first marriage his mother and sisters were the retainers of a family called Macha, but when he married Rigzin Chodon they were all presented to him by their owner – in writing, to avoid any future disputes about status – and so the whole family became nobility.

Tsarong gave a nice set of rooms to his mother, in one of our out-houses, and visited her often. Every New Year – usually on the third day, when all the official visiting had subsided – he would present her with a large sum of money. She used to say, 'You all have Chinese delicacies most of the time, so Mother will prepare a lovely Tibetan meal,' and she would produce the most delicious Tibetan delicacies, with about fourteen dishes, very good *chang* (beer) and tea, which would be served all day.

When Tsarong was a child his father died, but he had a step-father who was like a servant and cooked wonderfully — a nice quiet man. Tsarong's elder brother, Chola Dhondup Norbu La, became a trader and died of cancer at Gyantse on his way back from a trip to India. He was a shrewd man. After his death Tsarong helped his widow to educate the children.

3 Childhood in Lhasa

MY MOTHER WAS always in poor health after the deaths of my father and eldest brother but the religious teachings she constantly followed helped her in her sorrows and gave her much understanding of all living beings. Her ill health repeatedly disturbed her concentration, yet she always had the courage to meditate, read the scriptures and say her daily prayers.

When I was about six I had kidney trouble, my face and limbs became swollen and Mother called her doctor and nursed me herself. She put me by the window, wrapped in woolly blankets covered in green silk, and drew back the curtains so that the sun shone on me. Then she sat by me the whole day, telling me religious stories, and now and again she remarked that I would be lucky and devout. She gave me *tsampa* cooked in butter and sugar — a dish I loved — and let me play with her gold chain of tooth-picks and with her ear-cleaner, which had a beautiful jade ornament attached to it. This ornament got lost one day, but she did not search for it as she thought its loss might remove the evil interference from my life and help me to recover. Her loving care and the tender hands which she put on my head and against my cheek were such a bliss of comfort that I can remember it at the present moment. Gradually I got well and later the doctor told me how I used to say, with my hands folded, that it was through the goodness of the Lord Buddha, Mother and the doctor that I had recovered.

At that time Tsarong, Rigzen Chodon and Pema Dolkar were all living in the west wing of Tsarong House. One evening, when they were having tea, Rigzen Chodon had a colic and started to vomit. A moment later Pema Dolkar developed the same complaint, so the doctor was summoned and on his arrival given a cup of tea which he at once knew had been poisoned with aconite. My mother was called and everyone felt very surprised. The doctor said that if we children had had the tea we might have died, but luckily nobody was seriously harmed. The tea-cook was blamed, though the tea was always on a fire-pot in the corner of the hall, where anybody could have poisoned it, as buttered tea must be available right through the day for Tibetans because it is very bad manners not to offer it to every caller. His Holiness the thirteenth Dalai Lama advised Tsarong not to investigate, so all the gossip just subsided, but from that time onwards our tea on the fire-pot was always kept inside the living-room.

I loved my mother so much that I followed her everywhere like a dog until I was sent to school. She suffered greatly from constipation — owing to the heavy food she ate, I now think — and I used to wait for her a long time when she was in the lavatory. I made lavatory-paper for her by cutting into squares the paper we got from daphne bark, boring a hole for thread, which I also made from paper, and hanging it on the wooden screen around her lavatory. Any Tibetans who used lavatory-paper had to have it made in the home. I loved washing Mother's handkerchiefs, cleaning her silver spit-pot, handing over her religious objects when she was praying, lifting the door-curtains as she passed by, wrapping her cloaks around her and giving her milky tea in a lovely jade cup with a silver stand. I always put my forehead against hers, as Western people kiss, and gave her the cup with my two hands. She often teased me about my big head, saying, 'I prayed for a Mongolian-headed girl and it is you, my dear.' She had a big stone wrapped in red silk that made a noise, when shaken as though water were inside it and she once told me to pray to this gem for anything I wanted, as my wish would be granted. When I had prayed she asked me what I wanted and I replied, 'A silver coin'. She said, 'There you are, you can have your silver coin,' and she gave me one.

Most Tibetans sleep on beds about a foot high, made of mats stuffed with deer hair or straw, but I slept with my mother in a high, four-postered, canopied Chinese-type bed called a *dopi*, which had green silk covers and red frills. (Later this lovely green silk was utilised to make our blouses.) Sometimes I felt a little frightened when she snored, so I used to get up and kiss her and then she would stop snoring.

During these years my sister Tseten Dolkar often returned from her husband's home to live at Tsarong House and she used to play with me for hours every day. She was a tall, good-looking girl, with a very nice figure. At the age of sixteen she had married Horkhang *Dzasak*, the son of Horkhang *Shappē*, who, when accused of being pro-British at the time of the Younghusband Mission and imprisoned with his three *Kashag* colleagues, committed suicide. (The title *Dzasak* of Horkhang was similar to an English earldom and was one of the few hereditary Tibetan titles; the heir assumed it when he was old enough to be given a government post. Most Tibetan titles were conferred on individuals, for their lifetime, in recognition of personal achievements.) The Horkhang estate was large and Horkhang Dzasak was frank, generous and gay, though he read little. But Tseten Dolkar never loved him, so she often ran home. Her husband would then send her beautiful presents and beg her to come back to him, but she was always reluctant to do so. He used to pass Tsarong House nearly every day, on the way to his office, and sometimes my mother would look out and say, 'What a handsome person in passing!' Once

Tseten Dolkar looked – but when she saw Horkhang *Dzasak* she just threw herself face down on Mother's bed. However, she eventually went back to him and bore him two children.

In these days there were no public government schools in Lhasa. The two official schools were Tse School and Tsikhang, for young monks and laymen who were being trained as officials. Though all the lay government officials had to come from the aristocracy, monk-officials could be anybody, yet they always took precedence over their lay colleagues of equal rank and had the right to speak first; but sometimes they waived this privilege in favour of a layman of exceptional capability.

All the private day-schools in Lhasa were run by good and religious men who charged no fees but taught to gain merit. (Buddhists regard the providing of an education based on religion as very meritorious.) These schools accepted children from both noble and poor families and all were treated equally; a poor boy could become a monitor and beat the sons and daughters of the nobility, though complaints about the monitors could be reported to the master, who would investigate bullying and punish accordingly. There were about fifty private schools in Lhasa, each atended by seventy-five to a hundred boys and girls. Some students stayed at school for five years, some for only two or three years, depending on their ability. Boys and girls were taught the same subjects in the same way, but girls usually left school earlier because people felt that they did not need so much education as they were not going to serve the government – though many wives could influence their husbands on government work. If students chose to study further after leaving school they had to find their own teachers, either in one of the monasteries or among the officials, depending on the profession they wished to follow – medicine, astrology, art or trade. At that stage the most important subject was grammar, of which little was taught in the schools.

After requesting a schoolmaster to accept their child parents would select an auspicious day for the child to be admitted and prepare presents for the entry ceremony – which could be

My father in Kalon's *robes, September 1904.*

My mother and myself as a baby with maid servant. Photo taken by my father.

Street scene, Lhasa, showing old Tsarong House on the right. Photo: Ilia Tolstoy and Brooke Dolan.

Myself in 1923 as a schoolgirl in India.

My sisters, Tseten Dolkar (Horkhang) and Norbu Yudon Delarbten wearing Lhasa ladies' head-dresses of pearl and coral with jade and gold necklaces.
Photo: Colonel Leslie Weir.

On board a British warship in Calcutta in 1925, Tsarong, Dadul Namgyal and English friends.

elaborate or simple, according to the pupil's status The only essential equipment was a round mat to sit on, a wooden board, a bamboo pen, brown ink made from burnt barley and black ink made from soot.

When I was eight I went to Kyire Labtra school, where the master was Gendak Ugen La. Tsarong was already sheltering in our house a dozen boys – the sons of retainers – from Tsarong Estate and Lhanga Estate, who were going to the same school; one of the older ones, a son of the steward at Tsarong Estate, had already become a monitor. Some of these boys later became stewards, clerks, and traders.

On the day of admission children of the middle (traders') class and of the poor were brought to school by their parents, and children of the nobility by a senior servant. All wore their best clothes and the new student's family provided tea, and rice mixed with sugar, butter and raisins, for the whole school, including the master and his family. Usually the traders' rice was best as it had not been prepared by servants. The new student presented the master with an auspicious scarf and laid gifts on the floor of his room. The master then inaugurated the teaching by getting the child to repeat after him a beautiful prayer in praise of Jampal-Yang, the Lord of Wisdom, who is depicted with a book balanced on his left shoulder, holding aloft a sword in his right hand, to cut and root out people's ignorance. This prayer had to be memorised and said every day. It is very long, but the main verse is:

The impartiality of your love for all living beings,
Your voice like thunder waking up the sleep of the
    ignorant,
Your magic sword which cuts the root of all
    unhappiness;
From your loving knowledge, full of radiance,
Please light my dark ignorance with your sparkling
    light
To make me understand the teaching of Lord Buddha;
May you give me courage, and understanding of the
    great teaching.

Next the child sat close to the master, leaning his back to him, while the master auspiciously wrote out the complete alphabet, holding the child's fist in his; and for the next few days an older student did the same thing, until the child was able to write the letters properly by himself. (Clear hand-writing was considered very important for government work.) After the new pupil had read the alphabet once everybody enjoyed their feast and the school was given a day's holiday in honour of the occasion.

I was at school in Lhasa for five years. On my admission day the steward accompanied me and gifts were brought for the master and his family — a bag of rice, a bag of tea, two lengths of satin, of white silk and of red silk to make dresses, shirts and belts for the master and his wife, a hat for him, an apron for her, a scarf for each and one for the monitor. I went through the usual ceremonies and on the following day a lame girl was asked to help me practice writing. Being lame she leant all her weight on me, which was such a torture that for a long time I could not forget it. However, I learnt fast and was very happy, and Mother felt pleased to see me making good progress. Yet sometimes I was lazy and used to be beaten. Once I had not completed my writing exercise when suddenly the master's window was thrown open and we knew he was going to check our work before sending us to lunch. Each student had to show his writing and when my turn came I got hold of somebody else's good writing and showed this. The master looked me in the face and told me to continue writing after lunch. I was so frightened that I took my young sister and went to a relative's house and did not return to school, hoping that the master might forget about me. But next morning, when everybody was reading loudly, he called me and said that the most naughty daughter of the Tsarongs could not be controlled until she had been given a good thrashing. He called two boys to hold me down by the arms and legs, in the usual way, but I told him that I could take the whipping without being held and lay on the ground and pulled down my knickers. After four or five lashes I jumped up and ran home.

Some boys were sent to catch me, but I successfully hid from them in a baker's dark shop.

The children had to take it in turn to sweep the school daily, unless they avoided this duty by paying a small sum of money to all the other students. Only a few gave money, but noble children sent their servants to sweep. Some children always brought sweets and other titbits, which they shared with those who had none. Silence was strictly enforced, but if the master, his family and the monitor were all absent we became very mischievous. We attended school seven days a week and only had holidays on the fifteenth and the thirtieth of each month, on New Year's Day (in February or March), during the big religious festivals and during the week-long annual school picnic.

We were divided into two junior classes, who wrote on boards, and two senior classes who used paper. Tests were given twice a month, on the fourteenth and the twenty-ninth days. Marks and ranks were awarded by the master and we then stood in a line, according to our rank, and the boy with top marks hit all the other boys on their blown-out cheeks with a flat bamboo stick. The second boy hit all those below him – and so on. In a line of twenty students the last would receive nineteen slaps and this discipline made everyone work harder. The last in the class had to hit an empty tin to draw attention to his disgrace. Girls were slapped on the palms of their hands.

Occasionally I stayed at home instead of going to school and then my great protector was my father's sister, Yudon Nampon, who was known as Nampon *Mola* (grandmother) to everybody in Lhasa. She used to send a servant to the school with some sort of excuse and the master would respect her message. She was a tall, fat lady, gentle and religious, and I called her Nampon Ani La. (*Ani* means paternal aunt.) She never gossiped and had something good to say about everyone she knew. She was devoted to my mother, my sisters and Rigzin Chodon and had friends among the peasants, the traders and the nobles. As she had no children she adopted her cousin's son and her impartial love for her thirty-odd grand nephews and nieces won all their hearts. Whenever they had time these children would visit her and present gifts and although she had so many possessions we loved making clothes for her. I used to act a play single-handed in her room to make her laugh. She never once scolded me, but always praised me, and nearly every day she used to send her maid-servant to the school with dried apricots and dates and white sugar candy wrapped in green silk embroidered napkins. In later years we used to laugh together over my mischievous ways when I was a child.

School started at dawn and we were allowed home in the order in which we had come so some children came by moonlight and slept in the street, waiting for the door to be opened. The big, frightening dogs in the streets barked loudly at us but we noble children always had a servant accompanying us. After learning prayers of many kinds we memorised our tables, and the rules of grammar, astrology and medicine, before going home for our breakfast of *tsampa* dough with grated cheese and sugar, *thukpa* (thick soup) and sometimes boiled eggs, sometimes omelettes. On our return we practised writing, sitting cross-legged on the ground. Our wooden slabs were dusted with white chalk and ruled with a thread that had been pulled through a small woollen bag of chalk dust. At noon the roll-call was made and after lunch we again memorised rules until sunset.

Soon after I went to school Mother set out to visit the medical temple on Tsarong Estate, taking my younger sister with her because Changchup Dolma had not yet started school. A complete little fur outfit, lined with light green satin, was made for Changchup Dolma, and her small mule had a special child's saddle. It was sad for me to see Mother going and I envied my sister very much. Mother gave me sweets and silver coins and promised to bring back *chithang kotse* from Shigatze (this is a special Shigatze delicacy made of noodles fried in brown sugar) and *senchang* and *do-yo-ngarmo* (dried *chang* dough and sweetened fried wheat) from Tsarong Estate.

For this journey my mother had to wear her full ornamental

head-dress and robes, though she was riding a mule – it had two silken tassels under its chin because she was the *Lhacham* of a *Shap-pē*. She was attended by six servants, a cook and a steward to arrange for accommodation on the way. A small caravan of mules carried her bedding, clothes-boxes and food.

During the leaving-ceremony in the chapel the whole household offered her scarves to say 'good-bye and best wishes'. After the auspicious tea and rice had been served there was an early lunch of *shethuk* (noodles) to wish her a happy return home and that she might find everybody in good health. (*Thuk* means 'meet' and for this reason *shethuk* is always served before a departure.) Then she went to the chapel of our deity protectors, Palden Lhamo and Chugyu Gyalpo. (One monk was paid to attend constantly on these deities and make offerings to them and whenever the family were in trouble they sought the deities' advice by lottery. Rigzin Chodon told me that while my father was negotiating with the Chinese the attendant monk and the senior servants held a lottery and twice the deities advised that my father should go to India; but he would not heed this advice.)

On the way to Tsarong my mother was received in Shigatze by the Panchen Lama with the same honours as he would have accorded to a *Shap-pē*. At Delek Rabten she stayed with my sister Norbu Yudon, and after visiting Tsarong Estate she went on to Sakya, where the Sakya Lama received her very kindly. He suggested that she should take care of one of the *dumo* (she demons) of Sakya, who would then be her protective escort on her many journeys. So she took care of Hrikyila and was given a small mask of this *dumo* and instructions on how to feed her by burning *tsampa* and herbs. The Sakya Lama considered that my mother had enough religious power to control Hrikyila. There were many *dumos* at Sakya in a special temple – sometimes they are called *khandoma*, which means 'angel' and is a more polite way of referring to them. They were souls of women who had died in anger and had gone to Sakya, as only the Sakya Lama could control them; under this guidance some of them gradually became enlightened and purified. One friend of ours from Nanghatse was at Sakya after her death. All the *dumo* had their own images, decorated with their personal ornaments sent from home, and they were strictly confined by order of the Sakya Lama; but sometimes they were disobedient and went to Lhasa or other places and he was requested to call them back. They became a bit frightening when they were not under discipline.

Mother brough the mask of Hrikyila back to Tsarong House in a small silver charm-box. She spent the last night of her journey at Gyatso, a few miles outside Lhasa, with my sister Pema Dolkar and Tsarong. (At that time Tsarong sometimes moved to Gyatso, while working in the government mint.) Next morning Tsarong asked her what she had in her charm-box, which had a picture of Palden Lhamo on the front. He opened it and saw the frightful looking mask. Pema Dolkar then said that during that night she had dreamed that she was feeding her baby daughter at the breast – but the baby had the face of the mask. So Mother explained that she had taken Hrikyila as her escort only on the advice of the Sakya Lama.

When mother returned to Tsarong House Hrikyila was always in the small hall. She was fed by a mixture of burning flour in front of her mask and everybody was a little frightened of her, but nobody liked to ask Mother to return her to Sakya.

4 My Mother's Death

WHEN I WAS ten years old an agonising colic made my mother very ill. Her doctor got hold of two big black beetles, killed them by pressing them under the spit-pot, broke off their limbs, rolled them up in butter and gave them to my mother to make her vomit. I was looking on and she did vomit and brought up the bugs which floated in the basin. When she saw them she was very sorry that the doctor had taken their lives to relieve her pain but after saying special prayers for the poor beetles she felt a little better.

That year, when the officials' summer changing-dress ceremony was approaching – it always took place in the presence of His Holiness on the eighth day of the third month and was one of the occasions when new officials were appointed – Tsarong decided that Kalsang Lhawang, my lama brother, should join the government service as a monk-official. He was the only true heir of Tsarong and though he was not a steady young man it was hoped that he would be like his father when he grew older. On such important occasions families invited a capable relative or friend to arrange everythings and preparations were made for two groups of high officials to attend the ceremony – one to accompany Tsarong as Commander-in-Chief and the other my brother as a new government official. Both men also had an escort of about fifteen mounted servants and were wearing their best ceremonial winter dress, but on reaching Norbu Lingka they changed into their summer clothes, which were carried there by the servants.

The high officials' winter hats were made of black fox fur, their summer hats were of brocade. Their fur-lined winter robes were edged with strips of otter skin, about an half an inch wide, but their lighter summer robes had no edging. The Lhasa climate was quite cold in winter – though not so cold as some Europeans imaging – very hot in summer, and moderate in spring and autumn. During winter both men and women of all classes wore fur-lined dresses; lambskin was the most popular because it was inexpensive but those who could afford fancy furs used lynx, fox or rabbit. In summer women wore light sleeveless dresses, in spring and autumn padded dresses of tweed or serge and in winter the same with long-sleeved bouses. Our blouses were always brightly coloured and we wore aprons with narrow brilliant stripes of many colours and brocade around the sides. Our shoes of red boardcloth were beautifully embroidered with flowers and we wore tweed leggings, held up by garters, under our long robes. The men's robes were equally long, but most laymen tucked them up to knee length – only the officials had to wear them at ankle length. The officials' high boots were embroidered with blue and white silk stitching. Officials above the fourth rank wore red boots; junior officials wore brown boots.

When Tsarong and my brother left the house that day at about nine o'clock Mother, who was then convalescent, was up and dressed in her best. I remember well that she had on a dark green satin dress with a red silk blouse and her full headdress of pearls and corals. She took a little stroll on the terrace, with the aid of a walking-stick, and told me that she was glad she hadn't died and left two young daughters without a mother. I, as usual, was holding her hand and simply taking her loving words deep into my heart.

Then she went back to bed; my two aunts were with her – her own sister and my father's sister. Changchup Dolma and I and the other children of the household had been given a day off school and I went to play in the kitchen on the middle floor. Many relatives and friends were in the house, waiting to congratulate my brother on his appointment, and the cooks were busy preparing special meals. The maid-servants were wearing their full head-dresses, with ear-rings dangling down to their breasts. At about three o'clock in the afternoon, as I was having a cushion made for a game of *sho* (dice), I noticed much hustle and bustle of servants hurrying up and down stairs carrying fire in small pots for burning incense. All were looking worried and I began to wonder what was happening. I went to Mother's room to ask what all the fuss was about and to my great distress saw her breathing her last. I ran forward to grasp her but the relatives hurried me away and I never saw my beloved mother again. Changchup Dolma and I were at once taken to an aunt's house because Tibetans do not like a dying woman to hear the cries of her children, which may cause her great disturbance. Mother had been practising how to release her soul from her body, as the method by which this is done influences the next incarnation, but any disturbance by an earthly attachment might have prevented her from achieving the reincarnation for which she was aiming.

When Tsarong and my brother were informed they returned in great grief. Kalsang Lhawang wept bitterly and the whole household was tumbled into sorrow. The visitors who had been waiting happily with gifts and scarves were diverted to mourning and their congratulation turned to condolences.

Mother had died of a heart attack; she was then forty-eight. Pema Dolkar often told me of a dream Mother had when she was staying at Drepung Monastery just before my father's death. She dreamed of a lady dressed in green, and adorned with all her ornaments, falling dead on a bed. This dream, it was said, depicted the death of my mother to herself.

All the friends of the family helped with the funeral arrangements, as was customary, and joined in the performance of rites, making offerings and giving alms to the poor to gain merit for the deceased. An astrologer was consulted about how long the body should be kept in the home; this may be for two or three days, or even longer. Our custom is to leave the deceased untouched, in great peace, until a very holy lama has relieved the spirit of the body. When oozings are seen coming from the nose and mouth this indicates that the spirit has finally escaped and then the body is washed in medicinal herbs and spices, wrapped in white muslin, dressed in the deceased's best clothes, with a head-dress of five paintings of deities, and made to sit in the lotus position on a seat surrounded by a screen in one of the chief rooms of the house. Hundreds of butter-lamps are burned in this room; friends and relatives present butter for them and offer scarves and prostrate themselves before the body as a mark of homage. Lamas are invited to pray, the number depending on the status of the deceased, and they attend on the body, day and night, until the funeral takes place.

In Tibet, messages were sent to all the local monasteries on the day before a funeral, requesting them to burn lamps and offer incense for the benefit of the deceased. This ceremony was organised by friends who contributed money and butter; the butter was melted in large cauldrons and early in the morning, on the day before the departure of the body, many servants took small buckets of butter-oil to the monasteries and temples. They also took as offerings the belongings of the deceased – mainly clothes, which had been packed and labelled – to be distributed to as many lamas as possible, even up to a thousand. It was considered very important to send all the deceased's clothes to the lamas, who put them in front of the butter-lamps and prayed for their owner. These lamas then instructed the family to paint or build images of the Lord Buddha or one of the deities, according to their visions or predictions. Any jewellery the deceased had left might be sold to make special offerings, or distributed among the children, or kept as an heirloom; unless a will had been made the senior member of the family had the discretion to do what he thought best. (Lamas usually made wills, but few lay people did so. Mother's ornaments were divided between me and Changchup Dolma.)

Mother had wished to be cremated at Ratsak Temple, which belonged to her family, but her wish was not granted and this is one of my greatest regrets. In Tibet those who died during epidemics were buried, but the majority of the dead were given to the vultures and as a rule only lamas were cremated. After Mother's death the family were too upset to arrange anything and our friends just followed the usual custom. When the astrologer gave the exact date and hour for the disposal the servants carried the body to Ratsak. The procession was led for a short distance beyond the house by Pema Dolkar, as at least one member of the family must do this duty.

It is something terrible to see a corpse being given to the vultures; when I was grown up I once witnessed this ceremony. Early one morning I went with some friends to a place in Lhasa, near Sera Monastery, where the bodies of three ordinary people, which had been carried from their homes on the backs of friends, were placed on a huge slab of rock. (Relatives never attended this ceremony, but sent friends to represent them.) The six men who were to cut up the bodies sat by the rock and drank *chang* before uncovering one of the bodies and laying it flat on the slab, face downwards. About twelve yards away hundreds of vultures were waiting; these well-disciplined birds do not move until summoned. The limbs were then cut off and the hair pulled away to be burnt later; it came off very easily, leaving the skull all white. When the intestines had been taken out and hidden the vultures were summoned and while they were eating the men pulled out their big white tail feathers to make shuttlecocks for children to play with. The birds were then told to retreat and wait. After a while they were again summoned and allowed to finish the remainder of the body. Finally the bones were crushed and mashed up with the brains and intestines as it is essential that not a single speck of the body should remain. After their hard work the men again sat down to drink and eat, without even washing their hands.

Witnessing this rite was a dreadful experience for me. Yet I had been anxious to see it as watching such a thing is considered very beneficial to our spiritual development. No matter how happy and successful we are we become corpses eventually and some Tibetans keep a skeleton in their home as a reminder that we all must die. When we think of dying we feel less ambitious. For days afterwards I could not eat and I did not touch meat for nearly a month as the recollection of what I had seen was so awful. For a few days I had pains in all my joints and could not comb my hair because my scalp was so sensitive.

All this relates to the disposal of a poor person. For people of status there was a great ceremony, many lamas were invited to pray and the corposes were taken to a more remote and secluded site on a higher mountain.

For seven weeks after a death food is served as usual in the living-room of the deceased and prayers are offered in the house by whichever very holy lama officiated before the funeral. If the deceased was a man special rites take place every seventh day, if a woman, every sixth day. We believe that after forty-nine days the majority of people have been reincarnated but very holy people may be reincarnated sooner or very sinful people later. The images or paintings made to gain merit for the deceased must be finished before the forty-ninth day. After two or three weeks, according to the astrologers' calculations, the family have to wash their hair and bathe themselves; friends or relatives present the toilet requisities and new sets for hair-dressing, such as tassels and wigs. Even the banners and prayer-flags of the house have to be changed, but all these expenses are borne by friends, who in their turn receive similar help. The official mourning period is over on the forty-ninth day and a year later the anniversary of the death is celebrated by friends coming to offer scarves.

In Tibet, everything was done alike for rich and poor. Families were usually eager to spend all the deceased's possessions on these ceremonies and sometimes it was necessary to restrain the relatives from being too extravagant in their grief. Then kind friends would advise them, to save debts and troubles afterwards; some people were well known for their ability to help the bereaved in such circumstances. The workers' guilds had their own arrangement committees who organised the ceremonies and parties after a bereavement – and also on happy occasions, to celebrate births or weddings. These committees accumulated funds to be spend on the very poor.

After Mother's death the astrologers claimed that her end had been hastened because she had placed an inferior spirit — Hrikyila — on a level with her own protective deities. When I heard this I got very angry with the she-demon and, assisted by the school-boys who lived at Tsarong House, I went to Mother's empty rooms with a stick in my hand. Hrikyila's mask was still there and the boys and I called to her to get out of the place. The atmosphere was no longer frightening, as it had been during Mother's life-time when one could feel that there was something in the house and the maid-servants complained of being pushed without seeing anyone.

One night before Mother died Rigzin Chodon had an unpleasant experience. Her huge double bed — imported from India — was beside a wide glazed window, without a balcony, and when she woke after a disturbing dream she saw a woman gazing at her from outside the second floor room, leaning her forehead against the window-pane. She looked carefully to make sure that it was a reality, not a dream, and knew that indeed she was seeing, through the darkness, a Tibetan woman wearing a head-dress. She felt very much afraid, thinking that the apparition could only be Mother's she-demon, yet as she was alone she feared to shout in case Hrikyila might show her most frightening aspect. So she went far under the bedclothes and sweated with terror and said her prayers for a while. In those days many ladies slept with their wigs on and she felt very uncomfortable. (By about 1930 lighter wigs, which could be taken off every night, had become fashionable.) When she slowly looked out the woman was still there, in the same position, but at last she heard a cock crowing and remembered that her uncle, an Incarnate Lama, had told her that all devils and demons disappear at the first cock crow. Again she put out her head — and the woman had gone. She did not dare ask for the she-demon to be sent away, because my Mother was spiritually controlling Hrikyila. But after Mother's death

Tsarong invited another Sakya Lama to the house and asked him to take the mask back to Sakya. As the frightening atmosphere was no longer in the house, we knew that Hrikyila herself had already returned to her temple.

After mother's death I was brought up by my sister-in-law, Rigzin Chodon. I was a tom-boy and loved playing boys' games and wearing boys' clothes, which Rigzin Chodon gave me. I particularly wanted to be a little Khampa boy, so I wore a white Bure Khampa dress, a pair of Kongpo boots, a felt hat and a little dagger. Nobody recognised me as a girl and at parties people called me *Sekusho* (Prince). Among my school-mates were Surkhang *Shap-pē*, Phala *Shap-pē*, Neshar *Shap-pē*, Yuthok Lhacham, Kundeling *Shap-pē* and Surkhang *Dapon* — and they all still tease me about my Khampa outfit.

As we were now orphans I had to assert myself on my own and Changchup Dolma's behalf. Tsarong's steward controlled the household food and gave us badly cooked meals — such as omelette fried in rancid butter — like the meals that were being served to the craftsmen employed by the family. Once I threw the whole tray through the window into the courtyard and it nearly hit a servant on the head. Everybody thought that I had a very bad temper, yet it was only by behaving like this that I could get the things we needed. The tea sent to our school every morning was not well made. When we compared it with our friends' tea, by churning it in our cups to make butter, ours came out black while theirs came out creamy-looking, because having parents still alive they were well cared for. I used to get very angry about this and go home and fight with the steward, telling him to prove that we were not the children of the late Tsarong *Shap-pē*. I threatened that if our tea were not improved I would take my little sister by the hand and go to beg from our relatives. Then the steward feared disgrace, so we got much better tea and no more omelette with rancid butter.

In Tibetan noble households buttered tea was served early each morning and many people ate with it *tsampa* and grated cheese. Tibetan adults took two big meals daily, at about nine o'clock in the morning and five o'clock in the evening, and something light at bedtime, or tea only. For the morning meal everybody had *tsampa* dough and in noble households four or five different dishes, including dried meat and sweet cheese. The evening meal was the main one, consisting of rice or *tsampa*, with two or three dishes of meat and vegetables such as potatoes, radishes, cabbages or carrots. Since 1930 cauliflowers and tomatoes were also grown in Lhasa. Relatives and intimate friends stayed to meals whenever they liked and could ask for anything, and dishes of various kinds of sweets were always ready to be offered to visitors with their tea.

In the city houses of noblemen there were fifteen to twenty servants, according to the size of the family — one steward, one cook, one tea-maker, a few *chang*-girls (to brew and serve beer), two syces, one water carrier, one sweeper, half a dozen maid-servants and, if the house had a garden, one or two gardeners. People who were not wealthy had only two or three servants, who got no pay but worked and ate together with the family.

All government officials had to keep at least four horses. Those who had estates near Lhasa and could get regular supplies of their own food and fodder found it easy to keep many servants and horses; otherwise it was very expensive and some nobles got heavily into debt.

At this period Pema Dolkar lived at Gyatso and Rigzin Chodon spent most of her time on the country estates, so at Tsarong House everything was in the hands of the servants. But our aunts regularly invited us to their homes and sent us sweets and old friends of our parents often gave us money when we met them. This was very useful, as I sometimes got into debt. On the way to school there was a baker's shop run by a few Khampa women and the eldest, Nya Adon, made delicious pastries cooked in oil and stuffed with brown sugar. All the children bought these and they were my favourite delicacy. Usually I got them on credit, making a mark on the wall. Then I worried about having no money and longed to meet Detuk *Dzasa*, a kind monk-official who had been a friend of my father's and lived near the school. He always gave me two or three white *tamkas* when we met. (The *tamka* was then worth about ninepence.) If I got too heavily into debt I used to go to school by a round-about way to avoid Nya Adon's shop; she was so good that she never asked for the money, but I felt terrible when I could not pay her. We got two *tamkas* a day for pocket-money but some of that had to be spent on ink and paper. However, I made extra money by selling home-made readers to those who had none. I used to get hold of notes sent to Pema Dolkar by Rigzin Chodon and copy them many times on to sheets of paper: 'Dear Sister, I am sending two bricks of tea and a cake of butter, twenty bundles of *phing* (noodles), one packet of matches, two packets of candles, six cakes of soap, by Polala. Kindly accept and acknowledge. With much love and respect from Rigzin Chodon. Sent from Lhasa house.' Nobody ever made any comment, though numbers of students were reading aloud from these stupid readers – all with the same wording. I sold them for one *shokhang* each and made a profit of three *shokhangs* on one *shokhang*'s worth of paper.

One day my money worries were temporarily ended when the city magistrate, Mepon Gonthangpa – my father's brother – came to see me in his full uniform. He took off his hat in salute and gave me a packet of three *sangs* (thirty *tamkas*) and a basket of peaches. I was thrilled, but I burst out laughing because though he was seriously paying his respects to me, as my father's daughter, I felt that he must be joking. Later I was able to repay his kindness by helping a foolish son of his who was so stupid that when he wrote a love-letter to his girl-friend he called her 'Your Excellency'.

Even after he became a monk-official Kalsang Lhawang remained a worry to the family. He was about ten years my senior and once, when I was ten, he got me into trouble by taking me to a dance drama when the family was in mourning after the death of the Duke of Lhalu, who belonged to the house of the twelfth Dalai Lama and was a good friend of Tsarong's. That evening Tsarong heard that we had been to the drama and was very angry. He sent for me and asked if I had

His Holiness the 13th Dalai Lama. Photo: Colonel Leslie Weir.

The steps of the Potala Palace where my father was dragged from his office and killed in 1912. Photo: Colonel Leslie Weir.

The new Tsarong House in Lhasa, built in 1923.
Photo: Colonel Leslie Weir.

The dining-room at Tsarong House, myself with Pema Dolkar and Tsarong Dasang Dadul.

been there and I said, 'Yes, Kalsang Lhawang took me.' Then Tsarong caught me by the ears, put my head between his knees and thrashed me on the bottom. Pema Dolkar was shocked and told him that I should not have been beaten because I was only a child and I had been taken there by a grown-up. Tsarong also wanted to beat Kalsang Lhawang but as he had run away he escaped his punishment. Tsarong's quick temper always died down soon.

Kalsang Lhawang was tall – about five foot nine inches – and handsome, though heavily pock-marked. He was kind and polite, gay and lovable – and a true lama in the sense that he had no attachment to wealth. As a reincarnation of a lama of Drepung, he had been taken at the age of four to the monastery, where his strict tutor beat him so much that he made little progress with his studies. (All Incarnate Lamas get a certain amount of beating. Even the Dalai Lamas are thrashed by their tutors, who first have to prostrate three times before their pupils.) As a boy my brother came home only for the annual Monlam Festival, when he was treated with great respect and given his meals on a separate tray. But Mother visited him every few weeks.

Kalsang Lhawang was twenty when Tsarong decided that he should become a monk-official and return to live at Tsarong House. Usually Incarnate Lamas did not become officials or live outside their monasteries; but Tsarong hoped that having a government post might steady Kalsang Lhawang.

Like our father, my brother was a fine musician and played the banjo very well. He also had a good singing voice and composed many popular songs; one of them – 'Kalsang Lhawangla' – is still sung by Tibetans. Sometimes his satirical words hurt certain high officials, but in Tibet such songs were the equivalent of the 'free press' of other countries and nobody censured him. Being absolutely carefree he invited his young monk-official friends to his flat every day and night and had great fun with them. Some of those friends played the fiddle and the flute beautifully and often Changchup Dolma and I were kept awake by their music and the noise of their tap-dancing on the boards. This angered me, because we had to get up so early for school, but we were not allowed to go to the flat. Whenever I got annoyed and made a fuss everybody felt a bit scared because I was so quick-tempered, and my brother would then buy us anything we asked for—such as new brocade hats.

During the reign of His Holiness the thirteenth Dalai Lama the tea service for monk-officials was held daily just before sunset. Lay officials were invited only on special occasions, but all the monk-officials had to attend regularly at Norbu Lingka, where they were seated in order of seniority and given three cups of delicious tea and sometimes rice or pastries. A roll-call was held and absentees were fined or dismissed unless they had some good excuse. When going to such ceremonies, an official had to appear outside his residence in the costume of his rank, with the correct number of mounted servants. Most officials rode between their houses and their offices, but those who lived very near walked and those who could not afford to keep ponies wrapped up their uniforms and put them on outside their office door. When two mounted parties met it was customary for the junior to dismount and wait, hat in hand, until his senior had passed by. Equals remained mounted and, as they passed, each courteously waved the other on his way. My brother was very fond of ponies and kept lovely ambling horses.

For some time after his appointment Kalsang Lhawang had no special job and continued to enjoy himself, so Tsarong thought that if he had some big responsibility it might make him take more interest in work and he asked for Kalsang Lhawang to be given the most unpopular job of *Tsamshepa*. During the annual Great Prayer Festival the *Tsamshepa* had to pay twenty thousand monks a copper coin each every day for three weeks. To raise this money a tax had to be collected, but the *Tsamshepa* was given a good estate on lease at a low rent for three years as a reward for his hard work— which was very important, as the monks had to be paid without fail. The two head monks of Drepung Monastery had the authority to penalise the *Tsamshepa* however they chose if he did not do his job properly. Kalsang Lhawang knew all this, yet he gambled away most of the money that had been collected and only the faithfulness of his servants saved him from being penalised for they lent him what was necessary. My brother's best work was composing songs and enjoying himself.

After this, Tsarong tried another method to improve Kalsang Lhawang, by putting him in the office of His Holiness's Private Secretary — a nice understanding man — where he thought my brother would have to reform. The Dalai Lama gave his permission and a day was fixed for Kalsang Lhawang to begin this new job. That morning Tsarong was ready to take him to Norbu Lingka, but my brother was not at home. Servants were at once sent to search for him and he was found in the bed of a bad girl called Chinchang. The poor girl was imprisoned for having entertained a monk-offical, who was supposed to be celibate, and my brother was also locked up for a while. Tsarong gave him a beating, which I witnessed, and I felt sad and cried because I thought it was all owing to our having lost our parents so early. At once a report was made to His Holiness that Kalsang Lhawang was no more a monk-official as he had broken his vow of celibacy.

Everybody then thought very hard and when I was about twelve a marriage was arranged between Kalsang Lhawang and Tsarong's niece, Tsewang Dolma — a nice, tall, pretty girl. After the wedding Kalsang Lhawang decided that he wished to be a police officer; when this was permitted he felt very pleased with himself in his fine uniform, but about a year later he said that he did not like the job and stepped out. Then he announced that he wished to do some trading, so Tsarong gave him twenty thousand rupees as capital and he left for India. I believe he started to enjoy himself in Yatung and Kalimpong and after two months he came back with a few steel trunks full of rubbishy goods worth only about five thousand rupees. The rest of the money he had squandered. He was so fond of gambling and drinking that he also sold a number of his wife's ornaments.

In 1910 Powo Kanam Gyalpo, the chief of Poyul in south-
eastern Tibet, successfully resisted the Chinese invasion. He
then became too ambitious, refused to pay the customary
small taxes to the Tibetan government and prevented Tibetan
officials from entering his territory. The people of Poyul made
very fine hand-woven woollen cloth and traded – in Lhasa and
elsewhere – with rice, chillies, vegetable dyes, musks and the
skins of deer and fox. Tsarong wanted a peaceful settlement of
their dispute, to benefit everybody, so when these difficulties
had been going on for nearly ten years he decided that it might
help to give his sister, Tsering Dolma, in marriage to the ugly-
looking chief of Poyul. Everybody thought him very cruel to
do this, as the Poyul people are like tribesmen. I felt terribly
sorry for Tsering Dolma because she had always been so kind
to me, though I was only a child and she was nine years my
senior. She could have refused to marry the chief, but all
Tsarong's family were well satisfied with their promotion and
his brothers and sisters worshipped him like a god and would
never oppose his plans.

When the bridal party of Powo came to Lhasa they looked
most fearful, with hair hanging long over their shoulders,
tweed cloaks and hats, high Khampa boots and long daggers
on their waists. While they were staying at Tsarong House, the
schoolboys and I often made fun of them by saying, 'We are
the followers of Powo Kanam Gyalpo – if we don't use this
place [the garden] for a lavatory, where else to do our big
business?' Tsarong sent his brother Kyenrab to lead the bridal
party out of Lhasa and it was very sad to see Tsering Dolma
going off to Poyul.

Soon Tsarong advised his sister to persuade her husband to
come to Lhasa and request the government to take over his
territory and give him a substitute estate, such as an ordinary
nobleman would have, and the title of *Dzasa* or *Theji*. I
remember Kanam Gyalpo, Tsering Dolma and their attendants
coming to stay at our house, to discuss Tsarong's plan, but the
government thought that Powo Gyalpo was just a small man,
who could be put down any time, so they did not follow
Tsarong's advice and had a lot of trouble later on.

5 Schooldays in Darjeeling

BEFORE MOTHER DIED I used to tell her that I wished to go to the place where oranges are grown. She replied that that place is India and to get there one must cross a great snow pass, like a wizard's home, so I should not speak of going because the difficult journey could not be tolerated by children.

In 1920 Sir Charles Bell, the Political Officer for Sikkim and a close friend of the thirteenth Dalai Lama, came to Lhasa to visit His Holiness. Since Sikkim had been a protectorate of Britain for many years a Political Officer resided there and the Sikkim State consulted with him on every important matter. This officer also dealt with the government of Tibet on Britain's behalf and the Dalai Lama often invited him to Lhasa to discuss trade and any favour to be requested from Britain. Britain always had the policy to keep a good relationship with the Tibetan government and the friendship between the two countries was being strengthened each year until the British left India.

Sir Charles was accompanied by Mr. David MacDonald, the British Trade Agent at Yatung and Gyantse, who had accompanied the Younghusband Expedition to Lhasa and was very popular in Tibet. A luncheon party was given for the two men at Tsarong House and Changchup Dolma and I were thrilled to see Sir Charles who was said to have a red face, golden hair and a nose like a kettle spout. He was the first European we had ever seen and everybody peeped at him from every direction, whispering and giggling. His cook came ahead of him to prepare a chicken, because his health did not allow him to eat Tibetan food. This cook also made some buns which we were dying to eat, but until the party was over nobody would give us one. Mr. MacDonald's mother was Sikkimese, so he looked like a Tibetan gentleman with his moustache sticking up at both ends. He spoke fluent Tibetan and during the party left the dining-room and spent a long time playing with my sister and me. He gave us money and repeatedly said, 'You two should come to India and go to the English school in Darjeeling with my daughters.' Changchup Dolma was very shy but I asked many questions. I asked if we could get oranges and nice English biscuits and chocolates in Darjeeling, and he assured us that we could get even more than we mentioned. (At that time Tsarong was trying to stabilise Tibet's economy by dealing in gold with India to build up a national reserve.) When Changchup Dolma and I were small he was very fond of us and we were sometimes given Huntley and Palmer's biscuits and 'King George' chocolates that had been brought from India by Nepalese gold traders and presented to him.)

About a year after Sir Charles Bell and Mr. MacDonald had left Lhasa Changchup Dolma and I were asked if we would like to go to Darjeeling. Changchup Dolma took no interest in the idea but as I was most anxious to go I was told that I would be sent away to school in the following autumn. Mother's friends thought that I was just being sent as an experiment because both my parents were dead. I was very excited and at once went to school and told my news to the other children, who were most surprised.

All the preparations were made by Rigzin Chodon and I started to copy down English letters from empty biscuit tins and chocolate boxes to show off to my friends that I knew how to write English even before going to Darjeeling. I told Rigzin Chodon that I would like to ride a horse, not a mule, because only very good mules travel fast and they are much meaner than horses. When a rider is thrown a mule will kick him several times before running away. All was arranged as I requested and when the day came my things were packed and among my four menservants was Nyerpa Dorje, who had been my eldest brother's servant. That morning I did feel sad. I cried and as an excuse for crying pretended that I did not want to take my maid-servant with me, so she followed just behind and caught up with me at the end of the first stage.

It took us about three weeks to reach Yatung, near the Sikkimese border, where I was to stay with the MacDonalds until their daughters returned to school after the winter vacation. I felt very happy on my white horse with its Mongolian silver saddle and one silk tassel under its chin to show that I was the child of a noble family.

The first day we rode fifteen miles to Nethang, where we stopped in a village house. Every evening as soon as we got to our destination Nyerpa Wangyal brought out from Bhutanese baskets the food that had been prepared for my journey – *khabse* (pastries), sweets and many other delicacies of Tibet, including *bhuram garma*, our famous butter toffee made with brown sugar. Whenever we travelled all the best things were packed for us.

My evening food was dried noodles, dried yak-meat, boiled tongue and mutton, followed by salt buttered tea or sweet tea, whichever I preferred. My maid-servant sat by me and we ate together while the other servants ate out-side. Nyerpa Wangyal's arrangements for accommodation and food were wonderful. Whenever anybody in the family travelled he went too, so he was well used to doing this job. He had been my father's personal servant and was most faithful.

Every morning we had to start before sunrise to reach our destination not later than four o'clock. We spent the nights in villages, where we could find food, fodder and shelter. Being autumn this journey was very pleasant. After giving us our morning tea Nyerpa Wangyal would ride quickly ahead to prepare morning food at some suitable spot, which we usually reached at about ten o'clock. Wangyal would have put mats and a table in a sunny place and he served us with tea, *tsampa*, eggs, boiled meat and tongue. The riding ponies would have their bridles taken off and get good fodder. After an hour Wangyal again rode ahead and we followed. Each day we rode between twenty and twenty-five miles, according to the stages.

On the third day we crossed the Kyichu River in hide boats. At this season the water is deep so the animals had to swim across; their saddles and loads were taken off and put in the boats. The strong animals swam easily but the weak ones were roped and led across by men in boats. Otherwise the fast current might have carried them right away down the river, which would have made it very difficult for us to fetch them. It was so sweet to see the mules swimming bravely across on their own.

Next morning we crossed the very high Nyapsola pass, which took us five hours; it was too steep for anyone to ride over so Wangyal carried me on his back. (As a child I was rather lazy about walking and often had to be carried up and down the steps of Tsarong House. The water carrier used to wait at the gate and take me up the two long staircases on my return from school.) From the pass itself we overlooked the beautiful lake of Yamdok, so wide and peaceful, and lonely snow mountains could be seen far off against the blue sky. That night we stayed at the village of Pede, which stands by the lake, and in many places we saw peasants working hard in their fields, singing while they worked. Often we were able to buy peaches and walnuts in the villages.

A few days later we crossed the lonely Kharola pass. Even in its valley of glaciers there was a travellers' hut, where one could buy fodder, and in this shelter we had our morning food – noodles in soup, with powdered yak-meat. The weather was so sunny that we had a very pleasant ride, even through such a bitterly cold place. We spent that night at Ralung, a small, isolated village where we did not get good accommodation but only very smoky huts.

The next stage – Gapshi – was still more lonely, with black rocks hanging over the village and a dark river running by. In this region all the men-servants kept their guns handy to protect us from robbers. We had often heard stories of robberies around Ralung and Gapshi, so we felt afraid. Yet during all the many journeys I and my family made over this trade route to India nothing ever happened.

On the following day we reached Gyantse, where we spent three days on the lovely estate that Nyerpa Namgyal, one of our senior servants, leased from Drepung Monastery. (The servants of most Tibetan officials were well-off and worked for themselves while their masters served the government.) This pause was to rest the animals, who enjoyed themselves very much here. Namgyal entertained us with the best of everything and I enjoyed listening to the servants' stories or watching them playing *sho* in the park. While we were sitting around I once asked Nyerpa Namgyal about how my father had been killed, but he said, 'Dear, do not ask these things – forget them. There won't be another man like your father.'

From Gyantse we rode across the plains of Phari for five days and I tried to chase the wild asses and other animals such as gazelles. It was impossible to get near them, but I liked riding about. The servants used to say, 'We'll never get to our destination if we don't travel straight – and besides your poor pony may get sores on its back if you go galloping here and there.' Sometimes, I listened, sometimes I got angry and dismounted to play on the ground. The poor servants had a tough time with me.

Here, between the British Trade Agencies of Gyantse and Yatung, there were comfortable British rest houses but I was still taken to rented rooms in villagers' homes as the servants preferred this accommodation. It was so warm in the sun on the plain that I imagined we were nearly in India and told the servants that I was going to cut off my little pig-tails and remove my turquoise ear-rings. They said I was not to do so, as they had no orders from home to allow such things. This made me very angry and I went outside and played by the mountain and did not come in time for food. Next morning I made a fuss and would not get up in time, but nobody ever tried to scold me, as I was quite a child for defending myself. At the first word of a scolding I would say, 'You all bully us because we have no parents!' so everybody was afraid of me. When I saw the small dak bungalows at Khangmar I thought we were surely on the border of India and pretended to produce coloured drinks by filling empty Eno's Fruit Salt bottles with water and dissolving orange, red and green barley-sugar, that I had begged from Rigzin Chodon, in different bottles. This made me feel that I had already achieved some education.

Near the edge of the Phari plains we saw far off a man in a red jacket riding towards us. He turned out to be a servant from the British Trade Agency who told us that the Mac-Donalds were at the nearby Khambu hot springs but would be back soon to take me down to Chumbi valley. I felt happy and quite excited and after two days we reached the town of Phari and put up at the house of a family friend. Then we heard that the MacDonalds were already at the Phari dak bugalow, so the servants told me to change into my satin dress, new brocade hat and best boots before meeting them. When I met Mr. MacDonald I respectfully handed him a scarf. His daughters, Vera and Vicky, were waiting on the verandah to greet me, both looking sweet and pretty. They were wearing lovely navy-blue tweed coats, with black lamb's skin collar and cuffs, and at once I thought, 'I must have an overcoat like theirs.' But when I was given tea and biscuits I noticed that the biscuits were not so nice as those we got in Lhasa, and I began to wonder if all the things Mr. MacDonald had told us at the lunch party in Tsarong House were true.

Phari is known as the dirtiest town in the world and it is so cold that no grain ripens and the crop was sold to passing woolmerchants as fooder for their many mules. The beautiful Johmo Lhari, the Queen of the Snow-mountains, can be seen close by, and the local people said that by the blessing of the Queen of the Snow-mountains they got everything – fruit, vegetables and clothes from India, rice and chillies from Bhutan, grain from Gyantse and meat from Khampa Dzong.

We left for Yatung at nine o'clock next day. Bugles were blown in honour of the British Trade Agent who had a small military escort, and the Union Jack was carried before our procession, which made me feel quite important. As we approached the Chumbi valley the hills were very beautiful and during our descent they became more and more green, with many sweet flowers on both sides. We met bubbling streams and when we had to cross narrow bridges the servants dismounted and led our horses. We lunched in the small rest house at Gautsa and this was the first time in my life that I sat at an English table. I remember the lunch – roast meat and potatoes. As we were about to continue one of the Mac-Donald's sons, John, came in with a big gazelle that he had shot. He was a tall boy – nothing like little fat 'Daddy MacDonald' – and he had a very loud voice which seemed to fill the place.

The further we travelled the more I liked the pine-trees and the water hitting against the rocks and making such a terrific noise that one could not hear oneself talking. After riding between very close hills, following the noisy water, we reached the lovely little plain of Lingmathang, where the river calmed peacefully.

Towards sunset we came to the beautiful one-storied Western-style house of the B.T.A. It was painted brown and white and had a long, glazed veranda; the main door was surrounded by climbing roses. Yatung is only about eight thousand feet above sea level, so roses grew all over the garden and apples were hanging on the trees. I was thrilled to meet Mrs. MacDonald in a Nepalese dress made of Chinese gold-spotted brown satin, with a bright pink silk shawl around her shoulders and gold ornaments on her neck and ears – and the funniest thing to me was that she wore a ring on her nose. Annie, the eldest daughter, also looked beautiful in a white skirt and jumper with little pale blue square designs around the waist; though she was pretty she was not fair like Vera and Vicky. Mrs. MacDonald was the daughter of a Scotsman and a Nepalese woman.

The MacDonalds treated me the same as their own children, who seemed like my brothers and sisters. Later, Vera and I, particularly, became great friends. But Annie taught me a lot, from threading a needle to utilising sanitary napkins.

When I had presented a scarf to Mrs. MacDonald she caught my hand kindly and patted me and took me to the drawing-room. Soon the nursery-maid was told to give me a bath but I was so shy that I refused to have one for some days, until the maid insisted, assuring me that none of my host's daughters would come into the bathroom. After a lovely hot bath, with Lifebuoy soap, I changed my clothes and to my surprise found lice in my knickers and blouse, which I had been wearing day and night since leaving Lhasa. I begged Nani Ama not to tell anyone and to give the clothes to beggars. She promised not to tell, but I felt that she must have broken her promise because next day Annie bobbed my hair. Then she showed me the big catalogue of a Calcutta firm and told me to choose a hair-brush, comb, knickers and jumpers, which soon came by post. Gradually I was dressed in European style and gave away all my Tibetan clothes, but going to Darjeeling I had to use my own trunk, which was covered with hide. It smelled and this embarrassed me.

Before going home my servants spent a few days in the bazaar as the guests of Apa Enching, the famous host of many travellers through Yatung. When they came to say good-bye to me we all felt sad and my maid and I cried so much that Mrs. MacDonald said she could stay until I went to school. But I told her that she might return to Lhasa.

During my six months in Yatung, the MacDonalds did their best to make me happy by taking me to the local monasteries and cooking Tibetan food. Everyone in the town was very kind to me and I was not too homesick; but on New Year's Day I cried all the time, and though the Tibetan staff at the B.T.A. office came to offer me *Tashi Delek* flour, I just stayed in bed, refusing to go to a party to which I had been invited. I notice that all through my life I have had a very bad habit of getting my own way — even to this day. Now I am watching myself all the time, to try to correct this fault.

The MacDonalds were devout Christians who ran a day school in which Vera and Vicky taught English and two Nepalese teachers taught Nepali and Hindi. A few conversions were made, but they never tried to convert me. At this school they called me Dolma, which is the Tibetan name for the Indian goddess Tara and means 'Protector'. Then Annie asked me if I would like to be renamed 'Mary' before I went to Darjeeling, Mary being the Lord Jesus's mother's name. To me it sounded like Dolma, as Christ's mother is also a protector, so I accepted it and have since been known as Mary to all my friends.

In March 1922, I went to Darjeeling with the two MacDonald children, Pauline and David. It took us seven days to ride to Kalimpong on a very rough road; Annie accompanied us and we crossed the snowy sixteen-thousand-foot Jelap pass. In those days Kalimpong had no cars or electricity. From there we rode for another day to Ghoom, where we took the toy train to Darjeeling – it seemed a terrific size to me and I was very frightened when it whistled.

At Mount Hermon, the American Methodist boarding school, I was put in the kindergarten for a little time. During the first year I felt quite awkward, not knowing much English, but Pauline explained things to me in Nepalese, which I had learned at Yatung. Soon I was promoted to Class I where the teacher, Miss Hannah, always taught with kindness and a smile. The staff were fond of me and I became friendly with all the girls, who were mostly American or English, with a few Anglo-Indians but no Indians; as the daughter of Tsarong I was greatly respected by the Darjeeling Tibetans. I wore European dress and loved wearing my school clothes.

I was good at arithmetic and enjoyed most of the lessons but had no favourite subject. Though the school food was good I again got into debt through buying cakes and sweets. I was not really greedy, but it is easy to make friends when you have lots of delicacies. Moreover, I got no parcels from home, as the other children did, and since I preferred not to be always under an obligation to them I bought on credit from the Indian cake-sellers who came to the school with flat, wide boxes on their

heads. Two or three times a year Tsarong sent me a handsome
Tibetan money-bag containing a hundred bright shining
rupees, looking as though they had just come out of the mint.
He also sent Indian stamps in high denominations – five or ten
rupees – and I had a leather purse full of Tibetan coins. One
day the cake-seller wanted me to pay the fifteen rupees I owed
him, because he was going home to his village to visit his
family. He was furious when I offered him instead stamps and
Tibetan coins and threatened to report me to the Principal. (I
should have let him, as he would have got into trouble for
trading with the students.) At last he took the empty leather
purse as settlement.

We children used to go to a fruit seller near the railway
station to buy pears. This was forbidden, so when it was my
turn to go I put on my navy drill-bloomers and hid the pears
inside them. As I was half-way up the staircase, on the way to
the dormitory, I met the Principal, Miss Stahl, and at that very
moment one big pear fell out of my bloomers and rolled
downstairs, jumping and making an awful noise on one step
after another. She asked me what I was doing and as I moved
up one more stair another pear began to jump down loudly.
Again Miss Stahl asked, 'What's all this?' I screwed up my face
and stood still and said nothing. The Principal always liked me
and when she saw me screwing up my face she probably
thought I was going to cry, so she left me. The staff gave me
many privileges because I had come from Tibet. When the girls
wanted to go to the cinema they would send me to ask for
permission and the Principal would say, 'Of course – Mary
cannot see movies in Tibet.'

I went to church regularly with the other girls, took
scripture lessons and respected Christ. Yet I kept my faith in
the Lord Buddha and in Dolma as my karma deity – the
goddess who had been my protectress in all previous incarnations. Mother used to say that once you are protected by your
own deity neither devils nor witches can harm you. She also
taught me that when we pray we must pray not only for
ourselves and our loved ones in this life, but for all living

beings. So at church, and during prayers at school, I used to repeat, 'I pray to the Virtuous Protector, Portect all living beings from frightening destruction and death.'

After nine months at school our servants came to fetch me home for the holidays. It was the beginning of December and on Phari plains the blizzard nearly blew me off my pony. Everything got frozen, including the mask I wore to protect my face, and I used to cry a lot as chilblains and saddle-sores together are more than a child can bear.

At Yatung I heard that the Prince of Taring had come to stay with the MacDonalds. I felt shy of meeting him so I avoided the Agency house. On my way back to school next time Mrs. MacDonald gave me a good scolding for not having treated her more thoughtfully; I assured her that it was not that I did not love her and explained how shy I had felt about meeting the Prince.

At Gyantse the Tibetan Trade Agent told me that my family wanted to speak to me on the telephone from Lhasa. This 136-mile line had just been constructed at the expense of the Tibetan Government, with technical help from the British in India, and the T.T.A. had the only telephone in Gyantse. The line was so bad that we finished our talk by a few shouts, without understanding each other much.

On this journey I also refused to ride straight and often galloped after animals or stopped to skate on the ice. The kind old syce, Champa Tsering, always granted my requests. At villages on the way I used to make him paint his face, put a scarf around his neck, pretend to be an oracle in a trance and chase the village children. Then I would call the children back, explain that he was only playing and share my sweets with them. The day we got to Lhasa, Champa Tsering was very ill and shivering all over; the cook said that the real oracles were angry because he had pretended to be one of them. But he recovered after a few days.

Though I had been at a European school for such a short while I thought I was now very Westernised. From Kalimpong I had written to Pema Dolkar, telling her that I must always have bread or scones for breakfast, as I had forgotten how to eat *tsampa*, and saying that I would be sleeping on a bed and not on cushions on the floor. When I got to Lhasa my people did their best to serve food in the English style and I was given beds both at Gyatso and Tsarong House. I felt that I had learned a lot and was very superior to Changchup Dolma and all my old schoolmates. I showed off a great deal, always wearing my English overcoat, my school badge and my long boots – beautifully made by a Chinese shoe-maker in Kalimpong.

During that vacation I stayed mostly at Gyatso with Pema Dolkar and Tsarong, and one day a message came from His Holiness asking Tsarong if I had brought any fancy stationery from India. I had not even brought my school-books, much less fancy stationery, but Tsarong then said that I must pay homage to His Holiness and took me with him one morning, telling me to wait near the palace gate. For the occasion I wore my school straw hat over my bobbed hair, long boots and a padded purple silk Tibetan winter gown. Soon a servant called me and showed me into a room where His Holiness was sitting on a low seat. When Tsarong told me to prostrate I hesitated, as there are two methods and I did not know which was the correct one, but somehow I did the right thing by bowing very low three times, touching the ground with my forehead. When I had offered my scarf and an auspicious packet of twenty *tamkas*, wrapped like a snowball in a white cloth, His Holiness blessed me with his hands and catching hold of my ribbon asked, 'What does this mean?' Tsarong replied that it was to keep my hair back from my face. I was told to sit down, though Tsarong and the other attendants remained standing, and His Holiness questioned me about my school while tea and rice were being served. I had my little wooden bowl in my pocket and I took the tea and rice as I had been taught to do before leaving home. After about twenty minutes His Holiness told one of the attendants to give me sweets and I got the usual auspicious pastries for which I had a napkin ready in my pocket. When Tsarong gestured that I should rise to take a farewell blessing I received a big scarf and also a small one knotted by His Holiness's own hands and put around my neck to protect me from evil. I walked a few steps backwards, then turned and left the room. I felt very proud and happy to have met the Dalai Lama, as it is rare for a little girl to get a special audience.

During his years as Commander-in-Chief, Tsarong was very close to His Holiness and often took his small son, Dudul Namgyal, to see him, while the nun-nanny waited outside. Dudul Namgyal, then four or five years old, would be asked by the Dalai Lama if he would give him any of his toys — and the family joked for some time about the child once replying that he would give His Holiness his broken cock. At that period Tsarong was permitted to visit the Dalai Lama dressed in his old white tweed pants and coat, or in khaki like an ordinary soldier. During Chapshug, the autumn holiday of bathing, His Holiness enjoyed flying kites and Tsarong, in his scarlet silk suit, ran for them.

To celebrate Chapshug the government gave a feast to all officials and each one received delicious pastries, according to his rank. Some got about twenty pounds of pastries, cooked in butter, every day for three days — and for four days if they were *Kashag* members, and for a week if they were attendants of His Holiness.

During this holiday I often went to the Jokhang, our most precious temple, to take blessings from the holy images and books and other religious objects. The Jokhang was built about one thousand three hundred years ago by the Nepalese Princess, Balsa, who married our King Songtsan Gampo. When the King asked for the hand of this princess her father commanded her to go to Tibet and as part of her dowry she was given a most precious image of the Lord Buddha, said to have been blessed by himself. (The vacant seat of the image may be seen today in Nepal.) Balsa wanted to build a temple in Lhasa for this image so she asked Gyasa — the King's Chinese wife — about a site and was advised to build on a small lake in the city; but as Balsa had a doubt about this she consulted her husband, who confirmed, after prayer and meditation, that the lake was the correct site. To fill it up many goats carried loads of earth and stones on their backs, so in their honour we always had an image of a goat in the Jokhang. The three-storied building was constructed of wood and stone and its wonderful architecture was influenced by ideas from India, China and Tibet. The carvings of people and animals on the pillars supporting the roof were much like what one finds in the ruins of Bodh Gaya and in Sarnath. Balsa probably summoned some Indian architects to help, but the chief engineer was a Tibetan. The temple consisted of great halls, in which the monks assembled at Monlam, and many small shrines containing images of various Buddhas. It stood in the centre of Lhasa surrounded by the market-place, which was a mile in circumference. Many of the nobles' three-storied houses were built around the Barkor and their ground floors were rented to traders as shops. The Jokhang's entrance faced south-west. The outer court-yard was paved with stone slabs that shone because so many people prostrated there to atone for their sins by undergoing physical pain. Most of the government offices were in the Jokhang; the *Kashag* office was very small, but having had the blessing of the Religious Kings it was most precious and the government never attempted to build a bigger one. (The *Kashag* also had offices in the Potala and Norbu Lingka and *Shap-pēs* had to take it in turn to be at Norbu Lingka for a year to attend the daily tea service, along with the monk-officials, and to meet the Dalai Lama at His Holiness's convenience. The *Shap-pē* on duty had to entertain the whole *Kashag—Shap-pēs*, staff and servants—every Thursday, when they came to report on their work to His Holiness and to hold a meeting.)

The Jokhang's outer courtyard was overlooked by a number of rooms, including one from which the Dalai Lama watched religious activities. In the paved inner court-yard there was space for about ten thousand monks to sit, touching knee to knee, during the Great Prayer Festival. The pillars were then decorated with old satin and brocade, and the Dalai Lama had his own seat when he joined the monks at their prayers. The main temple was surrounded by many shrines filled with images and *stupas* (tombs) made of gold and silver. Between the shrines and the main building there was a paved way lined on both sides with thousands of little prayer-wheels which people would spin and spin. These were believed to have been placed there by King Songtsan Gampo and his two queens. All the walls were painted beautifully with scenes from the life of the Lord Buddha and in their leisure hours the people enjoyed looking at these pictures.

At the main gate of the temple there were tremendous stone slabs and one of them bore a foot-print of the thirteenth Dalai Lama. At the inner gate hung the big bell, inscribed in Latin, that had been brought to Lhasa by French Jesuits in the seventeenth century, and there were a number of large panels, inscribed with gold Chinese characters, which had been presented to the Jokhang by various Emperors of China. As one entered one saw a thirty-foot seated image of Champa, the Lord of Love, in the open centre of the building. People glanced at it on entering, but went around all the shrines before visiting it as Champa has not yet come to dwell on earth. Butter-lamps lit the temple's dark interior. The monk in charge had about a hundred monk assistants who were allowed to sell the surplus butter offerings and keep the profit for themselves.

The most important shrines had two-foot-high butterlamp cups of pure gold and silver. The images' crowns were of gold, studded with priceless diamonds, rubies and pearls, and their faces had been painted over and over with gold by rich worshippers. In the Jokhang there was also a great image of Chenrezig – the Lord of Mercy of whom the Dalai Lama is the reincarnation – built on a sandalwood tree that grew inside the temple.

One of the shrines on the Jokhang's first floor contained images of King Songtsan Gampo and his two queens. The King wore Gyasa's ring on his finger and people said that if one prayed to this ring one's wish would be granted.

On the third floor, on a verandah under the gilded roof, there was the *Lachag* (Finance) office and the shrines of many deities and of King Songtsan Gampo's ministers. The most important minister was Thomi Sambhoda, who was sent to India by the King, with sixteen companions, to study Sanskrit. He and his party reached Kashmir after a most difficult journey that took years; the King had given him gold to pay his teachers and cover all his expenses. He had as his tutors Lipi Kara and Devavidyasimha and he returned to Tibet with a full knowledge of Sanskrit, but most of his companions died in India.

For many years there had been a book in Tibet, that nobody could read, called *The Secret*. It had come from India and the Tibetan King, Tho-tho-ri, once dreamed that after four generations there would be a King who could understand this book; Buddhism was introduced to Tibet when Songtsan Gampo had in read by Sambhoda.

Sambhoda's image always held a book, because it was he who devised the Tibetan script, basing it on Sanskrit. Our written and spoken language is nothing like Chinese, though many people think that there is some resemblance. Tibetan grammar is very complex and the written language is often beautiful. Yet it has the advantage that one can write letters of importance without knowing grammar or spelling.

When Sambhoda was inventing the Tibetan alphabet, which has thirty letters, he found it very difficult to make the letters for six sounds. Not knowing what to do, and in despair, he saw a man in a dream and asked him where he was going – and the answer gave him the idea for the missing letters. Sambhoda is worshipped to this day and the book that his image holds was often touched by people – in particular children, to get his blessing and become as intelligent as he was.

Gyasa, the Chinese princess, had been sought in marriage by many princes, but our King won her through the skill of his minister, Gar-Tongtsan. It is said that the Chinese King arranged various contests for the princes and Gar-Tongtsan won them all. One of the two final contests was giving a turquoise with a crooked hole in it to all the princes and asking them to thread it. Gar-Tongtsan got hold of a small ant, tied a thread to it and let it make its own way through the hole. Ever since, when Tibetan girls marry their husband must give them an arrow, and they must have an image of Buddha or Dolma as part of their dowry.

Then the King challenged the princes to pick out the princess fron amongst many other beautiful girls, all dressed alike. He promised to give his daughter in marriage to the one who recognised her, so Gar-Tongtsan tried to bribe the princess's maid-servant with gold and asked her to give him a hint. She replied that if the King should know about it she would lose her life as a punishment. Gar-Tongtsan then suggested that she should speak through a copper pipe while he held an iron pipe in his mouth – to avoid the astrologist discovering their conversation. The maid-servant agreed and in this manner told the minister that a fly would be flying around the face of the princess all the time. When the contest was held all the princes guessed wrongly, but the Tibetan minister at once put his arrow on the right girl. As the skill of the Chinese astrologers was great the King urged them to find out who had given a hint to Gar-Tongtsan, but they could only discover that a person with copper lips had spoken to a person with iron lips.

From dawn to dusk, people visited the Jokhang. During religious festivals, and on the day of the full moon, they formed long queues and no matter who they were they had to wait their turn to pay homage at the shrines.

In the ancient temple, by the light of the Lord Buddha, I took a vow as a schoolgirl never to tell a lie or to harm anyone. This vow was taken in return for my mother's kindness, as she brought me into the world, and in memory of the love and worry she spent on us. So I took it on her death anniversary, the eighth day of the third month, and I renew it on that date every year.

In honour of my parents' memory Pema Dolkar and Tsarong had endowed the three big monasteries, where many monks said special prayers on the death anniversaries of my parents. Tsarong had also ordered from Calcutta large cast-iron cauldrons in which to melt butter, for the lamas who had been most helpful to my mother when our family was in calamity.

My return journey to school in Darjeeling was terribly cold and dangerous; in spring the passes are blocked by snow and one could easily get killed. The second year at school was much more enjoyable than the first and that winter holiday was spent with the MacDonalds at Kalimpong, where we used to have great fun. The Prince of Taring was then a pupil at St. Paul's School, Darjeeling, and was also spending the holidays at Kalimpong with his aunt, Rani Dorje. He often came to play with his friend, Joe MacDonald, bringing sweets from the market, and sometimes we went to play with him at Bhutan House. He was a quiet boy. I liked dancing and we used to put on records of old fox-trots and waltzes and dance and dance. I was the first Tibetan girl to go to an English school in India and the Prince of Taring was the first Tibetan boy.

My third year at school was the best. By then I was aged fifteen and I became a Girl Guide and enjoyed all the Guides' activities. I was in Class IV and made some good friends, many of whom are still my friends today. Sylvia Baxter, my closest friend, always came first in our class and helped me a lot in my studies. But I was not a girl who tried hard to learn; I just learnt as much as I could without making too much effort. Luckily I have a very good memory.

6 My First Marriage

DURING MY THIRD year at school many very worrying rumours came from Lhasa saying that the monasteries might attack Tsarong because they suspected him of being pro-British and were afraid that the reforms he wanted to carry out quickly would lessen their own power. He was then busy reorganising the Army, as he saw more clearly than anybody else how necessary this was for the sake of Tibet's independence. But his enemies accused him of wanting to become more powerful than the Dalai Lama and to take over the country himself. This made me feel very anxious about what might happen to my people should there be another conspiracy like the one against my father.

His policy as Commander-in-Chief made Tsarong many enemies, though as an individual he was loved and respected by most people. It had never been the custom for the big monasteries or noble families to pay much revenue to the government but, because of the great expense of maintaining a standing army, His Holiness and the *Kashag* set up a new office to revise the taxation system and collect a lot more money from monasteries and estates, according to their size.

The Panchen Lama's monastery, Tashilhunpo, owned huge estates and therefore had to pay high taxes. This was resented by the Panchen's officials, though the sixth Panchen Lama himself was a gentle, courteous man who would never have made any kind of trouble. For centuries the Chinese, in their efforts to dominate Tibet, had been trying to use the Panchen

Lama and his entourage against the Dalai Lama's court, and after His Holiness's flight to India in 1910 the sixth Panchen Lama's officials were very friendly with the Chinese—though the Panchen Lama himself refused to cooperate. When the new taxes were demanded these officials thought they were being punished for helping the Chinese and they feared worse punishments. So on the fifteenth day of the eleventh month of the Water-Hog year (1923) they ran away to China, after persuading the forty-year-old Panchen Lama to go with them.

The Panchen Lama's flight caused much distress and anxiety all over Tibet, as everybody realised that the Chinese might use the discontent of his followers as an excuse for again invading our country. It was all very sad, as there was nothing wrong with the friendship between the two High Lamas, though they rarely met because their entourages were not fond of each other. Four or five years earlier the Panchen Lama hed visited the Dalai Lama in Lhasa and they spent so many hours talking that it was said the Panchen Lama almost forgot the time he should be taking leave. When he did go the Dalai Lama himself carried a lantern in one hand and led the Panchen Lama out with his other hand and saw him off from the front gate. They were known to be on such good terms that even after the Panchen Lama's flight no one could imagine them being enemies. The Panchen Lama left behind a heart-broken letter saying that bad people had been misleading the Dalai Lama. After reading it His Holiness remarked that the Panchen Lama should have consulted his 'Father and Teacher' about his troubles instead of 'wandering away into uninhabited places, to his great peril, like a moth attracted by the candlelight'.

When I heard of the Panchen Lama's flight I became even more worried about what might happen to my people and I wanted to go home at once as I was afraid of being left alone in India without any support. But for some time I had to remain at school, despite my anxiety.

By 1924 Tsarong had succeeded in greatly strengthening the Tibetan Army. He, Lungshar and Kunphela—the three favourites of the Dalai Lama—were all very powerful then and some say they were extremely jealous of one another; but I know that Tsarong was not jealous of anybody. The older Army generals, who had served Tibet loyally for many years, were still campaigning in Kham.

Some of the young generals of the reorganised army had been trained by the British in Gyantse or India and they thought themselves rather important and progressive, which annoyed their elders. A Lhasa rumour said that the civilian and military officials were disagreeing, and this was proved to be true during a meeting of the *Tsongdu* (the National Assembly) when the taxation of the *Kashag* ministers' and the generals' estates was being discussed. The young generals, led by Tsarong, requested the *Tsongdu* to admit a military representative, but the assembly said that this unheard-of suggestion could not be considered; and Lungshar, the president of the *Tsongdu*, encouraged the monasteries to use Tsarong's request in their campaign against him. The Potala and Norbu Lingka Palaces were then heavily guarded by monks in anticipation of a military take-over and the generals, surprised by this move, at once armed their troops. But nothing happened, except that the military were accused of unlawfully interrupting the *Tsongdu* and two *Dapons* (generals) and one *Shap-pē* were dismissed.

Tsarong was then sent to inspect the National Mint at Yatung, and from there he and Pema Dolkar made a pilgrimage to India and Nepal. They arrived in Darjeeling during my winter holiday in 1924 and took me with them to Calcutta, Bombay, Bodh Gaya, Benares, Kushinaga and Kathmandu. As Tsarong was Commander-in-Chief of the Tibetan Army and Chief *Shap-pē* in the *Kashag* the British government gave him an official guide, Rai Bahadur Norbu Dhondup, Assistant Political Officer of Sikkim. But Tsarong was all the time on the alert, saying that the many Chinese in Kalimpong, who had been expelled from Tibet in 1912, might now take revenge on him.

In Calcutta the guide interpreted for Tsarong and I interpreted for my sister. Lord Reading invited us to lunch at the

Viceroy's House, where all the guests were much interested in Pema Dolkar's head-dress. Our friends Colonel and Mrs. Eric Bailey were with us.

Tibetans were then allowed to trade in India without taxation and Tsarong purchased much furniture, jewellery, one hundred and fifty Mauser pistols as gifts and for sale (our people were very fond of arms of any kind) and special presents for His Holiness – including a big chinese bowl and two parrots, one pure white.

At the huge store of Whiteaway, Laidlaw and Co., the manager took us over all the departments and gave Pema Dolkar and me a bottle of scent each. Tsarong and Pema Dolkar bought many things, but poor me – they did not buy anything for me. I used to get so fed up, because I had to go everywhere to intrepret. Whenever I had a little free time I would go to bed and sleep. Once I announced that I was going back to Kalimpong because it was all so boring for me, but one of the older servants said it would benefit me if I went to the sacred places and that this was a good opportunity, as our railway compartments had all been booked by the British government.

Our visit to Nepal was most memorable. In those days no Europeans were allowed past the frontier and little was known about the country. The railway stopped at the border town of Raxaul and from there the Nepalese government arranged our transport. Among the guides they sent to meet us was Baghadur, a junior officer who had lived in Lhasa as a child and gone to school with Samdup Tsering and Pema Dolkar.

Motor-cars were provided for the bumpy road from Raxaul to Chisupani Ghat, where we stopped the night at the Nepalese rest-house. From there each of our party of ten – which included Dudul Namgyal and his nanny – had a dandy carried by four or more strong men who took us over a long distance, crossing a high pass. Every night we camped in lovely tents and many Nepalese came to see us. At one place we waited all day while Tsarong went to see the Maharaja, Padma Samsher, who was shooting game in the forest nearby. The

Maharaja then sent his son, Mohan Samsher, and his grandson, to call on Tsarong at our camp.

The next day we crossed the pass from which you can see the beautiful old city of Kathmandu, with its many temples, spread our on the floor of a wide valley. A long line of high, snowy Himalayan peaks stretched out beyond the city for scores of miles to east and west. At the foot of this pass tents were pitched and when some generals came to receive Tsarong with chariots a salute of guns was fired and a guard of honour provided. We were then driven to a splendid palace surrounded by water; in the huge hall there were a grandfather clock, silver banded elephants' feet and beautiful sofas. We were given a room each, with pretty cotton-padded quilts covered with bright coloured silks. All the arrangements made by the State on our behalf were wonderful.

I had ear-ache, so a doctor was sent to me immediately; food was brought when we wanted it and our own cook prepared it because Pema Dolkar could never eat spicy foods; Nepalese money in silver coins was given to us as an allowance to spend during our stay. Lots of Nepalese traders who had shops in Lhasa came to call on us and Tsarong and Pema Dolkar visited the homes of some Nepalese who were close friends. They also visited Buddhist and Hindu temples, museums and a military barracks where the Nepalese displayed some of their artillery and the old Tibetan cannons they had won from us in 1855. The Nepalese Commander-in-Chief gave a banquet in Tsarong's honour at Singa Durbar.

I had to stay indoors most of the time because of my earache, but I did go to the Buddhist temples, where Pema Dolkar arranged for many religious offerings to be made.

After about ten days we left Kathmandu, being sent off with presents of kukris and other things, and were brought back to Raxaul with great show and pomp. On this trip Kadung Lhukhangpa, who later became Prime Minister, was Tsarong's A.D.C., as it was the custom for a *Shap-pē* to take one secretary from the *Kashag* whenever he went.

My wish not to return to school now fitted in with the

family's plans. They wanted me to know enough English to do their commercial correspondence and when I said that already I knew enough Tsarong agreed to my leaving school. I regretted not being able to finish my education in Darjeeling, but it would have been too difficult to remain there because of my anxiety about my people and the hard journey to and from Lhasa. Now I am glad in a way that I left school so young, because I was able to study Tibetan thoroughly as I could not have done had I taken higher English.

On our way back to Lhasa I nearly died of cold. I had put on only my school clothes and by the time we got to Phari I was very ill; so Tsarong went to visit a friend in Bhutan for a few days while Pema Dolkar nursed me.

When we arrived at Gyantse, where Mr. Frank Ludlow was then running an English school for Tibetan boys, he and his students were in line to greet us. This school had been opened the year before (1923) because His Holiness felt that an English type of education could help his people, but the monasteries feared that it might harm the Buddhist religion and put such pressure on the Dalai Lama that the school was closed in 1926. Most of the monks wer completely opposed to any change in the life of Tibet and to all influences from other countries. The great monasteries had such power that they sometimes objected successfully even to His Holiness's plans.

From every town and village along our route back to Lhasa some representative came to greet the *Shap-pē*. But then, at Chusul — only one day's ride from Lhasa — we got a bad surprise. Suddenly a special messenger arrived, bringing a letter from the *Kashag* to Tsarong dismissing him as Commander-in-Chief. This dismissal was given in a very polite way. I myself read the letter and it said, 'By order of His Holiness the Dalai Lama we have decided that the second-in-command, *Dzasa* Dumpa, can carry on the work of the Army headquarters as there is no anxiety in the country at the moment, so we need not a Commander-in-Chief.'

Tsarong did not show any sign of being upset when he received this message, but respected it courteously and remained serene and loyal to His Holiness. He always opened his letters carefully and he kept the unbroken seals of this letter on a big china plate hanging on the wall of his office.

When we reached Lhasa we realised that Tsarong's enemies had been working hard against him while he was out of the country. All the younger officers who supported him had been removed from the Army for various reasons that were not sensible – some because they had had their hair cut short while training at Shillong and Quetta, where the heat is great. Generals Dingja, Doring and Samdup Phodang had been demoted and ordered to put up their hair again as soon as possible. We heard a rumour that Tsarong's opponents had tried to persuade the Dalai Lama to remove him also from the *Kashag* and to confiscate all his possessions; but His Holiness was reported to have said that he could never be so mean to the man who had saved the lives of himself and his ministers.

Soon after our arrival home, an appointment was made for Tsarong to meet the Dalai Lama. With his precious presents from India – including the Chinese bowl, which had been packed with his own hands and carried over the passes on a man's back, escorted by a special servant – he left Tsarong House at nine o'clock one morning and only returned at ten o'clock that evening. His servants were fed at the palace and after this long chat with the Dalai Lama some people doubted His Holiness's being very much against him. But things became quite different. No personal letters were received from the palace, no delicacies were sent constantly and from that year Tsarong did not go up to the Pavilion during the Shotan ceremonies, to sit beside His Holiness, but remained in the *Kashag* tent as he had never done before. Still, letters and delicacies did sometimes come, and His Holiness was never too unkind to his hero.

As Commander-in-Chief, Tsarong had sometimes acted very strongly and independently. During 1923 a big disturbance had occurred in Lhasa and to deter the soldiers from trying to get ammunition out of the arsenal Tsarong ordered one man's leg to be cut off and another man's ear. (Those were very rare punish—ments in Tibet.) On a few other occasions he had ordered murderers to be shot and I remember seeing the condemned men being escorted to Dapchi plain by lines of soldiers. After his dismissal from the Army he was asked by the Dalai Lama through His Holiness's secretary, why he had put men to death when Tibetan law is against the taking of human life; he replied that he felt it would not be right to put the matter up to His Holineess who, as the spiritual leader, would then be in a most awkward position, since such punishments were necessary for the country's peace and discipline—so as Commander-in-Chief he preferred to take full responsibility. He was also asked why he had kept a military guard at Tsarong House, as though he were of equal importance to the Dalai Lama. To this he replied that the guard had been kept as a mark of respect to the Commander-in-Chief of Tibet, not to honour himself as a private individual.

Tsarong showed no resentment at any time because of his degradation and no one was able to shake the great loving relationship between him and the thirteenth Dalai Lama.

By this time Rigzin Chodon, who never bore children, had become a nun and left home. The first five children born to Tsarong and Pema Dolkar died as babies, so His Holiness advised Tsarong that it would be more auspicious for Pema Dolkar to live near a holy mountain beside Drepung Monastery, where her two other children—a boy and a girl, born in 1920 and 1923—survived.

In 1918 Horkhang *Dzasa* had died, during a very bad 'flu epidemic that killed thousands of people in Lhasa. He left my sister, Tseten Dolkar, pregnant and with great responsibilities. Her first baby had been a girl, so everyone was very pleased when a few months after her husband's death she gave birth to an heir to the title and the huge Horkhang estates.

Horkhang *Dzasa*'s nun sister, Ani Champala, had control of the treasury at Gyama Trikhang, the main Horkhang estate, and for some years she was not very helpful about administering the estate and refused to unlock the treasury, which held much gold, tea and silk. Although a nun she had had an illegitimate son, named Ngawang Jigme, in 1910. His father was supposed to have been a monk-official who once satyed in a flat in Horkhang House – one of the the biggest residences in Lhasa – while his own house was being built. Ani Champala was very ambitious for her son and when he was thirteen said that she would only unlock the treasury if Tsarong made a marriage agreement promising that in about twelve years' time Ngawang Jigme could have Tseten Dolkar as his wife – though she would then be thirty-seven. Tsarong had to give in, otherwise it would have been impossible to administer Gyama Trikhang. But meanwhile he himself married Tseten Dolkar. He had become very attached to her during the five years since her husband's death, for he often visited Horkhang House to help her administer the estaes on behalf of her son, Sonam Palber.

After this marriage, which took place in 1912, neither Pema Dolkar nor Tseten Dolkar showed any jealousy. They had the greatest respect and affection for each other and Tseten Dolkar often visited Tsarong House, though she never lived there, but received Tsarong in her own home. Eventually she bore him one son and six daughters.

Soon after my return from Darjeeling, at the age of sixteen, I was bold enough to become Tsarong's secretary and take charge of much important commercial correspondence at Tsarong House – in both Tibetan and English, though I had spent only three years learning English. Tsarong's business was big and successful. He traded with Mongolia, India, China, Japan and France. From India we imported sugar, kerosene, soap, medicines, sweets, crockery, cutlery, coral, turquoise, cloth, serge, cigarettes and tea; some of these things we exported to China. (Good money was made in this trade during the Second World War.) We imported silk and brocade from China and Japan, and Lyons brocade from Paris. To China we exported tweeds, herbs, musk, incense, dry blood from the horns of stags (for medicine), as well as the skins of sand-fox, leopard, wolf, marmot, otter, and the precious stone-marten; and we imported Chinese tapestries, satin, china, scarves, jade, tea, horses and mules. We also bought blocks of silver from Mongolian pilgrims and sent traders to all parts of Tibet to buy wool for sale in India.

People everywhere understood everything I wrote – even all the banks we dealt with. My English grammar did not matter much as long as I had the numbers, dates and places written distinctly. I also had to select auspicious days for doing business, so Tsarong called from the Government Astrological School an astrologer to teach me the necessary calculations. I learnt with great interest because I had already memorised the whole book of astrological rules at my Tibetan school. I still find this knowledge useful.

When letters came to Tsarong from the Dalai Lama I was made to copy them immediately because they were in His Holiness's own handwriting on four or five wooden tablets which had to be returned at once. These tablets – about nine inches by two, painted black and dusted with white chalk powder – were written on with a bamboo pen, which makes handwriting beautiful, and were tied with brocade or leather bands. The cover of each letter had a different painting and sometimes there might be meanings in those paintings if one could guess them. The Dalai Lama's letters were always short. They started, 'The purpose of my letter . . .' and ended, 'please bear in mind . . .'. This way of corresponding, which saved paper, was common amongst the Tibetan nobility but is not known in any other country.

At about this time my brother, Kalsang Lhawang, decided that he wanted to live on Tsarong Estate. He said, 'What could be better than working on one's own estate instead of leaving everything in the hands of the servants?' This plan was agreed to, all was arranged for the two weeks' journey and he set our for Tsarong with his wife and three small children – two sons and a daughter. Less than a year later he returned to Lhasa, saying that it was all right for him in the country, but the children needed a good school. The family then moved into their own flat in Tsarong House.

After a little time Kalsang Lhawang told Tsarong that if he

had a share in the family money and was given responsibility it would help him and his family. So he received a big amount of money, from which he replaced some of the jewellery that he had borrowed from his wife, years before, to pay his debts. The rest of the money he left with Tseten Dolkar, saying that he was going to be very good and not touch it until the children were grown up. But quite soon he went to her and said that it was silly keeping money idle and that he must make a profit by asking a real trader to do some business for him. He took all his money but just spent it instead of trading and went bankrupt.

I had been working as Tsarong's secretary for a year or so when he asked me to become his youngest wife. I told him that since he was then married to two of my sisters it would not be wise to marry him as he had enough wives already and was too old for me; I also thought that if I had many children it would not be good, all living together in Tsarong House. He reminded me that Pema Dolkar was not often able to stay at home and work on account of their children's health. As for Tseten Dolkar, he said that in about eight years' time, when she married Ngawang Jigme as arranged, he would be leaving her. He assured me, too, that as there was twenty-five years' difference in age between us I could marry again whenever I came across a suitable young man.

In this way Tsarong insisted that I should marry him and stay at Tsarong House to do all the correspondence; and he was so powerful and I was so young that I agreed. But I married him reluctantly and though he was so fond of me I was not at all happy. Our marriage was announced on a New Year's Day, but we had no special wedding-day as it was Tsarong's fourth marriage and I also did not want an elaborate wedding.

The office work was tremendous and Tsarong—whom I then called *Sawang Chenpo*, meaning His Excellency—was very strict; I cried many times when things went wrong. About once a week Tsarong visited Tsetsen Dolkar and I felt so happy because it was then a holiday. In the morning I used to ask the cook what food His Excellency had ordered, and if he said, 'Today you are having *phingde*' (noodles and rice), I knew that Tsarong was going to Horkhang House. Then I would play *sho* with Pema Dolkar, if she were at home, but next day I would always have some papers ready for Tsarong's signature and would wait very innocently.

Early in 1928 I became pregnant and had terrible morning sickness and sometimes fainted. Tsarong told me to wear a diamond brooch every day, because a diamond, or any precious stone, protected pregnant women from getting badly hurt by serious falls. I never felt like working and was advised to make holy walks so, with the help of Tsewang Dolma, Kalsang Lhawang's wife, I went to the Jokhang every morning and walked around the temple fifty times. The craving for food was terrible and then I got sick of everything I ate. Tsarong would never allow me to eat anything but home-made food; often our Muslim friends gave us delicious curry and rice, which I loved, but now it was forbidden. My mother's sister, our Dekyiling aunt, used to say whenever she met me, 'You were only a child not long ago and now you are going to have a child.' I never never liked her making this remark, because being pregnant I felt very grown-up; but it would not have been polite to object.

After six months I began to keep fairly well. Then one day the Samye State Oracle came to see Tsarong; they were close friends and whenever they met they talked for hours. (The Oracle was also a close friend of the Dalai Lama's.) Samye Choji came at about five o'clock and supper for the two men was taken to Tsarong's sitting-room on trays, while Pema Dolkar and I had our meal in the dining-room. At nine o'clock the men were still talking and I felt very tired, but I always stayed up respectfully until my elders were in bed. After supper I felt thirsty, so I drank a cup of cold milk.

The Oracle left at ten o'clock and a few hours later I had an unpleasant dream about getting into trouble with Tsarong for losing the receipt of a registered letter. I woke up and found myself with a severe colic and thought I was going to have a miscarriage. I called my maid-servant, who was sleeping in the next room, and asked her to fetch Pema Dolkar. Both Tsarong and Pema Dolkar came to my room at once and Pelma Dolkar said that drugs might be dangerous, because of my being pregnant, so she suggested crème-de-menthe, which always did her good. She gave me a small glass full and after about ten minutes the pain subsided a little. After a second glass I went back to sleep, but next morning I still had my colic so we called our doctor who gave me some very mild medicines. For a long time after I kept a bottle of crème-de-menthe always near me and could not drink milk; if I did the colic came back.

Tibetan babies were always born at home and as the time came near I trained my maid-servant, and Pema Dolkar got the baby outfit and blankets, and rites were performed so that the delivery would be safe. It was drawing towards winter, so wood-stoves were prepared in the delivery room, which faced south. Pema Dolkar and Tsaraong were both there to help me during labour and after twenty-four hours a big girl baby was born. One of our old maid-servants cut the cord and then the baby was washed, put in a warm cradle and given Tashi Delek *tsampa* to eat for good luck. My placenta was delayed for twelve hours, so our doctor was called. He made me get up and squat and in that way I was eventually able to discharge the placenta.

I then felt thirsty and took a cup of hot milk, hoping it would help me to produce more milk for my baby. However, it made me terribly sick that night, so without telling anyone I drank quite a lot of crème-de-menthe. This did help, but another complicated pain arose under my right ribs and it took the doctor a month to cure me. Yet I fed Tsering Yangzom for nine months. The Abbot of Ganden named her; Tsering Yangzom means, 'melodious long life'.

Tsering Yangzom was a beautiful baby. For the first three months she cried a lot but then she was very good and quiet. Although I was feeding her myself the maid-servant insisted on giving her a thin paste of *tsampa* and milk every day from birth, and from six months I gave her rice porridge and egg noodles. She used to love her baths twice a week. After their baths Tibetan babies are massaged with mustard-oil and then given a sun-bath while naked, with their eyes protected from the strong light.

I had a difficult time when she got measles at the age of eight months and had a cough for weeks; the house was full of lamas doing pujas and I had to order cough mixture from the British Hospital in Gyantse.

Tsering Yangzom began to walk when she was fourteen months and as a toddler she was very sweet and intelligent. She loved tiny puppies and would sit in the sun for ages keeping four or five of them warm under her little robe.

Some time before my marriage the government had sent representatives to Poyul to investigate the situation there, which was still being very difficult because Tsarong's advice had been ignored in 1920. One of the representatives — a monk-official from Kham — exploited the people so much that eventually they revolted and killed his servant. Tsarong's sister, Tsering Dolma, whom he had given to Poyul, came to Lhasa to seek help when Tsering Yangzom was a few months old. Tsering Dolma loved her new niece and her secretary, who was very intelligent, also thought a lot of my baby. He used to say, 'My wife and I wouldn't mind having a hundred babies like this baby.' I taught him English and arithmetic and he picked everything up quickly.

Eventually the government sent troops, under *Depon* Tana, to take over Poyul and the poor chief had to flee to Assam, where he died later. Tsering Dolma was left in Lhasa; she remarried happily, and the Tibetan government gave her a small estate in Chusul district. All the children in the family loved her because she was so full of fun. She was too afraid of Tsarong to say a word about anything in his presence, but among the rest of us she was always making jokes about him.

Tsarong was always greatly interested in the world outside Tibet and one of his most trusted friends was Surkhang *Dzasa*, the lay Foreign Minister. Though Tsarong had no Western education he was always with a map and knew the geography of the whole world. He received newspapers from many countries and had a pen-friend in Missouri, U.S.A. – Mr. William Englesmann, who first wrote to Tsarong for stamps and afterwards sent him *Life* and *Geographic* magazines. Tsarong used to say, 'My friend Englesmann never sends me his family pictures: I hope he is not an ugly-looking man' – and we all pondered our thoughts. But when the Englesmanns came to Mussoorie, India, in 1964 he was very handsome and Dorothy, his wife, was very beautiful. Life is such; in Lhasa we never dreamed of meeting them in India, after more than thirty years.

Both Tsarong and Pema Dolkar enjoyed gardening and grew the first cauliflowers and tomatoes to be seen in Lhasa. As soon as Tsarong came back from his office he would take a spade and work in the garden, wearing white tweed pants and coat. (This was after 1925; while he was Commander-in-Chief he had no time for such things.) My aunts and the old servants thought that his way of digging the ground with tools, wearing the clothes of an ordinary man, was an indignity. They said that he would bring bad luck by exchanging the luxurious life of the nobility for the modern behaviour of Communists. But nothing could shake his ways. It is not that he was not fond of satin and brocade dresses, because he had more robes than my father had. Having abolished my parents' debts, by skilful trading, he used to buy the best satin and brocade from India, China, Japan, Russia and France. After the death of Shatra *Shap-pē*, Tsarong helped with the funeral ceremonies and found that this minister had left few *chubas* or underclothes suitable for distribution to the lamas. Tsarong said that he would not let his own people be disgraced by such a shortage of clothes and ordered a tailor to make one hundred *chubas* of middle quality satin in different colours, one hundred white silk blouses and fifty red silk belts, which were all numbered and kept in readiness for his own death-ceremonies, being taken care of by Pelma Dolkar, as his senior wife.

Tsarong had a passion for nice things and collected old china, jade ornaments and good furniture. He was very curious about anything new and liked to buy cutlery, radios, watches and cameras; he loved photography, which my father had taught him, and had his own darkroom. He sent a boy to India to learn how to cook Western dishes and bake bread, buns and cakes; this cook taught many other cooks in Lhasa and so Western food and Indian curry and rice became well established.

Tsarong was an exceptionally shrewd businessman, which was his main motive for marrying me. Now I am glad that as his English-speaking secretary I had to undertake so much responsibility, because this was a very good training for me.

Though Tsarong had his enemies he hated nobody, not even those who plotted against him, and he was good and helpful to all, high and low. He often mediated for families who were having disputes and was fond of arranging marriages. He was popular among all the traders – Muslims, Nepalese, Bhutanese, Chinese and especially the Mongolian monks, as he spoke Mongolian, and loved their country. The thirteenth Dalai Lama also spoke Mongolian, and sometimes he and Tsarong used it as their secret language.

Tsarong had a great desire to help Tibet by opening schools, building roads and improving the Army to make our country really strong and independent. He did some great work, always with the Dalai Lama's approval, but unfortunately had the reputation for being pro-British or pro-American, pro-Japanese or pro-Russian, because he was keen that Tibet should have good relations with all countries. Most of the few foreigners who visited Lhasa were entertained at Tsarong House and in 1947, when the American writer, Mr. Lowell Thomas, came with his son, I was their interpreter. I remember Mr. Thomas asking Tsarong his opinion of the world situation: Tsarong replied that the big countries of the world have too much greed and want to devour each other.

Tsarong was a very kind-hearted man, though very quick-tempered, and nobody could turn him against anyone. He was good to children, especially his own: the strong man can yield to children just like that. His son by Pema Dolkar – Dadal Namgyal – was his soul; but once we saw him seriously chasing the boy with a stone, because Dudul Namgyal's dog nearly bit a visitor.

Though he was an eloquent writer, Tsarong was bad at spelling and grammar, unlike my father, so his secretaries always had to correct his letters. He was not afraid to talk in any circumstances. Sometimes, when he was being very frank at *Kashag* meetings, Pema Dolkar would remind him of the fate of our father. But he would say 'What will happen, will happen—and if my little bone and flesh are beaten, what matter?'

7 My Second Marriage

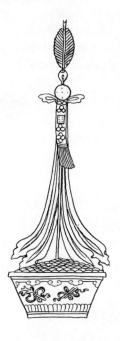

TSARONG WAS ABLE to have three wives at a time because he kept them separate and treated them without partiality. He respected the two seniors as equals and to me he was more a father than a husband – though he often asked for my opinions on important matters, because he knew that I had my own peculiar ways of thinking.

After Tsering Yangzom's birth I had a letter of congratulation, in English, from the Prince of Taring – Jigme, eldest son of Taring Raja of Sikkim. Along with it was a photo and another letter in English to my youngest sister, Changchup Dolma. (At that time Jigme was not able to write Tibetan very well.) He asked me to translate this letter to her, as he wished to marry her if she would like to have him. When I read the letter to her she just laughed and gave me no answer, but kept the letter and handed back the photo; I told her that I thought this would be a most suitable marriage, as I knew Jigme very well. I wrote at once to thank Jigme for his congratulations and assured him that I would write again as soon as I could get a reply from Changchup Dolma. I told him how happy I was about his suggestion and promised that I would advise my sister well, so that his wish might be fulfilled.

I next showed my letter and Jigme's photo to Tsarong, and told him about Changchup Dolma's letter, explaining that I considered the marriage would be very suitable. Tsarong thought, and then asked if I had been in love with Jigme while we were both at school in India. I replied that though we had met often, during our holidays in Kalimpong, we had never talked of love. But Tsarong said that if I agreed it would be even more suitable for me to marry Jigme, as we both knew English and could work together in the office at Tsarong House. He added that since there was such a great difference in age between him and me he would like very much to see me married to a nice young man for the sake of my future happiness.

I agreed that this was a good idea, so Tsarong wrote to Jigme's father, Taring Raja, proposing that Jigme should marry me, join the Tsarong family and come to live in Lhasa to help with the business until Dudul Namgyal grew up.

Taring Raja replied that it would be impossible to give his eldest son away to another family, but that he would be very happy if Tsarong consented to myself and Changchup Dolma joining the Taring family by me marrying Jigme and Chang-chup Dolma marrying his younger brother, Chime Dorje. He said that then he would not mind where Jigme worked.

Tsarong was very pleased and Pema Dolkar also liked the whole idea so they asked me to write to Jigme about the double marriage. As Tsarong thought it would be good if we all could meet soon he invited Taring Raja to bring his two sons with him when he came on his annual pilgrimage to Lhasa for the Monlam Festival.

When the Tarings arrived, in the spring of 1929, Jigme again wrote to me, expressing his own approval of the double marriage proposal and saying that he wished to see me soon. He sent his personal servant to Tsarong House with this letter and some English books. I showed the letter to Tsarong, who suggested a luncheon party at which the two families could meet and said that I should ask Jigme to come to Tsarong House whenever he wished to talk to me. I did this, but Jigme replied that he would not like to be so bold as to come to see me at this stage, though he was looking forward very much to meeting me at the party.

When that day came Jigme and I were delighted to see each other again. Changchup Dolma and Chime Dorje met then for the first time. Both were very shy, but they looked pleased with the meeting; Chime Dorje was even taller and more handsome than Jigme. Afterwards, Pema Dolkar asked Changchup Dolma if she would like to live at Taring Estate as Chime Dorje's bride and Changchup Dolma replied that she would be very happy with this arrangement as I would be in the same family. So before Taring Raja returned to Taring our marriage agreements were drawn up. After this my love affairs with Tsarong were cut off entirely because I did not want to have another baby before marrying Jigme.

The witness of our agreement was *Kalon* Dhokhar Ragashar, then a *Kadon* in the *Kashag*. The sealed agreement stated that 'By the great kindness of His Excellency the Tsarong, *Shap-pē*, his junior wife, Rinchen Dolma, will be married to the eldest Prince of Taring, Jigme Sumtsen Wangpo, and the Princess Changchup Dolma will be married to Prince Chime Dorje, second son of Raja Tsodrak Namgyal of Taring, the Prince of the religious King of Sikkim; and by the marriages of their children a great alliance will be formed between the Houses of Taring and Tsarong. In the case of Rinchen Dolma, her daughter Tsering Yangzom will be treated the same as the children of the senior Tsarong wives, and whether she be married in the house, by bringing in a bridegroom, or given away to another family, the full responsibility will be Tsarong's and not Taring's.' The marriage was fixed for the following year, 1930.

When the British Army came to Gangtok, in 1892, the King of Sikkim, Thutop Namgyal (Jigme's grandfather) fled towards Tibet, where he had a small estate, but on the way he was seized by the British and persuaded to return to Gangtok. He and his officials and his younger son went back but his eldest son, Taring Raja, and his brother, Lhase *Kusho*, were allowed to go on into Tibet. In Gangtok, the King found that the administration had been taken over by the British, aided by two of his Sikkimese opponents, who made things difficult for him. The British tried to force him to recall his son and brother from Tibet, but he replied that it was they who had driven them away and he said that he did not want to interrupt the studies they had started at Shigatse.

In the spring of 1892 the King decided again to try to get to Tibet, with his wife and some trusted officials. Instead of taking the usual route they went in the direction of Tingkye, the Tibetan district where an important Sikkimese official had already been welcomed and given an estate. There the King was upset to hear that the Tibetan local officials had told the people not to help any Sikkimese, so he had to go to Walung, in Nepal, where he spent five days thinking about continuing to Kathmandu. At Walung some pro-British Gurkhas arrested him and took him on a ten days' journey to Dhanakoti, where their C.O. told him that he had been arrested by order of the Nepalese government which had been requested by the British to return him to Sikkim. He and his party were soon handed over to the British Indian Police, who kept them near Darjeeling for a couple of months, before detaining them at Kurseong in 1893.

King Thutop Namgyal then petitioned the Governor-General of Bengal, Lord Curzon, and when his petition was investigated the British found that the King's Sikkimese opponents had been at the back of all the trouble. He was informed that the British government would reinstate him if he agreed to set up a government council and consult the British Political Officer before making any decisions. The King accepted this condition and on the ninth day of the ninth month of the Wood-Sheep Year (1895) he returned to Gangtok. He was a straightforward man who dealt fairly with everybody and never did any harm either to the Tibetans or to the British. All he wanted was to secure his hereditary rights.

When King Thutop Namgyal died his eldest son, Jigme's father, was asked to return to Sikkim and take the throne. But he loved Tibet and was happy with his small estate and quiet life there, so his brother, Sidkeong Tulku, an Incarnate Lama who had been educated at Oxford, succeeded instead. Sidkeong Tulku was very intelligent and quickly introduced reforms which aroused the anger of many Sikkimese landlords. He died in most mysterious circumstances before he had been ruling for a year. Again my father-in-law was offered the throne and again he refused it. His half-brother, Chogyal Tashi Namgyal – who had been born while his parents were in detention – then succeeded, in 1915.

All Taring Raja's children were born in Tibet. The Sikkim government sent him an annual allowance, and New Year and Summer Festival presents were exchanged. After my marriage to Jigme, Father-in-law told me that his brother visited once at Taring while he was King and felt not happy to see him living there. All Father-in-law's Sikkimese servants had taken leave, one by one, because they missed their daily rice, so Sidkeong Tulku asked Taring Raja to come back to Sikkim and promised that he would take all the responsibility of governing; but Father-in-law would not leave Tibet. Yet he loved his own people and the Sikkimese loved and respected him, as did the peasants at Taring, who worshipped him and regarded him as a true Religious King.

Tibetan wedding ceremonies varied a little in different provinces and were carried out according to wealth and social position, but whether luxurious or simple the principal traditional customs were the same. Unless a boy or girl had already fallen in love, and insisted on being married, all precautions were taken to arrange a suitable and happy marriage. (To upset one's family by an unsuitable marriage was considered most shameful.) A boy's parents carefully chose a good-natured, good-looking girl from a family in their own class. The girl's parents then investigated the boy's character and behaviour and a girl would not be given unless these were good. A happy relationship was considered very important, because divorce was thought bad for the children and for the reputation of the whole family. Many boys were given the privilege of choosing their own bride, but a boy's parents were extra careful if he was the heir. Then they chose from a number of girls, after consulting the family's and other deities, the lamas and especially the astrologers. The predictions of the deities and the lamas could be ignored, but when the astrologer calculated the horoscope on the basis of the couple's dates and hours of birth his forecast would be accurate if these dates and hours were accurate.

We Tibetans are very supersitious, which as Buddhists we should not be. We have a saying that very lucky people will be lucky always, and very unlucky people unlucky always; but most people have to seek for luck in the future, so marriages and other important events must take place on good days, which are found by looking into a horoscope. A marriage needs an auspicious day for two persons, when the star of the day and the persons' elements agree, and this is rather difficult to find. In family affairs only the senior member's horoscope matters. The stars of the days and the days themselves have formulae of elements, which are explained in books, and when these elements agree with the element of a person's birth-year this is an auspicious day. The prayer-flags of a house must be according to the element of the head of the family – for instance, if that person was born in a Fire-Dog Year the flag must be red. We also have to find out by horoscope in which direction people should face during important ceremonies and what colour their food should be. Tea and food must be offered to everyone at the beginning of any ceremony and the vessels must be full, and even at social or business meetings Tibetans do not like to talk before having a cup of tea. Such tea and food is called 'auspicious' and is said to bring good luck. The greeting scarves we offer to each other are also called 'auspicious' and the whiter and longer the scarf the better. We like ceremonies to be ended by people with lucky names – such as Tashi (Prosperity), Namgyal (Victorious) or Dondup (Successful).

In arranged marriages having the girl older than the boy was avoided if possible – particularly one year older. Neither was it good to have both the same age and if such marriages had to take place, because the couple were in love, special rites were performed to abolish the evil. The astrological rules explain that if a couple are the same age they may have financial difficulties or may not have children.

If there were only girls in a family they had more freedom to select their own bridgrooms; boys were introduced and many families desired their sons to join a wealthy and pretty girl's house. Girls were rarely forced to marry against their will and on the whole had the same rights as boys; but it was essential for them to be without any bad reputation and an illegitimate child was considered to harm the life of a girl – she might then lose her chance to marry into a nice, wealthy family. If by any chance an unmarried girl became pregnant it was kept a close secret. When nuns became pregnant they took baths in hot sulphur springs, hoping for an abortion; if this failed they occasionally threw the babies out to die, but such a thing was unusual in a Buddhist country and when it did happen the infants were usually found and adopted.

Though polygamy was practised for reasons of policy, to keep property in one family – or because the first wife proved barren – polyandry was more common. The custom was for sisters to share one husband or for two or three brothers to share one wife. In polyandrous marriages the girl had to be married in the name of the eldest brother, though it would be written in the engagement agreement that she was to be 'the wife of the son, or sons, of so and so'. The children of such unions always looked on the eldest brother as their father, even when it was known, because of his absence from home at the time of conception, that one of the younger brothers must be the real father. But most Tibetans are monogamous and some people voluntarily take a religious vow that they will have only one partner for the rest of their life. Both partners need not take this vow. When I married Jigme I took it and though I do not know whether or not he also took it I do know that he has been a faithful husband.

Tibetans consider that a marriage should be seen through to the end. If something goes wrong between a couple, it is an important duty for their friends to mediate and help both sides to straighten out and improve. In Tibet, if a divorce could not be avoided and the wife had one son, he would be the only legal heir – even if his father remarried and got other sons. Most divorce cases were settled through private mediation to avoid serious and prolonged lawsuits. The man had the right to retain all his possessions if he was serving the government, but if he had been in the wrong – ill-treating his wife or children, gambling too much, or being unfaithful – he had to leave the house and his sons inherited everything. The wife was entitled to take all her jewellery and a share of grain or money, according to the status of the family. If there were many estates and many children the wife might get an estate through mediation and do anything she wished with it; some divorced wives who remarried created new noble families. Usually, all sons remained with the father and all daughters with the mother, but if the husband had joined his wife's family he occasionally took what he had brought to the family, and a fair share of their possession, and left all the children with their mother. Whatever was arranged, a written agreement had to be made out in case of further disputes and the matter being taken to the law. If this happened everybody had to accept the verdict of the court. After a divorce, a couple could make it up and remarry should they wish to do so.

A girl or boy was invited to join a family by a friend or relative going to their home on an auspicious day with a good scarf, folded flat. The parents were informed ahead of the coming invitation and if their child agreed they consented and the *Nyenchang* or engagement party was arranged. (*nyen* = good relationship: *chang* = beer.) This could take place immediately or some time later, and for it the parents who were inviting the girl or boy into their family had to prepare the document, which began with prayers to a deity – may be a prayer to the Goddess of Health, asking her to bless the starting off of a new life for couple. The names of both sets of parents were mentioned and promises were given on behalf of the couple, saying that they would be faithful to each other, love and respect the parents, and treat the younger sisters and brothers and the family retainers kindly. The girl and the boy were granted the same rights. The girl promised to respect her husband and in return the boy promised always to give her love and never to be unfaithful. There was a witness to this agreement from each side and it was signed by the parents and representatives of both houses.

In the most usual cases – when a boy's family had chosen his bride – the boy's parents did not attend the engagement ceremonies in the girl's family prayer-room. They sent a representative with presents laid on trays which were carried uncovered through the streets by twenty or thirty well-dressed servants, watched by many people. (The poor did the same in their own capacity.) Among the presents there had to be auspicious tea and rice and loads of butter, wheat, *tsampa* and salt. As many as nine loads were sometimes left on the floor of the prayer-room, covered by pieces of brocade. A tray of presents for each member of the family was laid beside them – perhaps pieces of silk for dresses. The house was decorated with new flags and the managing committee escorted the boy's party from the gate to the prayer-room, where the members of the girl's family were sitting. The most important offering was the *Nurin* (Breast Price) which was always paid to the bride's family, even if her mother were dead – though it was meant to repay the mother for having fed the bride. This

Our wedding picture. Myself and Jigme with my mother and father-in-law.

The Taring family: Rani and Raja Taring, Taring Rinpoche, and in front, Chime, Kalden Wangmo and Jigme.

Tsarong Dasang Dadul when he was Commander-in-Chief and Chief Cabinet Minister of the Government of Tibet.

Shuksep Jetsun Lochen Rinpoche, a saint. She died in 1950 aged over 130 years.

Myself with my mother-in-law and sister-in-law, Kalden Wangmo.

money – is silver or copper coins – was wrapped up in balls of white cloth and sometimes as many as a hundred balls were put on trays. No fixed amount was expected, but the bride judged her value by the number of presents and the amount of *Nurin* received. The cost of the day's food was given by the boy's family in the same way, as food for everybody was prepared by the girl's family. Very special *chang* had to be offered to all the guests; if it turned out good this was considered a favourable omen. Those who had brought the presents were entertained for a short while before returning home with scarves around their necks. Then copies of the agreement, written on big sheets of Tibetan paper, were rolled up, wrapped in scarves and put on two silver plates on stands. (There was some wheat on these plates, as wheat is considered a very auspicious grain.) The agreement was read by one of the representatives, the two copies were compared, the boy's father's seal was shown to the girl's father and the two copies were finally signed and sealed. The witnesses had good scarves put on their necks to thank them and the whole ceremony was conducted in a most dignified manner.

The bride, dressed in her full costume, stayed in her own specially decorated living-room during this ceremony and auspicious tea and rice were served to her. The boy's representative went to put a long scarf around her neck, but no present was given to her because she belonged to the boy's house from that day.

Many beggars, and peons from various government offices, came to collect gifts of money and were given plenty of *chang*. Two meals were served to the guests and after an early dinner the boy's party rode away before sunset, having been seen off with great courtesy and scarves. The girl's father sent a folded scarf to the boy's parents to thank them.

After our engagement Jigme and I often wrote to each other. I was still working in Tsarong's office and one day he told me to sent Jigme one of the best fox-skins and tell him that I was busy working with fox-skins. We had heard that Jigme was fond of shooting and Tsarong thought that this might make him interested in the business and at the same time show him that I was fully occupied with work.

Meanwhile the wedding preparations were going ahead for Changchup Dolma and myself. Our dowries were arranged exactly the same in the numbers of dresses, blouses, underwear, footwear and jewellery, but I was also given two lovely diamond rings, fourteen other diamonds and a few bars of gold weighing about one hundred *tolas*. Servants were called from the estates to practise the wedding song and dance as it was customary to have a special auspicious song that kept the crying of the bride unheard. Many girls were married when they were quite young – about sixteen – and they cried a lot; in any case a wedding ceremony makes the bride sad at leaving her own home, no matter how happy she may be at the thought of her marriage. I was sometimes very sad at the thought of leaving my little baby, Tsering Yangzom, behind; she was about two years old when I left her. But Pema Dolkar loved her very much and Tsarong also took a great interest in her and carried her in his arms almost everywhere he went.

Changchup Dolma and I were to be married on the same day, for economical reasons. But at the time Changchup was suffering terribly from dysentery, so as there was no British doctor in Lhasa until 1934 she had already left to take treatment from the British doctors at Gyantse military fort. Our Nampon aunt, who had her own estate near Taring Estate, was to represent our parents at the wedding.

It was decided to have one representative and six official servants from each house to accompany our bridal party to Taring Estate, near Gyantse. Tailors were called, new dresses and hats were made for the servants and new saddles and beddings were prepared. Since it was to be an unusual bridal party, which had to go on a journey for seven days, I needed extra stores so sweets, biscuits, canned food, ginger wine and a bottle of crème de menthe were given to the steward in charge.

Before leaving Lhasa I had a three days' farewell party and all our friends came with presents. As the servants of a wedding party were well paid everybody was happy. The auspicious days for me to leave Lhasa and reach Taring Estate had been given by horoscope and the Taring's representative and servants came to Tsarong House on a fixed day.

I left early one morning and before my departure the astrologer came to draw many things in the palms of my hands, so that no evil spirit could harm me. He and I had been to school together and we had a good laugh while he was painting my palms. I had received a complete set of jewellery from Tsarong, but according to custom a full set of costume jewellery was sent from the Taring family and handed to me, piece by piece, by a young boy who had been chosen to suit the element of my birth year. When I was fully dressed I went to the Deity's room, to take leave of the Deity, and sat on a special high seat for about fifteen minutes while prayers were said by four monks. Then I was taken to the prayer-room, where another seat had been prepared and auspicious tea and rice were served. Here the servants sang the wedding song, which made me so sad that I cried. The family and the servants offered me scarves, said good-bye and wished me all the best – which made me feel even more sad. When the auspicious moment came I was told to get up and go to the Treasury House, where I had to leave a print of my left foot on a flat wooden box of wheat, in order not to take any of the family luck with me. Finally I was made to sit on a chair on the steps of the main house where an arrow decorated with five strips of different coloured silk, ornamented with pearl, turquoise, coral and amber, was put between my dress and the shawl at the back of my neck. This arrow had been given by Jigme to his representative the day the servants left Taring Estate and it meant that I now belonged to him. The arrow may not be presented inside the house because it would be bad manners to take something from a person within their own home. Usually it is worn all the way to one's new home, but my journey was so long that I removed it later that day at Kyitsal Luthing.

The sun was just rising when I left Lhasa. My pony was a pregnant mare – the horoscope indicates whether a mare in foal or a mare with foal at foot is best – but I left her at Kyitsal Luthing and took a horse instead. No bride would ride a mule because mules are barren. Many people had gathered to watch my departure, but I could not see anyone because I was covered with a white felt cloak to hide my jewellery from the jealous deities. The song of the menservants was carried on until at midday we reached Kyitsal Luthing, where Ragashar, a family friend, had a tent and lunch-reception for me.

Our family's representative was Tsarong's brother, Kyenrab. Up to Nangatse Tsarong had the responsibility of caring for the bridal party, from Nangatse to Gyantse Taring took charge. People everywhere kindly offered me *chang* and scarves, but in the villages the mothers were so superstitious that they put on their best clothes and with arrows in their hands prayed and circled round me, so that I would not take their luck, and as we rode away they shouted at me from the roofs of their houses, saying, 'All luck must remain! Do not take our luck!' I was sometimes still a child and I laughed and laughed with our gay servants, three of whom had been at school with me. The Chinaman amongst them was always asking for sweets because he smoked opium and was not very strong: he was to cook for us in Gyantse, as Tsarong had said that British officers would be eating with us there. The Tarings had also invited good cooks from Shigatse to help their cook.

For seven days in spring I travelled. Springtime had been chosen for our journey, so that no hail would damage the crops. (It was believed that bridal parties could bring very destructive hail-storms.) On the way I missed my baby so much that I envied even the sheep and goats going about with their babies. Still, I knew that I would meet her again and I was glad at heart to think that my life was going to be much happier.

At Phunling Shika, an estate of Nyerpa Namgyal's, Nampon Ani La and Changchup Dolma joined me. Phunling is about two miles from Taring Estate and we spent three days there waiting for the auspicious date to arrive; Changchup Dolma and I had great fun together. Before we left we were dressed in our full wedding costumes and had a short tea and rice ceremony with our aunt.

It was the custom in Gyantse for the local people to block a bride's door and say they would not let her pass by their fields. Their arguing was strong and lasted the whole night, but after giving them lots of money they let us go. Many women came with us, beating drums, ringing small bells and waving arrows in their hands as they went round both of us brides – which made us giggle even more than usual – and on our way past the fields men put fire right across the road and would not let us pass. Again our servants had to plead and pay them well until we were allowed to go by. (This was just a trick to get money; they would not really have stopped us had we insisted on continuing.)

At last, as the sun was rising, we reached Taring Estate, where the first welcome *chang* was offered by smartly-dressed *chang*-girls. After another few yards the second welcome *chang* was offered and monastic trumpets were blown on the roof-tops while about twenty women retainers greeted us by bursting into song. I felt both sad and happy at the same time, but Changchup Dolma began to sob like a child. Nobody could stop her crying, which distressed me and made me want to sob too.

After dismounting we stepped over loads of food-suffs – butter, tea, wheat, rice – covered with five-coloured silk. It was the right of the servants of the girl's house to divide all this between them. The bride's representative had to recite poetry before the bride dismounted from her pony; then a servant recited a poem of praise at the door, and another at the staircase. Coloured silk scarves were draped on the doors and stairs and left there until the wedding was over, when the servants of the bridegroom's house divided them.

My mother-in-law, in her full ceremonial costume, met me at the staircase with a pail of milk and took my hand. Since there were two brides to be welcomed, she was accompanied by an aunt of Jigme's, also carrying a pail of milk, to take the hand of Changchup Dolma. We at once went – all singing – to the newly built big hall, where we sat by seniority while tea and rice were served and Tsarong's representative handed Taring Raja, our father-in-law, a greeting scarf, folded flat, from the Tsarong family.

The Taring family, and their retainers and servants, then gave scarves to all. The Taring retainers were so happy about these marriages that they had volunteered to supply the *chang* for the wedding. (My parents-in-law were very good to their people and the mutual love between family and retainers was like that between parents and children.)

Because of having gone to an English school in Darjeeling, Jigme had short hair and was wearing a Mongolian hat, as was customary for all the few Tibetan nobles who had short hair, but Chime Dorje, having long hair, wore an official hat with a gold knob on the crown and silk tassels hanging over the brocade brim. They both wore official costume – yellow brocade robes with red sashes and long red boots.

The wedding party went on for about ten days. Soon after our arrival the ceremony on the terrace of the roof was performed. A tent was pitched there, containing decorated seats and offerings of water and *tormas*, all the banners and prayer-flags were changed and monks blew eight-foot monastic trumpets and beat drums. Our bridal banners were specially made of coloured silk, according to the elements of our birth years. My element was earth and Changchup Dolma's was iron, so a yellow flag for me and a blue one for her, both printed with prayers, were hoisted by our representative. This was a most important part of the ceremony. Before hoisting the banner the representative had to recite another poem, saying – 'Our daughter of the Tsarongs, who has married the son of Taring, will have equal rights with her husband. And by hoisting this banner of hers on the roof of Taring may this claim be known to all.' Sikkim State had sent a minister with a military escort, which presented arms when we arrived.

After the ceremonies friends came to greet us with presents. Intimate friends gave parties, each lasting a full day, which were held in the Taring's house though the food was paid for by the friends. The staff of the British Trade Agent at Gyantse, and the Commanding Officer of their British Army escort, came to these parties.

After about a fortnight Tsarong's representative and servants returned to Lhasa, with gifts and thanks from the Taring family to the Tsarong family. But our personal maids remained at Taring Estate with Changchup Dolma and myself.

8   Life on a Country Estate

TARING ESTATE WAS given to Taring Raja and his uncle in 1893, when they came to Tibet as exiles from Sikkim. It used to be enjoyed by *Dapons* (Army Generals) in place of a salary and was small compared with the estates of the old noble families and the monasteries. It was a very happy little place, though grain was always short. The main crops were barley, peas and wheat and we got only six times the seed – about four-thousand boxes of grain annually, which equals about two-thousand *maunds*. This was indeed a very poor crop. Our rice, sugar, cloth, matches, soap and iron were imported from India.

Out of the crops we had to pay land taxes to Gyantse Dzong and to the monastery of Gyantse, and we also had to pay for the performance of rites to abolish those evils and disturbances which may come now and again – such as epidemics and bad hail-storms. The main part of the rites payment was taken care of by the Taring family but the retainers also made contributions in kind. Twenty monks were invited to read the one hundred and eight volumes of the *Kagyur* (Lord Buddha's teachings), and there are many other rites, too, though we believe we can never avoid calamities which are bound up with our karma or fate.

At Taring we only had *dzo* to plough and cows for our milk; the *dzo* is a cross between a yak and a cow and the male *dzo* and because the retainers could not afford to keep their own we lent them ours and they paid us in kind or in service. The *dzo* ploughed in pairs and their heads were decorated with red wool and sometimes with little mirrors which could be seen reflecting the sunlight from a far distance. The wooden and iron ploughs — imported from India — were not strong enough to dig deep. Ploughing was done in autumn and spring because in winter the earth is frozen. Many fields were ploughed and left unsown for a year, for better crops; we utilised no artificial fertiliser and our best manure was human excreta. In lavatories the excreta was covered with ash and earth, and taken to the fields thrice a year. Cow and sheep dung also make good manure, but in central Tibet all such dung was used for fuel, as wood is so scarce.

The female *dzo* (*dzomo*) gives very nice milk — stronger than cow's milk, but weaker than the milk of the female yak (*dri*). *Dri*'s milk is very thick and most nourishing, because they graze on the highest mountains where they can get the most nutritious herbs. There was a small monastery above Drepung called Gephel Otse, where the eight ordained monks kept a herd of *dri* and send the curd to their patrons with their seal on the earthenware pot. The herbs on that mountain were said to be the most nutritious of all.

The life on Taring Estate was quite different from the fast life in Lhasa. Jigme and I enjoyed living in the country and were very happy. When I arrived at Taring in springtime the fields were growing, the birds were singing and we had our own sweet little summer house with a sitting-room and bed-room upstairs and a hall and lavatory downstairs. We went to have our meals in the main house, with the rest of the family.

Jigme's second eldest sister, Kalden Wangmo, worked hard in the house and took great care of us, coming to our room every day to ask what sort of food we would like. She was known as 'Goggles' to our British friends at Gyantse because she had big round eyes. She was a good singer and dancer and Jigme played the banjo and we danced every night.

Jigme's parents, then in their fifties, were most kind. There was a great contrast between our two families. At Tsarong House everybody was always doing business; here in Taring it was so peaceful, with Father-in-law reading or gardening, and Mother-in-law reading the scriptures, or spinning, or supervising the weavers. There were about six carpet weavers and three cloth weavers; what they made was used for the house or as presents. The Shema woollen cloth produced at Taring was one of the best. Very soft wool was collected off the necks of sheep and Mother-in-law used only fast vegetable dyes and knew exactly how to mix them. She turned out the most beautiful woollen aprons and pieces for dresses; the work was so fine that the family could get only one dress in a year, so each member took it in turn, year by year, to have a new dress. A length about ten inches wide could be drawn through a ring. This cloth can last you a lifetime and the more you wash it the brighter the colours become.

My mother-in-law was a good-looking, very big-built lady from the Dode family, which was considered to be the tallest in Tibet; their estate was also in the district of Gyantse. She had a placid nature, worked slowly and steadily and would never let Changchup or me work in the house as the Tarings wanted us to be free women and enjoy ourselves by doing whatever we liked. About thrice a month Mother-in-law's hair was dressed by one of the women retainers and this took nearly a whole day in front of the mirror. Both drank tea all the time and the hairdresser gave Mother-in-law the news of the village. Sometimes I sat by them and talked and made them laugh; nobody could make Mother-in-law laugh more than I could. Father-in-law – a small man, neither fat nor thin – often came to sit with us and joined in our silly jokes. He, Changchup and myself used to giggle and giggle whenever we were together. Father-in-law went down to Sikkim sometimes, on pilgrimage and to meet his relatives; the Sikkimese used to beg him to let them carry him on their backs where the roads were difficult, in order to get his blessing and have the satisfaction of serving him. Some wept and said, 'Our master has aged.' Everywhere they made bamboo shelters for him and joyously greeted him with oranges and *tungpa* (their national drink). Taring Raja did not serve the Tibetan government himself, but he took part in the New Year ceremonies in Lhasa and always looked forward to paying homage to His Holiness and giving him some of his nicest things as gifts. (After Sidkeong Tulku's death he had been called to Sikkim to receive his share of his brother's personal possessions, which were divided amongst the family.) He wished his three sons to serve the government of His Holiness, in whom he had great faith and confidence, and his most obedient sons did their best to fulfil their father's wish. Jigme's and Rigzin Namgyal's education was taken care of by the Sikkim State.

Though my parents-in-law were leading a retired life at Taring Estate they used to work hard before their children were grown up. Taring Rinpoche, Jigme's clever lama uncle, built Lingbu Monastery near the estate, and was Abbot. He took great care to make it a good monastery and the Sikkim State helped him generously. He also practised as a Tibetan doctor. The present Chogyal of Sikkim (*Chogyal* means 'Religious King') studied with Taring Rinpoche for about two years, from the age of twelve.

Chime Dorje and Changchup lived in the new main house. He worked in the fields, leaving at dawn to help our peasants to sow the seeds, and he used to go round the village solving people's problems. The Land Tax was collected in grain, some of which was stored and lent to our retainers whenever they needed extra. We ground large amounts of *tsampa* for the household at our mill and made mustard-seed oil in our own press; Chime supervised all this work.

Jigme was always making something at home, or painting,

or learning Tibetan grammar and spelling. He had a lot of memorising to do, because he had not been able to study much Tibetan when he was young, having gone to school in Darjeeling. Like his father, he is a talented artist and loves gardening. He is also handy at carpentry and used to make cupboards and bookshelves for our rooms. He is a good cook, so with his sister Kalden Wangmo's help he prepared special savoury dishes and cakes. (I was hopeless at both, and still am.) Together we built walls in the garden, and when the river was high we helped the retainers to dam it. Jigme worked really hard at these jobs but I used to offer to light a fire and make tea. Then Kalden Wangmo and I would play *sho* while everybody else worked. However, I always loved teaching so I organised a small school for my two younger sisters-in-law, the servants' children and two sweet orphan cousins of Jigme's who were being brought up by his mother. Whenever I got ill these children would come and worry and make my bed comfortable. Another pleasure of mine was sometimes bathing our retainers' children and cleaning their ears. I had a skill for taking out the wax with which the ears were often blocked; I used to put in glycerine and syringe the bad ones. I was very fond, too, of giving first aid treatment to anybody who needed it and I kept many patent medicines. The British doctor in Gyantse taught me how to give vaccinations and let me vaccinate all our retainers and their children.

Jigme's eldest sister, Rigzin Bhuti, was a tall, stout, religious girl with an extraordinarily sweet character. She married Ragashar Thokar—brother of the Queen Mother of Sikkim—who later became a *Shap-pē*. Their daughter is now the wife of Tsarong's son, Dudul Namgyal. Jigme's third sister became a nun, and the fourth married Numa, the son of an ancient noble family, and had two sons and two daughters.

Jigme owned two very good greyhounds—Shiva and Shila—that he got from a British officer in exchange for a valuable Tibetan dagger. He used to go on the big hills with them to chase hares, and he also took his double-barrelled gun and shot burrels and gazelle occasionally and hares, partridge and duck very often. I did not like his shooting, but I said nothing for some time. My maid, Doma, used to say, 'The younger Prince is so good – he works and comes back and stays with his wife in the evenings. But our Prince is always out to shoot, which is very cruel. It is the way of living of a poor hunter and a prince should not behave like that because his livelihood is good.' When she felt very sad she would say – 'Why have you left your beautiful house!' Then I told her that I did not like to check Jigme at once, but that one day I would ask him to stop shooting. I also told her not to feel sad, because if we were not content at Taring we could easily go back to Tsarong House. The day I left Lhasa, Tsaarong said, 'In case you are not happy at Taring you may call servants and ponies and come back to Tsarong House. Your home will ever be at your own disposal.' But he also wished me a very happy marriage.

Eventually I asked Jigme to give up his shooting, as it was not the gentle work of a prince. He replied that he liked to hunt with his greyhounds and that the gun had been given to him by his uncle, the King of Sikkim. He said, 'The servants get good meat and hare's meat is very tender.' His mother also did not like Jigme's shooting, but treated him as the eldest son, with full respect; otherwise she could have stopped him, because he would have done anything at her command. The Taring children always had the reputation for having wonderful natures, and I found that this was true.

After some time Shila died, and as I always refused to go hunting with Jigme he stayed at home more and more. When I married him I found that he read the scriptures and performed rituals much more than I did, so I used to ask him, 'Are you seriously following the teachings of the Lord Buddha or are you simply passing your morning hours this way to amuse yourself?' He would reply jokingly that it was I who made him a lay person and didn't I remember that on our wedding day he still had short hair and wore an orange shirt. He said he had learned all the rites from his uncle, Taring Rinpoche, with whom be had lived for about two years at Taring Monastery. During our arguments I would tell him that animals love their lives and that no matter how small they are, or ugly, they do not like to die. I used to say, 'They cannot talk but they love their wives and children. To separate them is a great sin and it is no use doing your morning prayers if you behave like that.' One day he shot one of the two wild ducks who lived by the pond behind Taring House and for several days the other duck hovered around, crying for its companion. Jigme saw this and was very much moved. Then he said he was going to give his gun to his father – and he took it up to the main house and handed it over to him.

A few months later, the servants said that a very funny bird had perched on the huge Taring poplar tree, which was said to be over two hundred years old. We looked, and Jigme told me that it was a black duck and must be a bad omen, as no such bird would normally perch on a tree. He said, 'Let me get my gun from Father and bring it down' – to which I agreed, because I thought he would not be able to shoot it as it was on the highest branch. So he got his gun and with a bang brought down the poor bird. We found no similar birds in Gyantse, but later in the pond at the back of Potala we saw many of them.

After that Jigme did not go shooting regularly, but often on our journeys he was very much tempted. Once when I checked him – by saying that shooting should only be the work of a poor man, to earn – he got angry and galloped to the next stop, leaving me behind with a few servants. I caught up with him two hours later and he was smiling and saying that he had only come ahead of us to make the fire and have tea ready.

Six months after our weddings Changchup had a relapse of her old illness and developed chronic dysentery. This was a great worry and sadness for the whole family, yet it was wonderful to see Chime nursing her with such devotion. She died while Jigme and I were having a holiday in India and when in Kalimpong we heard of her death and felt terribly upset.

Shortly after our engagements had been arranged Taring Raja dreamt that one of the banners on the roof of our house got burned and fell down right in the courtyard. As he suspected that something bad might take place in the family he had special rites performed to avoid mishap. When Changchup died he knew that this dream had been a bad indication.

A few years after Changchup's death, when Jigme and I were living in Lhasa, Taring Raja sent an old family friend to ask me to marry Chime Dorje as my second husband, for the strength of the family. I refused, saying that I loved Jigme too much to have any other husband, but I suggested that Chime should marry one of my sister Norbu Yudon's daughters instead, so he married my niece, De Kyongwangmo, and they had two sons and three beautiful daughters.

The life at Taring was unforgettable. Since I did not conceive I was like a schoolgirl, playing always, though everybody else worked so hard. But I did work sometimes in a small vegetable garden and every week all Tsarong's foreign correspondence was sent to us and we translated the letters into Tibetan and sent them back to Lhasa, where Tsarong wrote the replies which he sent to us for translation into English; then we returned them to Lhasa for Tsarong's signature and finally he sent them back to us to be posted with the British post from Gyantse. It took quite a long time for people to get their answers.

At the New Year, harvest and other festivals Jigme, Chime, Kalden Wangmo, the servants, the retainers and myself used to dance through the night till dawn. I enjoyed this gay life, which we did not have in the city. Every month there was the hoisting of the prayer-flag, and then the retainers brought big earthen jars of *chang* and danced and sang until they had emptied them. They had different songs for threshing, reaping, sowing, ploughing – Tibetans can do no work without singing, which helps to lighten their burden.

Women sowed the seeds in the springtime and Kalden Wangmo used to help with this work. I do not say that all our Tibetan noble ladies were the same, but it is fairly accurate that both men and women worked hard on their estates. Life in a town is much easier, so we owed a lot to our farmers, herdsmen and nomads.

At least once a month Father-in-law invited the British Trade Agent from Gyantse and his staff to lunch. In summer the water from the river was always muddy-looking, so when guests came someone was sent right up into the mountains for clear spring water. Both my parents-in-law were very particular about *chang* and tea. Jigme and I were often invited to spend a few days at the British fort at Gyantse where we enjoyed ourselves playing tennis, riding out into the hills and dancing in the evenings.

Father-in-law once sent Jigme and me to do the annual account at Dopta, another small estate, five days' ride from Taring, which had been given to the Sikkim royal family by the Tibetan government. During my engagement to Jigme his monk-uncle had asked the Dalai Lama, through Lungshar — who was a friend of Taring Rinpoche — to give him this estate for his monastery. Tsarong was in the *Kashag* at that time and saw the petition. He came home looking rather upset and said, 'Taring Raja is about to lose Dopta Estate. We must call him to Lhasa at once — but in the meantime I shall write to His Holiness.' He told me to get a nice scarf and he wrote 'Taring Rinpoche is asking for Dopta Estate for his monastery. Since Taring Raja has taken refuge in Tibet, kindly do not give the verdict until he himself comes to Lhasa.' Then he wrote to Taring Raja and all these letters I had to copy after he had drafted them. Soon Taring Raja came to Lhasa and asked the government not to give Dopta to the monastery: he pointed out that it had already been given to the Sikkim State, who had granted it to him. The Dalai Lama said, 'Since Dopta has been given to Sikkim State, if the Chogyal of Sikkim agrees, Taring Rinpoche may have it for his monastery.' Taring Rinpoche at once went to Sikkim to see the Chogyal, who decided that Dopta must be left with Taring Raja because he had children to inherit it — otherwise, on the Rinpoche's death it would go to the monastery, which would not be right since it was Sikkimese property. So Dopta remained with us. Father-in-law was very much hurt, as he considered that Taring Rinpoche had not been a kind uncle to the children.

Group of Tibetan army officers, Tsarong seated centre.

Group of Tibetan noblemen's sons with Dadul Namgyal, Tsarong's son, centre. Photo: Colonel Leslie Weir.

(Following page) A Monlam Festival ceremony being celebrated in the courtyard of the Jokhang. Photo: Major George Sherriff.

From our Dopta Estate we got about a thousand *maunds* of grain, fifteen *maunds* of butter and fifty *maunds* of wool every year. We had a few thousand sheep and about a thousand yak there, with our own nomads. There were also some houses for the two hundred or so retainers who grew grain; several of these families invited us to dine when we went there and gave us very nice food. But most of the people were nomads and Jigme and I camped beside their tents. They owned land, yaks and sheep and many of them were quite well off. Their huge mastiffs with red eyes were very fierce and barked with all their might. They were usually tied up, but the loose ones attacked our ponies and once Jigme had to fire his pistol to frighten them back to their tents. The thirteenth Dalai Lama was very fond of mastiffs and always had them guarding the palace doors. There were two types – long-haired and short-haired. The best mastiffs came from the small district of Duchung, near Gyantse, and when our great friend Dingja was governor there he used to send dogs to His Holiness. I remember the Dalai Lama writing personal letters to Dingja, asking him to give offerings to the spirits at Duchung because the mastiffs from there were getting ill and dying.

When Jigme and Chime decided to live separately Dopta Estate was given to Chime as his share of the family property. I feel very happy to look back now on that wonderful time at Taring Estate. I say to myself that I was lucky, because many wives do not get on with their in-laws. I took a vow right from the beginning that I would serve Jigme's parents most lovingly, since I had had no opportunity to serve my own mother and father. There is nothing more meritorious than to serve one's parents – especially one's mother, who suffers so much to bring up her children and gives us the best love we ever get.

9   Intrigues in Lhasa

WHILE JIGME AND I were enjoying our happiness on Taring Estate, poor Tsarong was having a difficult time in Lhasa. His rivals continued to plot against him, spreading false rumours and urging the Dalai Lama to degrade him further; but His Holiness was always reluctant to be unfaithful to his hero and it was only in 1930 that he removed him from the *Kashag* and left him with no power. Tsarong broke the news to Jigme and me by sending a telegram asking us to address his letters *Dzasa* instead of *Shap-pē*.

It puzzled many people that Tsarong's enemies were able to divert the Dalai Lama's confidence from him. However, those enemies were led by *Tsi-pon* Lungshar, who was such a cunning man that he made His Holiness doubt Tsarong a little; the thirteenth Dalai Lama was so powerful that nobody could persuade him to do anything against his will.

Lungshar was an ambitious man, from a poor noble family, who had spent a few years in England supervising the four Tibetan boys who went to school at Rugby. During Tsarong's absence from Tibet in 1925 he came close to the Dalai Lama as his adviser and it was said that Lungshar and Dumpa *Dzasa* – His Holiness's nephew, who replaced Tsarong as Commander-in-Chief – often told His Holiness that Tsarong was only strengthening the Army to make himself ruler of Tibet. Rigzin Chodon told me that she had heard that Dumpa shed tears in the presence of His Holiness, saying that he could not bear the responsibility if Tsarong succeeded in taking over the country – and that Tsarong had already built a palace for himself. (This was the new Tsarong House, built in 1923, which some malicious people said was even finer than Norbu Lingka.) Dumpa *Dzasa* took opium and was very slack in his work and it was rumoured that Lungshar had schemed to have such a weak person made Commander-in-Chief.

Lungshar was very clever at sorcery. He was all the time doing magic to destroy Shatra *Tsi-pon*, the son and heir of Shatra *Lonchen*, because Lungshar had achieved a marriage between his own eldest son, Chapase, and the daughter of Shatra *Lonchen*. It was said that he thought if Shatra *Tsi-pon* died Chapase could take the name Shatra and would be all in all in Shatra House. (The Shatras had a house like a monastery, and many estates, and were one of of the greatest noble families.) Shatra *Tsi-pon* was about to become a *Shap-pē* when he died of a very peculiar illness, after getting attacks of pain five or six times a day. Then a sorcerer's object was found on the flat roof of Shatra House, over Shatra *Tsi-pon*'s living-room. It was a figure of Shatra *Tsi-pon* kneeling down naked, holding a scorpion on his head – this Shatra *Tsi-pon*'s widow told me. However, the Shatra servants, who were like members of the family, backed the baby son of Shatra *Tsi-pon*, as the only heir of the house, and were able to have Chapase and his wife sent away by letting them have one of the family estates.

Lungshar had also made most of the trouble between the Dalai Lama and the Panchen Lama – both good men – and after the Panchen Lama's flight to China in 1923 Lungshar sent Tsogo *Dapon* to pursue him and bring him back alive or dead. When the people heard this their hearts broke in pieces and they all called Lungshar a wizard. They said that he was the incarnation of Khanpo Palden Dondup who in 1862 aroused feelings of rebellion in Drepung Monastery, causing the monks to lead a civil war. The Lhasa people then composed a song:

Lungshar was not a hunter,
Tsogo was not a hound,
Panchen was not a deer.

In August 1930, Colonel Leslie Weir – the Political Officer of Sikkim – visited Tibet with his wife and their daughter, Joan Mary. It had been planned that I should accompany them to Lhasa, to act as Mrs. Weir's guide and interpreter, but when they heard of Tsarong's degradation they decided not to take me. Colonel Weir wrote to Mr. Howell – then Foreign Secretary in the Government of India – from Lhasa: 'The degradation of Tsarong *Shap-pē* is attributed largely to his having been too friendly with foreigners and I believe the Dalai Lama told him so. Every official lives in mortal dread of the Dalai Lama and to save himself from Tsarong's fate is chary of showing outwardly too great a friendship for us ... Tsarong *Shap-pē* has very privately written me reassuring me of his friendship but, in view of recent events, he wants us to keep entirely away from him. We did not bring Mary Tsarong from Gyantse to help Tyra as we had planned – it would not have been wise.' I had been longing to go to Lhasa with the Weirs, but at that time we were all in anxiety.

Shortly after Tsarong's degradation from the *Kashag*, His Holiness set up a new government department, called the *Trapchi Lekhung*, to take care of the mint, the paper currency factory and the ammunition factory. Before this, separate departments had dealt with these three things and Tsarong had been in charge of the mint. Now he and a monk-official named Kunphela were put in charge of the *Trapchi Lekhung*.

In olden times we had only silver coins in Tibet and some of these were cut in pieces to use as change. Later the government minted copper coins for smaller denominations. Ten *kar* made one *sho*, ten *sho* made one *sang*, ten *sang* made one *tamka*. Because our old *tamkas* were pure silver many were taken out of the country by traders and sold. We had plenty of good quality gold, though little of it was mined, so the government also minted pure gold coins – which remained in Tibet an even shorter time than the silver coins. In 1925 two officials from the mint were sent to Calcutta to buy printing presses and learn how to use them. After a lot of paper currency had been printed Tsarong said that this was not good for the country and suggested that we should have a gold reserve. So every year three hundred small slabs of gold, each weighing twenty-seven *tolas*, were put away in the Potala. This gold was imported from India – along with silver and copper for the mint – because our own mining was not well developed. Nepalese traders did most of the dealing and some of them were robbed and killed in Zara, a lonely, frightening place about four days' ride from Lhasa. After that we had a joke whenever we talked about dividing anything – 'First kill the Nepalese, then divide the gold.'

Kunphela, Tsarong's colleague at the *Trapchi Lekhung*, was by this time one of the most powerful men in Tibet. He started as a very intelligent boy from a poor peasant family and while still a young monk was doing the difficult work of carving wood-blocks, for printing religious books, at Norbu Lingka. In 1925, when Tsarong ceased to attend daily on His Holiness, Kunphela became the Dalai Lama's most influential attendant. He could have been a clever statesman, had he had a good education, but as it was he did not know much about government work, though he was very active and ambitious. Like many other people, he respected Tsarong's great knowledge and experience of government affairs and consulted him often on important matters. Tsarong felt no jealousy or resentment towards him and always advised him as best he could.

About eighteen months after my marriage to Jigme he was offered a job in Gartok, as British Trade Agent, by Mr. Williamson, the Political Officer of Sikkim. At the same time the Tibetan government telegraphed to say that Yuthok *Kadon* (my mother's first cousin) was bringing to Gyantse twenty-five soldiers out of the five hundred men of His

Holiness's bodyguard regiment, for training by the British there as machine gunners. Jigme was informed that the Dalai Lama wished him to be their interpreter and also to be trained, and then to come to Lhasa. Since he could not disappoint His Holiness he refused Mr. Williamson's kind offer.

During the three months' training course Captain D. Marshall was the instructor, and Jigme and I were given quarters in the British fort while Yuthok *Kadon* stayed in the town with his sister, Kyipup. At first we all enjoyed ourselves, making many new friends and going to parties, but after two months we suffered a great sadness.

One morning Yuthok told me that his wife – a niece of the thirteenth Dalai Lama – had given birth to a daughter and had had an easy time; but just before lunch a servant came running to ask me to tell Yuthok that his wife had died. Yuthok and I hurried to her with the doctors, who could do nothing. His two small sons and an elder daughter had also been brought to Gyantse, so we were in despair. I took care of Yuthok and his elder son, and Kyipup looked after the others. The baby girl lived for only a year.

Many young Tibetan women died in childbirth, mostly because they could not discharge the placenta. The peasants took birth for granted, like animals do, and women shepherds often had their babies in the mountains and cut their own cords with sharp slates. Tibetan doctors had no method of dealing with bad presentations. The woman who went through childbirth naturally usually came off best, but sometimes mothers were given drinks of hot *chang* or a cup of hot melted butter with musk, and these treatments produced many complications. Midwives were taught to put more blood on the children's side of the cord before tying and cutting it, because it was believed that the more blood the child had from the placenta the healthier it would be. It was also believed that childbirth caused a lot of infection and some people avoided visiting a new mother until her room had been disinfected by a lama sprinkling holy water and saying special prayers. As soon as a child was born a pinch of *tsampa* and butter was put in its mouth to wish it a happy, prosperious and long life. Mothers often had nine or ten children and every married person considered that it was good to have many children. There is a Tibetan proverb – 'No matter how beautiful a wife may be, she must have a child in her lap.' Twins were common in Tibet; triplets came but seldom and three boys were considered very auspicious. There was no birth-control, but some of our noble wives went down to India to have birth-control operations. After childbirth, or during any illness, the sick person was not allowed to sleep in the daytime because our temperature rises while we sleep. So someone stayed always in the room, to guard the patient from sleep.

When we returned to Lhasa from Gyantse we found that Kunphela had become very influential indeed. Even if he said, 'East is West', everybody had to say 'Yes' because the Dalai Lama trusted him so much. He was then recruiting a new regiment, called *Drong Drak Makhar*, from among the younger sons of well-to-do peasant families and from a few noble families too – as reinforcement for the troops on the eastern border, where the Chinese were then being very troublesome. He was so ambitious that people thought he wanted a special regiment for his own purposes, but he never admitted this. Jigme was made the junior *Dapon* and Yuthok the senior *Dapon* of *Drong Drak Makhar* and a big barracks was built at Dapchi, near Lhasa. Ngawang Jigme, the illegitimate son of Ani Champala – who had been educated well by Tsarong – was one of the thousand young men who were now being compelled to become ordinary soldiers. When something is the custom people do not complain, even if they do not like it; but this regiment was a new idea, that nobody liked, being imposed on the country. Soldiers had always been those who wanted to join the Army, yet everybody was so afraid of Kunphela that instead of complaining aloud they just wondered how long his harsh influence was going to last.

There were then only two cars in Lhasa, both owned by His Holiness, and every day Kunphela came to the barracks in the Austin, driven by his friend, Tashi Dondup. (The barracks were near the *Trapchi Lekhung* where Kunphela was working with Tsarong during those years.) Kunphela was so fond of his regiment that he himself paid for gold badges for the *Dapons'* hats and ordered complete British uniforms from Calcutta for Yuthok and Jigme. All the soldiers' uniforms were made with great care and the men were fed well — sometimes delicious dried yak meat was brought from the Norbu Lingka for their cauldrons. They got the same pay as ordinary soldiers — about twelve shillings a month — but in other ways were given all sorts of special treatment; yet they were never happy.

While Yuthok was advising Kunphela about recruiting, Jigme was training the men to use machine-guns. Long after, Lhalu *Shap-pē* — Lungshar's son — often teased Jigme about the way he used to make the recruits run with tripods on the Dapchi parade ground, getting their pants torn by the tripod pins; he said he could never forget the hardship of that time. Once Kunphela had a junior officer lashed because he complained that the recruiting system was unjust. The only way to escape conscription was by giving bribes or knowing one of Kunphela's favourites.

During this period, great romance activities were going on in our family. My cousin Yuthok had fallen madly in love with Surkhang *Shap-pē*'s sister, Dorje Yudon, whom he later married. Ngapo *Shap-pē* died in Kham and his beautiful young widow, Tseten Dolkar, came back to Lhasa. She was a grand-niece of the thirteenth Dalai Lama and a niece of Yuthok, whose home she often visited. There she met a number of young officials — all hoping to marry her — and among them were Surkhang *Dapon* and Ngawang Jigme, who was now a very handsome, shy young man. The time had come for Ngawang Jigme to marry my sister, Tseten Dolkar, according to the agreement drawn up, when Ngawang Jigme was thirteen, between his mother, Ani Champala, and Tsarong. But in the meantime Tseten Dolkar had had seven children by Tsarong so she refused to marry Ngawang Jigme, though Tsarong reminded her that the marriage had been agreed to by all. She said, 'I will not remarry any more and have so many children of different fathers.' Therefore Ngawang Jigme was free to marry the other, younger, Tseten Dolkar, if he could get her. His main rival, Surkhang *Dapon*, was capable, but again the concern of the servants of the house influenced things. They believed that Ngawang Jigme would be the best choice, as a shy man suits servants; and also Tseten Dolkar liked him very much. So he married her and eventually became Ngapo *Shappē* and they had twelve lovely children — four boys and eight girls.

After spending nearly two years away from my little daughter, I was very happy to be with her again. But Jigme and I wished to live in a small house of our own, so Tsarong permitted us to build one in the compound of Tsarong House and there we stayed for some years. (Later, Heinrich Harrer and Peter Aufschnaiter lived for a year in this house.)

After my marriage to Jigme I did not conceive for more than three years. I was not keen to have another baby, because I had had such a difficult labour with my first one, but as Jigme was longing for children we consulted a very holy lama, one of my mother's religious teachers, who lived as a hermit in a cave near Lhasa. When we asked if it was our karma to have children he prayed and then said that he felt we would have some wonderful children, by the blessing of our deities. He gave me a charm and told me to wear it always. A document was given with it, saying that if it were worn by old people and infants it would protect them from evil, and if by a woman who had not conceived she would bear children. The hermit also advised me to pray to Dolma, my karma deity, and asked us both to perform certain rites. We did all he told us to do and a few months later, in 1934, I became pregnant.

I was sick for the full nine months. At the time I was taking lessons on the *yangchin*, but after a while I could not bear the sound of it, so I gave it up. I had a big appetite for radishes, and it was springtime, so Jigme and I strolled all over the place to see every vegetable garden, and went from door to door asking people if they had new radishes. Finally we did get some and I relished them. (Tibetans believe that much walking exercise should be taken during pregnancy.) When I developed this longing Pema Dolkar at once planted radishes and said they would be ready in a fortnight, as she had some special quick-growing radishes from England. But by the time they were grown my craving for radishes had gone and instead I was craving *mingduk*, a famous delicacy of monks which was given to High Lamas after they had passed their examination in dialectical debate; it was made of rice boiled in butter with meat, raisins, and dried apricots. Pema Dolkar said that she would get her cook to prepare some for me, but though I enjoyed it I could not look at it again for another four or five years.

At this time our closest friend was General Dingja, one of the three army officers who had been sent to Quetta and Shillong for military training. He was a brother of Rigzin Chodon, of Delek Rabten (my sister Norbu Yudon's husband) and of Tsawa Tritrul, and his wife was Tsarong's sister Yangchen, who bore him three beautiful daughters. He was stout, round-faced and full of fun – a very fine man, intelligent and broad-minded. Everyone enjoyed his company and Tsarong and Dudul Namgyal loved him. When we were living in the compound of Tsarong House, Jigme and I just could not do without him; he had his breakfast and dinner with us nearly every day and we spent our evenings playing card-games and laughing. When he went to the *Kashag* for information only Jigme and I knew that under his khaki Army greatcoat he was wearing his pink nightpants, tucked into his knee-boots. Once he told us that in the *Shap-pē's* scretaries room, when he was being pulled here and there in play, his pink pants were discovered – but as most of our officials of all ages were full of fun nobody minded. He used to tell me that I was like one of the fatty little boy-monks who beat small drums in the New Year procession, and I used to call him the monk who carried the big, huge drum and skipped on the way, dropping balls of *tsampa* from his pocket. Once when Mr. and Mrs. Williamson (Mr. Williamson had succeeded Colonel Weir as Political Officer in Sikkim) were at a party at Tsarong House, Dingja put on a full lady's costume and gave a short dance that made the Williamsons roll on the carpet with laughter. He was such a humorous-looking man that any little movement of his would make a party merry – no one can imagine how gay life was in Tibet. General Dingja's wife was good-looking but very serious; usually nothing could make her laugh, yet sometimes even she laughed, with a hoarse voice, at one of her husband's gestures or jokes.

On the night of the thirteenth day of the eleventh month of the Water-Bird Year (17 December, 1933) Dingja brought us the sad news that His Holiness the thirteenth Dalai Lama had left for the Heavenly Field, at the age of fifty-eight. We were very much shocked, because we had not heard that he was ill; some weeks earlier he had caught a cold, which continued to worsen until he died. As Dingja was then the City Magistrate he had to inform the whole city of Lhasa that very night and the whole country as soon as possible. lights were burned inside every house and on the roofs; the flags and banners of all houses and temples were brought down; officials put on their mourning dresses and took off their ear-rings; women took of their gaily striped *pangdens* (aprons) and all their ornaments. (The ornamental *pangden* of a Tibetan woman is considered most important and is only taken off on the death of a Dalai Lama. We say that our husband's life is connected with our *pangden* and if a woman loses it she must perform rites, as the loss may be a sign of illness or bad luck for her husband. This is a traditional custom and has nothing to do with our religion.) Next morning people flocked to Norbu Lingka to pay homage to the Holy Body and everyone wept at having lost their great ruler and lama.

The thirteenth Dalai Lama was such a strong and strict ruler that during his reign there was little corruption and the monasteries were well disciplined. By playing off China against India he preserved our independence; capital punishment and amputation, which had been common in some regions, were forbidden – except for high treason; a law was made against the demanding of free transport by officials; the rate of interest charged by money-lenders was limited and if landlords neglected their land others were given the right to use it. Doctors were sent to many rural districts and women in childbirth and sick animals were given free treatment. Gambling, drinking and the smoking of opium and tobacco were forbidden, as His Holiness believed that these pastimes made men weaker and wasted a lot of time and money. The ladies of the poorer officials were forbidden to borrow money. The ladies of the poorer officials were forbidden to borrow money to buy elaborate costumes and ornaments; these ladies used to get badly into debt because it had become so difficult to move in high circles without displaying expensive dresses and jewels. These reforms were not liked very much by many of the rich, but most Tibetans considered the thirteenth Dalai Lama the best ruler we ever had. After His Holiness's death, while the two Regents were in power, all the good rules were relaxed and there was much corruption among the officials, who were very fond of mahjong and neglected the duties of government.

I went to Norbu Lingka with Tseten Dolkar and we offered scarves. All the people of Lhasa were allowed to pay homage and after a month or so the body was taken up to the Potala and left in one of His Holiness's private rooms until it was well preserved. (Salt was the main preservative used in Tibet for embalming.) Then it was enshrined, covered with sheets of silver and gold to give it the form of a *stupa*. The roof of the temple where it was to be placed needed repairing and heightening, so the government organised a special committee to look after this work. The tomb became beautiful; it was studded with His Holiness's precious stones and with many donations. I contributed a large turquoise and a few pieces of amber. We sometimes went to see the tombs of the Dalai Lamas in the Potala and the thirteenth's became the most valuable one.

A few months before he died His Holiness had written a letter telling his government to work harmoniously and sincerely to keep Tibet independent and not to be 'like brass masquerading as gold, putting off today's duties until tomorrow'. He mentioned that the spread of Communism in outer Mongolia was a great danger to Tibet and described how monasteries were being destroyed and how Jetsun Dampa's reincarnation had been disallowed by the Communist officials. He also foretold that eventually Communism would come to Tibet, either from within or without, if all the officials did not work hard and remain united.

The Dalai Lama's unexpected death caused great confusion in the government. *Tsi-pon* Lungshar longed to have all the power himself, but he knew that Kunphela was in the way and that to get rid of him it would be necessary to disband his special *Drong Drak Makhar* regiment, of which Jigme was junior *Dapon*. He secretly urged the thousand soldiers – who had all been recruited against their wishes – to resign, and three days after His Holiness's death the whole protesting regiment appeared in front of Norbu Lingka, while the *Kashag* was meeting. The *Shap-pēs* promised to consider its request in due course, but ordered it to get back to its job – guarding the nearby Mint – without delay. However, all the men deserted their post and returned to Lhasa, which was very worrying for Jigme and Yuthok.

Then the representatives of the three big monasteries – who at that time were being influenced by Lungshar – suggested to the *Tsongdu* that the deserters should be replaced by monks. But Trimon *Shap-pē* said that it would be silly to have monks acting as soldiers and he instructed half His Holiness's body-guard to take up duty at the Mint post and to shoot anyone who tried to stop them doing so.

Next day Lungshar called a meeting of the *Tsongdu* to consider the unexpectedness of the Dalai Lama's death. Kunphela and two of His Holiness's personal attendants were blamed for keeping the illness secret and not giving the Dalai Lama sufficient medical attention. They were exiled to Kongpo, away in the south, and then all the men of the *Drong Drak Makhar* regiment gradually took leave and the regiment was no more. Soon after this, Jigme became one of the Treasurers of the government of Tibet.

Within a week of the Dalai Lama's death the *Tsongdu* drew lots to select a Regent from amongst Ganden Tri Rinpoche (the Abbot of Ganden Monastery), Reting Rinpoche (an Incarnate Lama of Reting Monastery) and Phurchok Rinpoche (an Incarnate Lama of Sera Monastery). The three names were enclosed in identical balls of *tsampa* dough which were carefully weighed on a scale before being put in an urn. Then the urn was rolled round and round, very quickly, until one of the balls jumped out. Reting Rinpoche's name was inside; and a nephew of the late Dalai Lama, Yapshi Langdun *Lonchen* (*Lonchen* = Prime Minister), was appointed his lay colleague.

Reting Rinpoche was a famous Incarnation who had been born at Dakpo in south-eastern Tibet, to poor peasants. At the age of three he drove a wooden peg deep into a large rock near his parents house and when asked why he had done so said that he was expecting a caravan of guests from afar, to take him home, and that the peg would be needed for tying their horses. Soon the search party did come, recognised him as the reincarnation of Reting Rinpoche and took him to his monastery. His parents and family were also looked after by the monastery. (This always happened in the case of a poor reincarnation, but if a reincarnation were born into a rich family, his people spent more on him than the monastery did.) Reting Monastery was three days' journey north of Lhasa – a very sacred place, full of juniper trees, and the local people were nomads. Reting Rinpoche was only nineteen when he became Regent – a nice young man, pleasant and friendly to talk to, though completely inexperienced in politics. He often sent traders to China to purchase satin and porcelain – some for his own use, the rest for sale in Lhasa.

Early in 1933 Tsarong had been granted a year's leave from Lhasa, to go to our estates of Tsarong and Lhanga, so he was away when the Dalai Lama died. He came back to pay homage to his master's body and said to me that had His Holiness not granted him leave he would have lost his own life, because if he had been in Lhasa he could never have refrained from giving the Dalai Lama a few aspirin to reduce his temperature – and therefore would have been accused of poisoning him. He was really thankful for his escape and took this great act of foresight on His Holiness's part as a reward to his faithful servant.

Between 1912 and 1934 there were no Chinese officials in Tibet. But the Chinese government took advantage of the thirteenth Dalai Lama's death to send General Huang MuSung at the head of a mission to offer religious tributes and condolences to the Tibetan government – who could not refuse a mission with a religious purpose. After the official ceremonies, General Huang Mu-Sung insisted that the mission must be stationed permanently in Lhasa. Our government, with great difficulty, persuaded the General himself to leave, but two of his liaison officers remained behind. Before his departure, the General gave big presents and medals to the Regent and the officials. As the *Shap-pēs* were worried about accepting the medals they discussed the matter with Tsarong, when he came to a *Kashag* meeting on business from the Mint. He advised them to give an honorary title of *Dzasa* to the General, and to give the other officers lower titles and presents of official costumes, with compliments. In this way the Tibetans would be treating the Chinese as equals, not as overlords. The *Kashag* accepted Tsarong's advice.

During the absence of the Dalai Lama the Reting Regent asked Tsarong to rejoin the *Kashag*. But Tsarong refused, though he offered any other service he could give, and he occasionally visited the Regent with presents and invited him to Tsarong House for whole days, which were spent playing darts or sitting in the garden. Tsarong was wise to keep out of politics at this time, because some very unpleasant things were happening in the government.

After getting rid of Kunphela, Lungshar tried to control the whole country by replacing the *Drong Drak Makhar* regiment with monks who would be faithful to him. When Trimon *Shap-pē* successfully opposed this plan Lungshar collected a group of young officials who were on his side, called them *Kychog Kuntun* (Happy Union) and said that his group wanted to reform the government offices. Soon Trimon *Shap-pē* was warned that Lungshar meant to assassinate him, so Trimon told the Regent and took refuge in Drepung Monastery while the *Kashag* was arresting Lungshar. When he was arrested Lungshar, in fright, took off one of his boots, removed a piece of paper from it and swallowed the paper. (Many people witnessed this.) His other boot was searched and another piece of paper found, on which was written a magic spell meant to destroy Trimon *Shap-pē*. Lungshar was imprisoned and an enquiry into his behaviour showed that he had been planning to overthrow the government, so he was condemned to lose his sight and be imprisoned for life.

Poor thing! I feel as sorry for him as for my own father and I am ashamed that our Buddhist country gave such a punishment. Yet it was not the fault of the whole country, but was done through the personal jealousy of a few people – the cause also of my father's death. During that time the Regent was young and his lay colleague, Langdun *Lonchen*, was not a very strong person.

Lungshar's elder son, Chapase, was also exiled because of his father's treason. It was very sad that he was thus separated from his family. His sweet daughter, Sodonla, looked just like her grandfather, Lungshar, and eventually, married a nice boy who took her family name. Chapase's wife died some years after he was exiled to Kongpo, where he had married a peasant woman by whom he had some more children. After many years he returned to Lhasa with his second family and Sodonla looked after them.

Lungshar's younger son, too, was for a time degraded; but later, by the kindness of Lhalu *Lhacham* (the Duchess of Lhalu), who had adopted him when he was about fourteen, he became Lhalu *Shap-pē*. He was very ambitious and when he went to Chamdo as Governor he took Robert Ford – an Englishman – with him to set up a wireless station. Lhalu *Lhacham* was Lungshar's junior wife and, despite his life sentence, she had him released and kept him under gentle care until his death. She was a great friend of Tsarong's and used to say to him, 'You are a saint. You did no harm to my husband, though he was so jealous of you, wasn't he?' She knew that Tsarong had always been good to Lungshar's sons and that they liked him. Tsarong never considered Lungshar his enemy but other people, in speculation, did think so.

When the search for the fourteenth Dalai Lama started there were many indications that he would be found in the east. Clouds with auspicious shapes appeared in that direction and on such occasions Tibetans always watch the various appearances of clouds. Also some antirrhinums grew unexpectedly from the base of a pillar on the east side of the Jokhang, the State Oracles presented their scarves east and the body of the thirteenth Dalai Lama, which had been seated on a throne facing south, after a few days turned its face towards the east.

In the meantime every pregnant woman was having hopes and I, who had conceived so long after my marriage to Jigme — and then only after visiting a very holy hermit — was much teased by my friends. We used to discuss what would happen if the Dalai Lama were born to me. Dingja said that until the child was big enough to be taken care of by the government the most senior attendant of the thirteenth Dalai Lama would have to come with a yellow satin laundry-bag and take away the baby's nappies to be washed respectfully. As usual, Mrs. Dingja was really serious about it, and the hermit's prediction that we would have some remarkable children made me wonder, but I was not ambitious, as it is difficult to be the parents of the Dalai Lama. I felt a bit frightened that Jigme or I might die because we would not be able to bear our good fortune.

Then our daughter was born — and Dingja came to see me, with his hands on his mouth, pretending to be very upset. 'Disgraceful,' he said, 'it is a girl!'

Pema Dolkar again nursed me through the labour, sitting holding my hands for more than ten hours. Sometimes we sent Jigme out of the room, because we say that if the child be a girl it takes longer to come in the presence of its father. But Jigme would only stay out for five minutes before returning. When the baby arrived Pema Dolkar cut the cord, with Jigme's help; everything was sterilised and we treasured the scissors afterwards. Then Dr. Bo Tsering was called from the British Agency, as it took another ten hours to discharge the placenta; after his visit everything was all right and we sent a telegram to Jigme's parents. It was a very happy occasion.

Sometimes the mother is sponged with soft *chang* dough, which is said to be very refreshing, but I never took this *chang* bath. It is our custom to celebrate a child's birth on the third day if it is a boy and on the second day if it is a girl. The main idea is to disinfect the place and a relative or friend must inaugurate the ceremony. After two days Pema Dolkar inaugurated our ceremony by burning incense and sprinkling milk around the room; auspicious tea and rice were prepared and we waited for the visitors, who came at a fixed time. (It is best to call on this day, though some call later.) Many friends and relatives poured in with presents and scarves for the baby and its parents. The presents were a small bag of *tsampa*, a cake of butter, tea, *chang* and a full set of baby-clothes – a little *chuba* (gown), blouse, hat, belt, a pair of boots and napkins. A scarf and a packet of money were always given to the midwife or nanny.

I was able to go out by the second week and we took our baby on the customary visit to the Jokhang for her to pay her first homage to the Lord Buddha. She was carried on the nanny's back, wrapped in a soft maroon blanket with a big silk patch in the centre, specially made by Mother-in-law. A little black mark was put on her nose to protect her from evil spirits while she was out. Many gold and silver charm boxes, a tortoiseshell and a *sipabo* (a holy picture which can be as big as a *thangka* and is often carried like a banner before people) were sewn on a brocade belt and put round her to protect the little life from all harm. We did not have a set like this, but Pema Dolkar lent us hers and after the birth of our second daughter we gave it back to her and it was used for her grandchildren. On our way home from the temple we visited Tseten Dolkar for Ngodup Wangmo's first outing. On this occasion a big party was always given by the grandparents or some relative and the child was greeted with *tsampa* and *chang*. When the family left the host put a scarf around the baby's neck.

The Ganden Tri Rinpoche named our child Dondup Dolma, but nine years later we had to change this name when she became very ill with typhoid. Then a lama renamed her Ngodup Wangmo. The British doctor, Dr. Terry, treated her and praised me for nursing her well. Any lama could be asked to give a name, by sending a messenger to him or taking the child with a scarf. Also anyone could request the Dalai Lama for a name, which would be given on a paper with a seal. This custom applied to all babies, rich or poor.

The mothers of poor babies had to get up sooner than I did to do the cooking and shopping. Among both rich and poor most fathers were very helpful with babies – but some were not, and only gambled while their wives worked. Jigme was very good.

A few years later the Williamsons came to Lhasa, and Mrs. Williamson was so fond of Ngodup Wangmo that we nicknamed her 'Peggy' after our friend. While in Lhasa Mr. Williamson became very ill and the British government wanted to send an aeroplane to take him to Calcutta, but the Tibetan government refused to allow an aeroplane to land in Tibet because the monasteries felt that this would be inauspicious – so Mr. Williamson died. The government was very sorry and all his Tibetan friends were sad. I was the only Tibetan woman who could speak English so I spent the night with Mrs. Williamson and accompanied her to the funeral next day. Many officials came to convey condolences and the coffin was given a guard of honour. I still regret that our government did not allow the aeroplane to land.

After eighteen months I became pregnant again and though we had hoped for a son we thought our second daughter, Yangdol, was also very sweet. Then I took off my charm and did not conceive any more.

One year after His Holiness's death, Reting Regent went to

the sacred lake at Chokhor Gyal and spent several days praying there, seeking guidance about the discovery of the fourteenth Dalai Lama. The Regent and some of his attendents saw many indications, through reflections on the surface of the lake, and search parties were sent to various regions; others of his attendants saw nothing. During the following year the precious and true two-year-old reincarnation of the Dalai Lama was found in a peasant's house in Kumbum (northeastern Tibet); but for political reasons – that region was then under Chinese domination – the discovery was kept a great secret.

In 1933 my brother Kalsang Lhawang's wife, Tsewang Dolma, had looked for a divorce and got it. She then married a Khampa trader and died in Kham of some gastric disease at about the age of twenty-eight; we heard that she had also been suffering from a mental illness. Kalsang Lhawang married a poor Khampa girl who looked after him well. It was terribly sad to see him with no money left and he used to get money from all his sisters whenever he needed it. He liked Jigme very much and Jigme shared his clothes with him, and Tsarong also did his best for my brother, who was the only true Tsarong heir, but Kalsang Lhawang enjoyed life as he wished. Pema Dolkar brought up his sons and I brought up his daughter; the younger boy did not do well but the elder was a good student. The girl was very intelligent but for a time, when she was about eighteen, had delusions which were a form of religious mania.

At the age of thirty-six – three years after his second marriage – Kalsang Lhawang developed liver trouble because he drank so much. Tseten Dolkar and I went to see him when he was very ill and he died on the night of our visit.

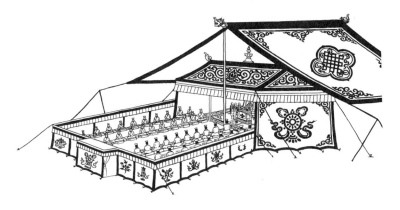

In 1937 THE government sent Jigme to India, to take delivery of arms and ammunition, and I accompanied him. We met Mrs. Williamson again in Gyantse; she was on her way to visit her husband's grave, bringing an engraved headstone all the way from England. Our two babies were left at Taring Estate with my niece – Chime's second wife – and Mother-in-law.

We broke the journey home by spending a lovely week at Shigatse – where General Dingja was then Governor – with my sister Norbu Yudon. As she had married Delek Rabten at the age of nineteen, when I was only five years old, I saw much less of her than of my two other surviving sisters. We sisters were all very close and particularly Norbu Yudon was devoted to me. She was a gentle, feminine, hospitable lady, slim and good-looking, and she loved her mother and the family and came to Lhasa once every year to see us, with many presents. When I was at school in Darjeeling she used to send me various gifts to give away to my friends – silver cup-stands, ink-pots and pen cases. She was clever at making pastry and stringing jewellery and had a small home industry, using vegetable dyes to make the most beautiful yak-hair blankets and aprons; all her relatives were generously provided with these lovely things. In her early years Norbu Yudon worried terribly over everyone of us because she was so kind. Once when a relative died she cried so much that I had to remind her how we eventually laughed an danced again after the tragedies of our parents' deaths. I said she would destroy her health by behaving in that manner and she then became much better. After taking religious teaching from the famous lady-lama, Lochen Rinpoche, her understanding of karma became high and she stopped worrying too much. While with her teacher she often went into trance and all the other disciples then heard her reciting many wonderful verses though the beautifully poetical words she uttered were not remembered by her when she was herself. Always she was possessed by the same spirit – the she-deity Lhama Yudonma, who is one of the protectors of our religion and was constantly with the saintly lady-lama, Lochen Rinpoche.

Norbu Yudon's husband, Delek Rabten, was ten years older than her and as a senior official of the Panchen Lama held the title of *Theji*. (A *Theji* and a *Dzasa* are of equal rank, but *Dzasas* are seated above *Thejis*.) Delek Rabten was a very learned and religious person, well liked by the Panchen Lama and much respected by Tibetans of all classes. He and Norbu Yudon were deeply devoted to each other and by their conduct in their public and private lives they set a very good example. They had two sons and three daughters. The eldest daughter married Chime Dorje, four years after Changchup Dolma's death. The second became a nun at Lochen Rinpoche's nunnery, where she nursed and served the lady-lama for many years, and the youngest girl married the Reting Regent's brother. Their two sons became government officials.

After leaving Shigatse we stayed with my sister-in-law, Rigzin Chodon, at Lhuling Estate for about ten days. She was then meditating but was very happy to meet Jigme and the babies. This was my last meeting with her; she died two years later. At Lhuling, Ngodup Wangmo was nearly shot when one of Jigme's orderlies, while talking to a maid-servant who was attaching sheets to the babies' blankets, leant against a pillar on which a loaded pistol was hanging. When the trigger touched the pillar bang went the pistol, very near where Ngodup Wangmo was playing.

During 1937 there were many rumours in Lhasa about the Regent wishing to resign. Reting was a young man who enjoyed games and having good food – unlike the thirteenth Dalai Lama, who had lived very economically, spending little on himself and only having one dish at each meal. (The present Dalai Lama also lives simply. Usually, whatever wealth a Dalai Lama gets is accumulated to be spent on his tomb, and all his expensive robes are handed down from previous incarnations.)

The Regent was very intelligent and soon learnt to ride a motor-cycle and take photographs. Jigme was introduced to him by Tsarong and they became so friendly that Jigme visited him often – mostly to take photographs – and Reting greatly enjoyed his company; but Jigme had absolutely no interest in politics. Reting sent his younger brother to me to learn English. Thubten Gyaltsan was a very sweet boy, but not very clever at learning.

Occasionally, all our family went to pay homage to the Regent, and on our return from India in 1937 Jigme went to stay with him for a month or so at the lovely new summer palace he had built for himself near Reting Monastery. Tsarong, Pema Dolkar and I were also to have gone, but at this time both Tsarong and Tseten Dolkar became very unwell. Tsarong was too ill to nurse Tseten Dolkar as he wished to do, so I looked after her instead, remaining constantly with her, day and night, for seventy-three days. One night when I was having a nap, leaning against her knee, I dreamed of a monk who poked me hard under my armpit and was trying to show me a Russian pocket-watch in black case. When I woke up I had a pain under my arm and Tseten Dolkar was taking her last breath.

Early in 1938 we heard that the Prime Minister, Silon Langdun, was retiring from active politics, though he would remain Prime Minister in name. The *Kashag* and the *Tsongdu* had been very much against the Regent's resigning and they hoped he would settle down more happily to his job if Silon Langdun, who was not very capable, resigned instead and left Reting free to make important decisions quickly. Langdun seemed pleased to be freed of so much responsible work, but some people claimed that he had been forced to resign and for a while the atmosphere in Lhasa was fearful and uneasy. Then the tension disappeared, because Langdun was not anxious to make trouble.

At about this time Pema Dolkar's gall-stone suffering became very severe and Tsarong had to bring her down to Calcutta for medical treatment – taking both her son and daughter. They travelled as far as Sikkim in a dandy and the British representatives in Lhasa kindly let their doctor – Rai Sahib Donyot – accompany the party to give morphine injections on the way. At the time Lord Anderson had just died under operation, so Pema Dolkar absolutely refused to have her operation. She took oral treatment and had to stay on a diet for the rest of her life.

Jigme has a talent for architecture and is clever at drawing and any work requiring practical skill. During the Earth-Tiger Year (1938) he was busy helping Tsarong to build the first iron bridge in Tibet, about seven miles outside Lhasa. Tsarong supervised all this work himself and Jigme was as obedient to him as to his own father. While the work was going on Tsarong and Jigme camped at Trisam, where there were many estates belonging to Drepung and Sera Monasteries. The Abbots and the retainers asked Tsarong to investigate their very old debts, which had accumulated so much, by the addition of interest every year, that both parties were in great difficulty. (The official rate of interest on money was twelve per cent and on grain one-fifth or one-sixth of the amount borrowed.) As Tsarong always liked doing something useful he gladly helped by arranging for the retainers to repay only the original amounts they had borrowed. He did this as his side work, with great enthusiasm, though it was such a tedious job. He was helped by the staff of government workers – including Jigme – who were busy with the bridge at the same time.

When the bridge was finished Tsarong made a motorable road along the Nethang precipice, about ten miles from Lhasa on the trade route to India. This precipice overhung the river and had a terrible narrow path, about two miles long, going up very steeply for hundreds of feet and then going down very steeply.

Sometimes donkeys and mules slipped off with their loads and died. To construct the road Tsarong imported from India a small railway and a big pulley, which had to be carried over the Himalayas, in little bits, by mules. He then filled up part of the river with rocks and made a wide road, sixteen feet across. Even before any wheeled vehicles came to Tibet this road was enjoyed by thousands of donkeys, yaks, mules, horses, men, women and children.

That same year Jigme and I decided, on Tsarong's advice, to build our own house in Lhasa. Tsarong felt that the city was going to expand so quickly that later we would find it difficult to get a nice place; and in time this prediction was proved correct. We asked for Metok Dumra, a four-acre site on the outskirts of the city where my father once ran a government tannery and where many other houses were built afterwards. At that time most people were afraid to build on the edge of Lhasa because we had lots of thieves.

In consultation with Mr. Hugh Richardson — then British Representative in Lhasa — Jigme drew the plans, and while he was out of Lhasa for a month, visiting the Regent, I supervised the building, which took about eight months to complete. First we put up a huge wall around the site, which surprised everybody, as Lhasa houses were not isolated in big compounds. We sent a man to get good wood from Kongpo, in the forested region of southern Tibet, and I myself went to the river banks to buy the wood that used to be sent into Lhasa floating on the Kyichu River. I took deliveries of stones from donkey-men who drove loads into the city for sale at any building site. We also had special masons cutting stones in a nearby quarry, and though we had two horse-carts of our own I had to hire extra transport — mostly donkeys. I saw to it strictly that neither the labourers — retainers from our Dopta Estate — nor ourselves were cheated. If not carefully watched they would have caused us extra expense and it was equally important to treat them fairly once they were satisfied the work was well done. They got good food, which I shared with them; this was once reported to Reting Regent, who told Jigme that he had heard I ate with our retainers. It was nice to watch them working, and to chat and joke with them. my face and hands were well tanned from staying outside all day and I enjoyed this work very much.

Our overseer was a retainer named Samdup, who also came from Dopta Estate. He had become a doctor and was most popular in Shigatse and Gyantse before moving to Lhasa. I did all the bargaining and counted all the stones and slates and gave him receipts. He worried greatly over the expense because some money was missing, but I told him I knew it was a mistake that couldn't be helped as he always did his best. The day we finished building all our accounts were paid up. Then we employed many artists to paint the elborately carved interior pillars and the walls and furniture.

As soon as Taring House was completed we asked Jigme's parents to come to live with us, because we Tibetans consider it a very important duty to care for our parents in their old age and every elderly Tibetan liked, if possible, to live in Lhasa in order to visit the Jokhang regularly. They agreed to come and it was wonderful to have them with us for the first *Losar* in our new home.

Losar is the Tibetan New Year, which is celebrated on varying dates in February or March. It is not very easy for foreigners to understand the Tibetan calendar and it is impossible to work out a conversion table between our month and day, and the Western month and day, in any one year. (For this reason I don't know which Western date is my birthday.) The first difficulty is that our lunar year is supposed to consist of twelve thirty-day months – which only add up to three hundred and sixty days, so an extra month is added every third year and put in anywhere among the twelve months that is considered auspicious for a particular year. The next difficulty is that there are really three hundred and fifty-four days in the lunar year, not three hundred and sixty. So certain days have to be left out and there are squares on our calendars with no number but only the word *chad* (cut off). That day of the month does not exist. Also, to avoid unlucky days some dates happen twice and one finds numbers repeated in two consecutive squares, to make up for *chads* elsewhere in the year. Towards the end of each year a new calendar is worked out by the State Astrologer and no one knows what dates the next year will have until it has almost begun.

Tibetan months are only numbered, instead of having names. But the seven days of the week are called after the sun, moon and five visible planets, as in the West. The peasants liked to name their children after the day of birth, for example Pasang (Monday) Dolma, if a girl was born on a Monday, but the nobles never did this.

In olden times, our calendar was based on a twelve-year cycle and each year was called after an animal — mouse, ox, tiger, hare, dragon, serpent, horse, sheep, ape, bird, dog and hog. Then, in the eleventh century A.D., a sixty-year cycle was introduced by combining the names of these animals with the five elements — wood, fire, earth, iron and water. One element goes with two successive animals and to make quite clear the difference between the two successive element years 'male' is added to the first and 'female' to the second. Therefore the Wood-Female-Ox Year follows the Wood-Male-Mouse Year. This cycle is called *Rabjung* and it started in A.D. 1027. A single year is called *Lokhor*.

The hours of the day and night are also named after the twelve animals:

Midnight: Mouse	Midday: Horse
After Midnight: Ox	After midday: Sheep
Dawn: Tiger	Afternoon: Monkey
After Dawn: Hare	Evening: Bird
Sunrise: Dragon	Sunset: Dog
Forenoon: Snake	After dark: Hog

Our new year begins with the rising of the new moon in the

Western month of February or March, depending on when our extra month has been added. We always considered well how to bring good luck for the New Year while saying good-bye to the old year. The exchanging of food gifts, and the giving of presents to poor friends and relatives, started about ten days before New Year's Day. The house flags and banners, and the white frills around the outside of our windows were changed. (The new frills could be put away after the celebrations, but the new flags had to remain until well worn out.) *Khabse*, the *Losar* pastries, were made in many varieties and put on the family altars, with every other sort of food that could be obtained. Four or six *khabse*, each a foot long, had to be offered to all who came to greet a family. Monks and poor people loved getting *khabse* so the big houses prepared two or three thousand pastries, cooked in butter or oil, and for a week the smell of frying was all over the city. A couple of days before the New Year, big trays of *khabse*, were sent to foreign friends, with a scarf, as their share of the *Losar* celebrations. It was customary to return the scarf, with thanks. Friends who came from a distance had to be given everything to facilitate their New Year.

The *Losar* cleaning was done very thoroughly. All the glass doors of the shrines were wiped and some families changed the brocade or satin clothes of their deities' images. About two weeks ahead, barley and wheat were sown in pots to decorate the altar and by *Losar* they had grown four or five inches and looked beautifully green and fresh. *Tsampa* flour and wheat offerings were put in specially designed wooden boxes, with two compartments; these were piled full, to look like mountains, and two small banners, decorated with gold and silver paper and cloured butter, were stuck into them. A bowl of *chang* went with this *Tashi Kele* (Good Luck) offering. In every Tibetan home, on New Year's Day, people took a pinch of each grain and threw it in the air – first the wheat and then the *tsampa*. The remainder of the *tsampa* was taken between the thumb and first finger and tasted. The *chang* was also sprinkled in the air, with the fourth finger, as an offering, and a drop was taken on the tongue. The head of a sheep, decorated with coloured butter, was always put on the altar to mark the New Year.

On the last day of the old year everybody prayed to expel all evil from the house, and the government and the monks organised ritual dances at the Potala Palace and other monasteries for the same purpose.

For three days people visited each other's homes to give New Year greetings, but did not stay long – though close friends might stay. Elderly people sent their sons or daughters to greet friends on their behalf.

It was important to get up as early as possible to greet the New Year. After the *Tashi Delek* ceremony, boiled sweet *chang* was served in every home. Then people sat in their family prayer-rooms, in order of seniority, after prostrating to the deities and offering them scarves; the younger members of the family offered *Tashi Kele* scarves to their seniors, and the servants offered them to their masters. The servants' scarves were returned to them on the last (third) day of *Losar*, when they were given *chang* and enjoyed themselves dancing and singing until dawn.

After the home celebrations everybody went to the Jokhang and queued to visit all the shrines. Thousands of people used to line up and everybody except government officials had to stay in their place in the queue; the officials could go ahead because at sunrise they had to attend a celebration at the Potala in the presence of His Holiness.

The first day celebration took place on the top terrace of the palace, where the Dalai Lama (or the Regent) led the prayer. It was very cold up there, as nobody was allowed to wear scarves and not all ceremonial hats cover the ears. The high officials' ceremonial breakfasts were sent from their homes and they ate in the hall after the prayer on the roof; this meal had to consist of traditional foods and the senior officials were each given a square wooden table and their food was taken from their servants by a junior official. Tea was provided by the government. (The junior monk and lay officials brought their breakfasts with them in bundles.) We took great care to send the best food, because it was usually shared with friends; I used to pack Jigme's breakfast in a small silver dish, wrapped in a white napkin.

During the morning all the officials went to Nechung, where the State Oracle would be in trance, and wished him *Tashi Delek*.

On the second day of the New Year – called King's New Year – the foreign representatives were entertained at the Potala, where special dances were performed. In the hall a great feast of *khabse* was given and people were allowed to grapple around a whole trough of dried yak-meat; His Holiness's giant escorts dispersed this crowd, when it got too rough, without thinking of their own safety.

The Dalai Lama always had about six men, over six feet tall, as his personal guards. When a very tall unmarried man was found anywhere in Tibet he was presented to His Holiness, provided that he would agree to become a monk, but nobody was compelled to accept this honour. These tall men were mostly Khampas without much education. Their duty was to guard His Holiness's rooms and keep order during ceremonies. They were padded out well across the shoulders to make them look bigger, and they had loud voices and often roared, 'Keep quiet!' to the crowds.

In 1955, during a *Monlam* tea service at the Jokhang, when *tormas* were being distributed among the officials Tsarong stretched out his legs to take paper – to wrap round the *tormas* – from the pocket of the trousers which he wore under his yellow robe, when one of the giants whipped him on the back for stretching out his legs. Tsarong did not mind in the least; he said it was the man's duty and complained to no one. But the news of what had happened quickly spread all over Lhasa, even before the family heard it. Tsarong's children were very sad, and so was Pema Dolkar. I consoled her by saying that these men were not educated – had Tsarong been hit by an official in a good position it would have been another matter – and I asked her to ignore the incident. When the young Dalai

Lama heard about it he immediately sent Tsarong a letter on wooden slabs, like the thirteenth Dalai Lama used to do, apologising for the mistake of his giant guard. Then everybody in the family was happy and there were no more rumours; that letter was just like pouring cold water into boiling water.

There was a special place behind the Potala, called Zongyap, where on the third and last day of *Losar* officials went to enjoy archery, singing, dancing and *chang*. It was always long after sunset when they returned home, tipsy and happy.

Fireworks of every kind were allowed during *Losar*, but then came the twenty-one-day *Monlam Chenmo* (the Great Prayer Festival) and fireworks were prohibited.

Monlam began on the third or fourth day of the New Year, depending on whether or not a day was missing in the first month. This festival celebrated the Lord Buddha's victory over the malicious spirits who tempted him during his meditations. Over twenty thousand monks came to Lhasa from all the nearby monasteries, including the three greatest monasteries of Tibet — Ganden, Drepung and Sera — where only a few monks remained as caretakers. During *Monlam* the two City Magistrates of Lhasa had no power and discipline was kept very strictly in the city by the two chief monks of Drepung, helped by a full staff from the monastery. Nobody was allowed to ride a horse in the *Barkor*: even *Shap-pēs* had to go on foot. No woman was allowed out without her full costume and head-dress and the streets and public wells were kept very clean, because the two chief monks were responsible for the health of the visiting monks and thousands of citizens and pilgrims. All the monks appeared four times a day, going to the Jokhang, and at certain times no monks were supposed to be seen on the streets; if any did appear, they were thrashed then and there. They were so well disciplined that most of the time one hardly noticed them.

During *Monlam*, tea for twenty thousand monks was served three times daily at the Jokhang. The *Lachag* office, where Jigme worked as one of the treasurers, had charge of the supply of tea and butter. There was a special big tea-kitchen, with several huge cauldrons, attached to the temple, and for months before-hand fuel had to be collected. Many people gave tea and butter, because to feed holy monks is considered very meritful. To be lucky in this life and in the next incarnation – apart from reaching Nirvana – we believe that you have to accumulate much merit, by making offerings to the deities and helping holy lamas and doing merciful acts, in charity.

About two months before *Monlam*, those who wished to give tea or butter had to report to the *Lachag* office, where a list of the benefactors was made and each person informed of the date was made and each person informed of the date on which he was to bring his offering. Poor people could bring even a little slice of butter and contribute it to a cauldron to make the tea richer. The tea-makers had a hard job, standing by the cauldrons with huge sticks stirring the boiling tea. They were used to it, but the heat of the steam could not be borne by most people.

Monlam was greatly respected by the government, the people of Lhasa and the many pilgrims from other parts of Tibet and neighbouring countries. Everybody gave contributions of some kind to the monks, who were so busy praying for the happiness of all living beings, and especially for the prosperity of Tibet and the flourishing of Buddhism. In Tibet there may have been good and bad monks, but such holy crowds were considered to be like an ocean in which you may find both stones and gems. The government gave the monks tea, rice and money three times a day; even the poorest contributed as much as they could, and got the same merit as the rich who contributed a great deal.

It is said that one day during the Lord Buddha's lifetime, kings and many rich people in India made offerings and burnt thousands of lamps while Buddha was preaching. There was also a poor woman who had no money, yet wished to offer a lamp of prayer. She got a goat's hoof, cleaned it thoroughly, bought a pennyworth of oil and offered her lamp among the many others. She then sat in the audience and prayed to the Lord Buddha and her prayer was:

Let me light my lamp at thy feet,
Let the light be shown in my wisdom
To help me help all living beings take the road to Nirvana.

After some time, when all the other lights had burnt out, her little light was found still burning strongly. His disciples asked the Lord Buddha why this was and he replied that it was owing to the great prayer the woman had said. She was then enlightened and became a saint.

During *Monlam*, anybody could write notes requesting special prayers and throw them among the gathering of monks. The notes were then thrown up an up to the various chief monks who were sitting on tiered seats; and finally one of the head monks read the notes and led the requested prayers.

On certain days His Holiness or the Regent attended the prayers, and Ganden Tri Rinpoche, the Abbot of Ganden Monastery, attended every day, like all the other High and Holy Lamas.

The different monasteries had their own accommodation in the city, yet it was hard to imagine where all the monks stayed. Every morning and evening religious debates were held in the Jokhang and on a platform facing the Barkor. Once, during one of these public debates, a traveller asked a Muslim trader, who lived in Lhasa, what the monks were doing. The Muslim replied that he heard there had been a great dispute about religion while Buddha was living and he supposed the monks were still trying to settle their differences.

On the night of the fifteenth day of the first month we had the great butter festival, when the whole Barkor was decorated with butter offerings and flickering butter lamps. For these offerings of butter was coloured with powdered dyes and they were most beautifully sculptured, with the figure of a wealthy, laughing fat man on the front of each. The monks were specially talented at doing this fine work and some of the offerings were forty feet high; many monasteries and noble houses had to make these offerings as a duty. Sometimes the Dalai Lama would come to see them and all high officials were compelled to inspect them. The Dalai Lama awarded prizes for the finest work.

The monks returned to their monasteries on the twenty-fifth day and before leaving Lhasa every monk had to take a stone to the river, to reinforce the dykes – a tradition that went back to the summer of 1562, when Lhasa was flooded.

Immediately after *Monlam*, very holy lamas performed special rites for many days to abolish evil, and on a certain day they burnt *tormas* (cone-shaped religious sweets) and cast them out to expel all malicious spirits who might harm the religion or the country of Tibet.

Jigme was always very happy when *Monlam* was over because, as one of the treasurers, he had a big share in the great responsibility of feeding the monks and distributing their money. At three o'clock every morning he had to go to the Jokhang and three times daily the monks had to be paid from four different doors. But he always said he did not mind this work as he was serving the monks.

On the twenty-first day of the first month the annual races were rehearsed. Some were for men, some for horses with riders and some for horses on their own. Each official sent a number of horses, according to his rank, and every animal was branded on its neck so that after the final race they could all be checked. Four days later the races took place; the men ran for about two miles, the horses with riders for about three miles and those without riders for about five miles. When a gun was fired they all started at the same time in three groups from three different places and each group had its own stopping place, where men stood to check the winners. The men's race would make anyone laugh because some competitors were old men and some were small boys; on their backs or chests they wore the names of the nobles who had sent them. If the government horse did not come first in the race without riders the stable managers were fined. The Dalai Lama and the *Kashag* watched the races from a room in the Jokhang, and though Tibetans liked gambling so much there was no betting because these races were organised by the government. Once Tsarong's horse, named Gyatso, won the race and was then presented to Tsarong's great friend, Mr. Ladenla, the famous Buddhist scholar who spoke ten languages fluently; later Gyatso won many Governor's Cups in Darjeeling.

On the twenty-second day of the first month we had the ceremonial Army roll-call. It was the duty of young noblemen to become in turn commanders of the cavalry — *Yasor* — and though this was an expensive duty it could not be avoided. (Jigme was excused only because we had no estate of our own.) Two important nobles led the Army, which was divided into two sections called the Right and Left Lines. They and the *Shap-pēs* each had to provide twenty-four mounted men in full armour; the *Dapons* each had to provide thirteen, the sons of noblemen seven — and so on. There were over a thousand mounted men and every one of them had to show their skill separately.

The junior government officials took part in this contest every three or four years, when forty or fifty new officials had entered the government service. They had to practise for months before-hand, because the contest was so difficult. As the horses galloped along a straight road that had high banks — to prevent them from going astray — their riders never touched the reins, but had to hit three targets fixed at about thirty-foot intervals. Very quickly the horsemen aimed at the first target with muzzle-loaders, slung their guns over their shoulders, drew bows and arrows from their respective cases, aimed at the second target, returned the bows and arrows to the cases, took out their spears and aimed at the third target.

The junior officials' horses were well saddled and decorated and had their manes and tails plaited with coloured silk. Jigme took his turn in 1938 and though he practised his skill well he was not interested in the decoration of his horse, so it was I who attended to this. Most of the wives and relatives were very enthusiastic about the contest.

At the end the two Chief Officers were supposed to demonstrate their skill in the same way, but they could be excused. From 9 a.m. to 5 p.m. all the lay officials watched from special tents and were served with a good lunch and the best tea and *chang*. The Lhasa public also enjoyed this display; spring was just beginning and everybody loved being out in the countryside.

Two days later the Army took part in the city show, when the infantry gave a display of old-fashioned drill. Then the Chief Officiers, in their brocade uniforms, sat on high seats placed in the street in front of the house of a nobleman called Thonpa. Hundreds of friends greeted them until they were covered in scarves: and sometimes one could judge, by the number of scarves, which had the most friends. While the infantry were active the Chief Officers received tea and lunch from Thonpa and the cavalrymen were fed in the street by friends; they got so drunk that when they started to move again they could hardly keep their seats on their horses and the spectators enjoyed this sight.

Monlam ended on the twenty-seventh, when the government gave a day-long party for the *Shap-pēs* and lay officials. They had archery contests, and whoever hit the target was given a scarf. Apart from the horsemen-archers, we had two other forms of archery in Tibet. In late spring and summer many officials — young and old alike — went after office hours to play whistling archery in the parks. Their arrows had small wooden boxes, with holes, near the head, and the whistling sound was part of the pleasant atmosphere of Lhasa in summer; our house being on the outskirts of the city we often heard it. The target was about ten inches in diameter, stuffed with sawdust and pinned to a thick curtain. When it was hit — from a distance of eighty feet or so — it fell down. The other from of archery was practised during *Losar* and *Monlam* and consisted of seeing who could shoot an arrow farthest. For this contest, each arrow had the archer's name on it; these arrows were made out of fine seasoned bamboo, because bamboo gets lighter as it gets older. The winner got a horse as a prize from the government; it was presented in front of the *Shap-pēs* – covered with a brocade saddle-mat and wearing a scarf. There was some betting on these *Monlam* archery contests and the *Shap-pēs* enjoyed getting a bit intoxicated. On that day they used to wear *soksha* – the hats of officials' servants – which meant that everyone was of equal rank and all relaxed together to end the Prayer Festival. Late at night the *Shap-pēs* would come home – like brides being taken to their new homes – with the government band playing and singing beside their procession and long scarves around their necks.

After *Monlam* the two City Magistrates again took charge of the law and Lhasa was run as usual. The City Magistrates were not half so strict as the two chief monks and the people could once more appear on the streets without being frightened. The monasteries had the best system of organisation in Tibet and the monks always kept strictly to their routine. As long as a man was dressed in monk's clothes, no matter what sort of person he might be, a true Buddhist would respect him deeply.

In the summer of 1939 we heard that His Holiness the fourteenth Dalai Lama had been recognised and as the news spread that he was on his way to Lhasa the happiness of all Tibetans was indescribable. The city people, especially, got very excited, and the government sent officials to meet His Holiness's party at different stages. When we heard that it was going to take a hundred days for the party to reach the city, everybody felt impatient – yet there was much to be done. The government was painting the palaces and preparing accommodation for His Holiness's family, the monasteries were making banners for the procession and Tibet's foreign friends were eagerly awaiting the great occasion. (The Chogyal of Sikkim asked Jigme to present his valuable gifts, on behalf of Sikkim State, to the new Dalai Lama. These gifts included two beautiful horses. Poor Jigme was in charge of them and was very worried in case they should die before the ceremony.) Nepalese, Bhutanese, Chinese, Mongolians – all were getting ready to receive His Holiness. The yellow satin Peacock Tent, which is only used for the reception in Lhasa of a new Dalai Lama, was taken out and mended; because of being stored for so long it had many holes. It was about fifteen feet high and had a yellow silk lining and a silk top; it covered an area of a hundred square feet.

It was traditional to have the reception-camp for a new Dalai Lama at Rigya ground, three miles from Lhasa. Every official, monk and lay, had to have his own tent in this camp, so many people were making new tents. Some of the old noble families had nice tents, but Jigme and I had to have one made, which was very exciting, though it was difficult to get this done in time because all the tailors were working hard on tents, banners and new clothes.

When His Holiness's party arrived at Rigya, on 8 October 1939, the officials had their tents pitched around the separate tents which the five-year-old Dalai Lama had for sitting, sleeping and dressing. Nearly everybody in Lhasa – officials, lamas, men, women and children – came to Rigya, where His Holiness gave his first audience in the Peacock Tent. All the traditional activities, from prayers to folk-dances, took place. There was a big distribution of pastries and dried fruit, and from a huge trough of dried yak-meat everybody was allowed to grab what they could. (This was supposed to bring prosperity.)

His Holiness's party stopped at the camp for two nights, and on the twentieth-five day of the eighth month of the Earth-Hare Year (1939) left for Lhasa at sunrise – the time appointed by the State Astrologer. The little Dalai Lama was carried right at the centre of the procession in his palanquin, which was borne by sixteen junior officials in green satin dresses with red tasselled hats. The *Lonchen* rode in front of the palanquin, wearing a Mongolian-type dress and a silk tasselled hat with gold bands. Immediately behind rode Reting Regent in his best robes, on a horse led by two junior officials and draped in brocade with a gold knob between its ears. The procession was headed by the State Astrologer, in a white satin dress, carrying the banner of *Sipaho*. Then came junior monk-officials and junior lay-officials; important people like *Shap-pēs* and *Tsi-pons* were nearest to His Holiness. The senior official who was in charge of the palanquin walked beside it, and His Holiness's family and the foreign representatives followed the high officials that preceded it. The order of the procession was read out before its departure from the camp and His Holiness's giant monk escorts and monk secretaries took care that everybody was in their right place.

The private servants of the officials — each had six or eight servants — wore their best dresses and red caps and went ahead of the procession to prepare things for their masters. As the procession started, a famous drum — the *Da-Ma* — was beaten, a special flute was played, monastic horns were blown on the monastery roofs and this music was heard by all. The *Da-Ma* drum — introduced from Ladak, a Buddhist province in northern India — and the peculiar flute, called *Suna*, that goes with it, were used only on special occasions. To Tibetan ears, those two instruments combined produced a sound of great dignity and happiness. Men rang many little bells to accompany the *Da-Ma* and *Suna* and the band had about twenty small boys attached to it as folk-dancers. This dancing group had lots of privileges, including their own school, and these peasant boys were brought up strictly and much respected; their daily uniform was green tweed with white and red spots and little yellow caps. They were called *Gartrukpa* and their headmaster was known as *Garpon* and counted as an official of the fifth rank. They danced in the Potala during all big ceremonies and if capable could become officials; most of them became clerks in the *Tsechag* and *Lachag*. Many of these boys — and many stable-boys — became His Holiness's personal attendants.

In the procession, two *Da-Mas* with different tones were put over a well-saddled pony draped in silk satin and led by a man dressed in a black skirt and brocade jacket with a white ring of cloth on his head. There were six of these ponies, carrying a dozen drums, and the drummers beat both drums at the same time and made beautiful music. The drummers and flute players wore brocade dresses, white blouses, flat tasselled hats and long gold ear-rings.

On the death anniversaries of Tsongkhapa, and of all the

Dalai Lamas, the *Da-Ma* was beaten on the roof of the Potala and heard by all in Lhasa. The atmosphere felt wonderful on these occasions; almost everybody was on the housetops, burning of lamps and praying. Tibetans consider the celebration of all festivals important and try hard to bring luck for their own future by praying to have many more people living in happiness. Their main idea is to hope for the best always and they believe that to celebrate with high spirits and gaiety brings good luck.

When His Holiness arrived the whole of Lhasa was decorated with the best flags and silk banners blew in gay colours everywhere. Both sides of the road were marked with white and yellow chalked lines and lined with incense-burners every thirty yards. Rows of monks stood by the road and army regiments with their bands provided a guard of honour. There were windows on all sides of the palanquin and His Holiness looked out to see the people greeting him – they were so happy, some praying for his long life, some crying through joy. The proudest men were those who had searched for the reincarnation, Kyitsang Rinpoche and Kunsangtse Dzasa. They wore their best travelling dresses to look more prominent. The *Gyayap* (the special title of a Dalai Lama's father) was dressed like a *Shap-pē* but the *Gyayum* (His Holiness's mother) wore her own Amdo regional dress, which looked beautiful. Everybody was very happy to see her, and at the same time amused by her costume.

After the procession had left the camp we rode quickly ahead, to watch the Oracle meeting His Holiness, and saw the whole procession again. When His Holiness reached the city the State Oracle, in trance, wearing his full costume and looking very fierce (when in trance his own face was worse than any mask) met the little Dalai Lama and offered him a scarf by putting his head right against His Holiness's head. To everybody's surprise His Holiness was not a bit frightened, but put the scarf on the Oracle's neck as if he knew him already. The Oracle then walked beside the palanquin until His Holiness entered the Jokhang, with his family and all his officials. A high seat had been raised for him in front of the chief precious image of the Lord Buddha and the lamas and monks prayed while we went into the other shrines to offer scarves to the chief deities. Next His Holiness was taken to the shrines in Ramoche Tsuklakhang and then to Norbu Lingka, where the Regent, the *Lonchen* and many officials, lamas, monks and foreign representatives sat in the hall to witness religious and folk dances. All presented scarves to His Holiness and took his blessing and were given tea and pastry.

The Dalai Lama stayed in Norbu Lingka until an auspicious day had been arranged for him to go to the Potala; his parents stayed at Gyatso and later a big house was built for them beside the Potala. They also had a small house near Norbu Lingka, where the *Gyayum* spent most of her time, and while His Holiness was little she saw him as often as she wished.

11   Tibetan Customs and Beliefs

WE WERE VERY happy in our new Taring House – Jigme's parents, Jigme, myself and our little daughters. We had a fine view over the broad green plain, surrounded by bare hills, on which Lhasa is built. To the north are holy hills and on their slopes were many beautiful, ancient monasteries, always looking peaceful and serene. Beyond the river, to the south, was the Bumpari hill, where people hoisted flags and burnt incense; every morning we could see smoke rising in the air from this hill – which meant that someone was praying for themselves, for every living creature and especially for peace in the world. There was one bad mountain to the south called Chakyakarpo. After *Monlam* the soldiers used to shell Chakyakarpo, with a black tent as target, to subdue the evil spirits for the New Year.

From our house we also had a wonderful view of His Holiness's main palace, the Potala, standing on a solitary hill about five hundred feet high, at the edge of the city, facing south. The huge red and white building really looks more like a fortress than a palace and has gilded roofs that glitter beautifully in the clear air and bright sun. The middle part was painted dark red, being the centre of the religious life of Tibet; it contained His Holiness's living rooms, many temples, shrines and tombs, and a monastery for about a hundred monks. The two wings were painted white, and contained all the most important government offices, special prisons for very important prisoners and accommodation for some of the lay officials. There were also a number of big halls where various ceremonies and meetings were held, and several courtyards where the *Losar* monastic dances took place. Often monastic trumpets – eight or ten feet long – were blown on the rooftops and every day at noon two conch-shells, one having a higher note than the other, were also blown and made a peculiar sound called the 'Ee-Uu'.

Below the west wing was a yellow house where the State Astrologer lived and nearby stood the Kagyur Press, which produced many religious books. Below the east wing was the Army headquarters and within the great walls were the second city magistrate's court, the prisons and His Holiness's stables.

Behind the Potala, at the foot of its hill, a small stream runs into a lake about two hundred yards long, and in the middle of the lake is a tiny island on which was built a temple called the Lu Khang (House of the Serpent). Every year, on the fifteenth day of the fourth month (the Lord Buddha's birthday) about fifty coracles made of yaks' hide were brought to this lake and many people in their best costumes rowed round the island, singing and dancing. (The dancers laid planks across their boats and took musical instruments with them and their music and the tapping of their feet could be heard from quite far away.)

Pema Dolkar used to prepare a picnic of many vegetarian delicacies – being a very holy day, no Tibetan ate meat – and she and I rowed around in one boat, with the children, after first visiting the temple to pray. It used to be so lovely. There was much romance in the air, because young girls would be looking for their lovers in other boats – and everyone was looking out to see their friends. The boats moved slowly and sometimes came close to the bank, so that one could smile and chat with those one knew amongst the watching crowds. All the officials in their ceremonial costumes were being rowed around and when the *Shap-pēs'* boat passed it looked very serious, compared with the other gay parties, as the monk-*Shap-pē* was there. On this day Jigme and his three *Lachag* colleagues and their clerks were even more important than the *Shap-pēs*, since it was the duty of the *Lachag* office to entertain all the other officials. The thirty clerks prepared special butter tea, and a drink made by boiling raisins and cooling the liquid, and sweet rice with raisins. We much looked forward to seeing Jigme floating by in his ceremonial robes; the children used to get very excited and shout, 'Pala! Pala!' when they recognised him.

As the crowd went home that evening many people paid a visit to the elephant who lived behind the Potala. He and a companion had been presented to His Holiness by the King of Nepal in 1937 and when we knew him he was quite old and his companion had already died. His name was Langchenla; *Langchen* means elephant and *la* is the honorific. Every day he went to drink from a well in the grounds of the Potala and once when I was riding home from Dekyi Lingka I heard his bell going, 'Ting! Ting!' and next appeared Langchenla. I became very frightened, in case my little pony might bolt, so I jumped off and let my reins go. But Langchenla passed by nicely and I had no trouble.

Around Taring House we had vegetable gardens and we leased some of them, keeping the best for ourselves. Jigme loves gardening and as soon as he got back from his office he worked hard with a spade—just like Tsarong. He did a lot of experimental grafting and budding and layering and all his new fruit trees flourished; later many people in Lhasa followed his example and successfully grew apples, peaches, cherries, pears and walnuts. We also had grapes in a greenhouse.

Soon our annual income from apples was about £200. The first ripe fruits were presented to the Jokhang and to His Holiness; then we sent some to all our relatives and friends and preserved about a thousand apples—by burying them in sand, three feet underground, ready for the New Year, when we again distributed them. People very much appreciated beautiful red apples in winter. The remainder we sold—some to our servants, who re-sold them at a good profit.

To spare Jigme home worries I took full responsibility for running the household and gave the best possible care to my parents-in-law. We usually got up at sunrise (between five and six o'clock), said our prayers and made offerings at the altar, lighting butter-lamps and burning incense. (Many took early holy walks with their dogs, going right round the Potala or the Jokhang.) Then I went to see our cook and give him whatever he needed, from the storehouse, for the two big meals of the day. Most noble families bought rice, sugar and flour in bulk, but marketing for meat and vegetables was done daily by the steward or cook, who kept a daily account of his purchases. At Taring House I did the accounts. Many brought all the butter they needed from their estates, but we bought ours from other people. In our kitchens there were big mud stoves, which were dyed black, oiled to make them shine and studded with amber or turquoise. We used wood stoves for heating the living-rooms but wood was scarce and expensive in Lhasa, so the poor people burnt dung.

Every morning, when Mother-in-law had finished her prayers, I went to ask after her health and enquire what meals she would like that day. Sometimes she mentioned special dishes, but usually she said, 'Whatever you like, my dear.' Then I asked Jigme if he wished to have anything special. We always had special food on Saturdays, when Jigme was not at the office, because on that day friends or relatives were sure to come. On some Saturdays we visited other houses for the whole day, but mostly Jigme spent his spare time working in the garden. It was our custom for the visits of close friends to last all day and for the visitor to have both main meals with his host.

I seldom went visiting, except to see relatives, but when I did visit my friends would not let me go, even if I said that Jigme would be home from his office—instead, they sent for him to come to join us. I was lucky to have won the love of my friends and relatives, who were always very good to me. Even those who were not my relatives would consult me about their private affairs. As I never used cosmetics the younger ladies enjoyed doing up my face at parties with their powder compacts and lipsticks. They would say, 'Oh, you look so greasy – please put on some powder!' While they played mahjong I sat beside them, watching, and they all laid side-bets, so that I might win something. They were a bit embarrassed to make high bets in my presence because I was against this, and also against playing the whole day.

Most Tibetan households kept more servants than we did, because we tried to cut expenses by keeping only the very necessary ones. Whenever we needed extra help we called servants from our estates or borrowed them from relatives or friends. We had a maid-servant for Mother-in-law, two men-servants for Jigme (they always had to escort him whenever he went out), one tea-cook, one general cook, one assistant cook, one syce, two gardeners, two muleteers and one man-servant for myself. Unlike most Tibetan ladies, I never kept a maid-servant of my own after my first maid-servant and her husband were put in charge of one of our small leased estates – but my man-servant escorted me everywhere and did my washing and many other jobs. I also trained a young girl to help me look after the children, but until they were three or four months old I bathed and dressed them myself. At night the older one slept in a cot by Jigme's bed and the younger one in a cot by my own bed. Sometimes in the middle of the the night I would take the baby into my bed and change her nappies whenever they were wet. I never troubled the maid in the night but at sunrise, when she took the babies away, I slept deeply for another two or three hours and I used to enjoy this sound sleep.

Every Tibetan lady had a maid to help care for the babies and some of these girls became the family nanny and were respected by children as their second mother. Mothers handed down their well-experienced nannies to their daughters or daughters-in-law and the great nurses had the full history of the family and would tell the children stories beginning,

'When your father (or mother) was small . . .' Everybody – including the friends of the family – would respect the 'Mamala'. I used to love my Mama, and Dudul Namgyal's nun-nanny was very powerful at Tsarong House, because Dudul was the only Tsarong heir. She had been one of my mother's maid-servants, but later she became a nun and so was known as Ani Chungki. She accompanied Dudul to school every day (the same school as I had been to), and every half-hour or so, she burnt incense to keep him healthy; she would hardly ever allow anyone into his room and when we were admitted she would not allow us to sit on his bed. Dudul began to smoke when he was about eleven, but Ani Chungki did not mind: she even encouraged him to buy a long rubber tube for his pipe. She used to say to him that he could smoke because his grandfather (my father) had smoked and 'another man like him would never be on this earth – the man who could make a hole in rock!' Pema Dolkar was very good to Ani Chungki and also to Tsechog, who had been my own nanny when I was small and now looked after Dudul's sister. Ani Chungki was well known to all and greatly respected because she was so influential at Tsarong House.

While Jigme was a *Dapon* I took much interest in his uniform – polishing and brushing his boots, belts and leggings and making his buttons shine. Jigme was never proud of himself and cared nothing about his Tibetan clothes or his military uniforms. I also cared for his horse and saddlery, as his military saddle had to be kept shining. I was longing to get a beautiful horse for him after his lovely grey pony died, and through a friend I was lucky enough to get a fine dun horse from the Reting Regent's stable, in exchange for a black fox-skin which I had brought from Calcutta. Genuine black fox-skins to make hats for monk- and lay-officials, were greatly valued by Tibetans.

I did some trading regularly to increase our income. We had about twenty pack-mules of our own who went to India once a year, with loads of wool which were sold for Indian currency, and they brought back all the stores we needed for the year, as well as cigarettes, patent medicines and tea. These goods I sold to the Lhasa shopkeepers, showing them the cost of the goods in India and receiving profit according to the prevailing prices.

In autumn I sometimes went to Taring Estate to inspect the crops and settle accounts with the steward. Our retainers there loved us to come and I used to see what I could do to help them if they had any difficulties.

After building Taring House we leased two small estates near Lhasa — one from the Army headquarters and one from the Ragashar family — to provide us with grass, grain, fuel and eggs. Otherwise it would have been very difficult to feed six or seven horses in the city and get enough fuel for the household. We had faithful retainers on both estates who enjoyed being put in charge and cared for the fields well. The rent we paid for the Army estate went to feed eighty cannon- and machine-gun mules. Every ten mules had two soliders to take care of them; the soldiers were paid by the government but it was essential to keep a good relationship between them and us.

Another of my duties was to see that everybody in the household, including the servants, got new clothes when they needed them. All Tibetans — except the very poor — employed tailors and we used to have several working in the house almost right through the year. The senior tailor was a clever and really fine man who belonged to the guild of government tailors; we often had most interesting talks.

Always, one of my main interests was teaching, so I gave tuition in Tibetan spelling and grammar and in English to my daughters and to the children of relatives and friends. I still enjoyed giving first-aid treatment and sometimes beggars came to Taring House for me to cure their sores. Whenever my nieces or any of the maid-servants were having babies I nursed them and many babies were born into my own hands. But my chief interest was studying Buddhism and trying to understand the false or illusory nature of all things. This is such a difficult study that I invited famous lama scholars to the house and learned from them.

(Previous page) Myself with my daughter, Ngowang.

Myself with Jigme. Photo: courtesy of James Cooper.

Myself in full Tibetan costume with my two daughters.

Gyantse, town and fort.

Lord Buddha found the truth by contemplating the realities of life and recognising the transience of our existence. The teachings of every sect of Tibetan Buddhism were: abstention from all evil, performance of good acts and the purification of the mind. This doctrine is based on the Eightfold Path:

1 Right Understanding (To be free from superstition and delusion)
2 Right Thought (High and worthy of the human intelligence)
3 Right Speech (Kindly and truthful)
4 Right Actions (Peaceful, honest and pure)
5 Right Livelihood (Bringing hurt or danger to no living being)
6 Right Effort (In self-training and self-control)
7 Right Mindfulness (To have an active watchful mind)
8 Right Concentration (In deep meditation on the realities of life).

Lord Buddha was the one who carried this teaching into perfect practice. Many of his followers make an effort to copy him and go on pilgrimages to bring about feelings of religious awe and repentance. We make offerings and say prayers to reduce our desire, hatred and malicious thoughts. At least all Buddhists believe in deed and consequence, and this belief helps them to try to avoid sin. We are taught that:

By oneself alone is evil done,
By oneself is one defiled,
By oneself is evil avoided,
By oneself is one purified,
No one can purify another.

The true teaching is concentrated in a small lump, but understanding is difficult and practice still more difficult. Even though Tibet was a Buddhist country the true practice of our religion was not easy, therefore people performed rites and went through many formulae to take the right steps gradually. But you find God, or Truth, in yourself – if you study. Mind is very important; if we do not cultivate our minds there can be no spiritual advance, and kindness develops intelligence. People cannot really believe anything unless they find it out for themselves. Many Tibetan Buddhists believed just because they were taught certain things; it is easy to do what you are told, without making any effort. But others search, find and then believe. Truth exists; it doesn't matter whether the Lord Buddha or Jesus Christ leads one to it. It is there, and the great teachers are like guides helping us to to reach it. We Tibetans do not object to our children studying every religion; it is good to put many dishes before people, who can then choose which they like best. Moral discipline has to be very good to maintain happiness; without religion we think too much of ourselves.

Buddhists believe absolutely that the human life is the most desirable. In it one may combine reason and faith and earn the privilege of leaving the transient life and dwelling forever in Nirvana. Therefore Buddhism teaches that suicide is the greatest sin and if one takes one's own life, through anger of fright, one cannot reincarnate as a human being for five hundred lifetimes. Of course it is not so if one deliberately gives up one's precious life for others.

As the love of life is with all, neither humans nor animals like to die. So the Lord Buddha has said, 'All beings long for happiness, therefore extend thy compassion to all.' When we are ill we take medical treatment and pray and perform rites so that it may be successful. In Tibet we also saved some animals' lives by sending the belt of the patient to the slaughter-house, throwing it over a sheep or goat and leading the animal home on it – often paying a little more than the ordinary market price. Sometimes the animal was taken right inside the Jokhang to let it have a blessing from the Buddha. These animals could be presented to the Jokhang, where there was a special place for grazing them, and the monks could use their wool and manure. I often saved animals' lives when children in the family got sick. If the real time has come for an animal to die nobody can do anything about it, but it is sad to see one being taken to a slaughtering-house where its life will have an unnatural interruption. The animals always know what is going to happen to them.

Once, when I was riding into Lhasa from Sera Monastery, I met a Tibetan Muslim taking a nice fat sheep to be slaughtered by the stream. The poor sheep was so reluctant to go that the man had had to tie a rope around her and drag her, sometimes hitting her from behind. I just could not bear it. I dismounted and begged the Muslim to sell her to me and buy meat from the market instead. He told me that he had been fattening her for a long time and that now she must be killed because he was going to have a feast for his family. Again I asked him to spare the life of the animal; since I had seen her I could not let her be killed because it was possible to save her and the merit would come to us both. I told him that though the sheep couldn't talk we could see how she was feeling — and just put that feeling to ourselves. The meal only lasts for a little while and then what is there, except that you have filled your tummy. I said, 'I am willing to pay a good price, and although you are a Muslim surely we all have the same feelings.' After a long argument the man sold me the sheep and I took her to one of our estates.

In Lhasa we had more than a thousand Tibetan Muslims who originally came from Kashmir. Their wives were mostly Tibetans wo had been converted to Islam, and there were no objections to these conversions; but we never saw a Muslim becoming a Buddhist because Tibetans respected all religions equally and made no effort to convert. The Muslims do not believe in rebirth and they carried out their practices of fasting, and taking no interest on money lent, very strictly. Buddhism teaches that mortification of the body is not so important as control of the mind and knowledge of one's self.

We Tibetans are very superstitious, contrary to the Lord Buddha's teaching. We have a proverb that if one is superstitious enough even an empty house may be robbed. Our superstitions have developed through observing that certain indications are repeatedly followed by the same consequences. If one spills any food accidentally on departing from home for a

distant place this is considered unlucky. If one is met accidentally, on departure, by someone carrying a full vessel of water
or tea this is lucky. If a raven who always lives away from
people nests over your home this is a bad omen. A small book
has been written to interpret the sounds of the raven, who is
considered to be a bird of the deities. Ravens make two sounds
and first you must find out in which direction the bird is
facing. A low clacking sound means good luck – one is going
to have a gift, or a guest, or success of some sort; but if the
raven makes a big barking sound it indicates some misfortune.
A sparrow nesting in the house is a good omen, but bird-
droppings falling on a person's head bring bad luck. To dream
of an eclipse of the sun or the moon is considered to be an
indication of the death of a king, a lama or a parent; to dream of
a sunrise is good, but a sunset is bad. People are advised to
observe their dreams while they are meditating. If a person
who is earnestly meditating on the realities of life dreams that
he is wearing new clothes, or crossing a bridge, or having a
bath it is considered that he has achieved the purpose of his
meditation.

On the fifteenth day of the fifth month (June – July) the
whole of Tibet went out on picnics. This was called the World
Prayer, as everybody prayed then for the happiness of all living
beings all over the world. Shops closed for many days and in the
evenings government officials came direct from their work to
the riverside, where in lovely tents their families were waiting
for them. Everywhere one saw people playing games, or
enjoying music and singing, and during this festival the Taring
family always arranged a three-day party for friends and
relatives; we had a routine that during other festivals Tsarong
and our friends gave the parties. As Tsarong House was near
the river, with beautiful flowers and fruit trees, we used to
pitch tents in the garden and relatives would bring their
bedding and spend days with us. It was lovely to sleep in the
garden and get up early and have your morning tea brought to
you while special birds sang in cages hung on the tent ropes.
On the first day of the festival every family burnt much

incense and hoisted many prayer-flags. These – and various other Tibetan religious customs connected with weddings, births, deaths and so on – are not real Buddhist activities, but remnants of our original animist religion, called Bön.

When Padmasambawa, the great Indian saint, came to Tibet at the invitation of King Trisong Detsen (A.D. 742–797) he was attacked by Bön spirits who opposed his mission to spread Buddhism in Tibet. With his powerful magical formulae he soon subdued those spirits and made them take an oath to defend the new religion – and so many of them were drawn into Tibetan Buddhism. The Bön customs of burning incense and hoisting prayer-flags were also continued, only the flags now have Buddhist prayers printed on them, so that the wind may read them in countless multiplications.

Buddhism suffered during the reign of King Langdarma (A.D. 803). King Ralpachen, one of our three most religious kings, was doing much for the country's new religion when he was greatly opposed by his brother, Darma. A man named Be Gyator killed Ralpachen – while the King was relaxing and drinking *chang* – by twisting his head around until his neck was broken. Then Langdarma took the throne, Be Gyator was appointed Chief Minister and many other pro-Bön people became government ministers. They made new laws to destroy Buddhism, sealed up the principal temples and broke all the images. It is said that the Tibetan custom of officials putting up their hair in knots, plaited with red ribbons, was started by Langdarma to hide his horns – the sign of being a wizard. The hairdressers were threatened that if they told about the King's horns they would be killed. It is also said that Langdarma had a black tongue. Ever since, when Tibetans meet high-ranking persons they scratch their heads and put out their tongues to show that they have neither horns nor black tongues.

Langdarma made the Buddhist monks choose whether to marry, to carry arms or to become huntsmen. Death was the punishment for remaining Buddhist. But Langdarma was able to wipe out Buddhism only in Central Tibet and not in the more remote parts of the country.

Eventually things became so bad that a hermit – Lhalung Paldor – who was meditating in a cave at Yerpa, near Lhasa, decided to do something. He set out for Lhasa, wearing a black hat and a black cloak, with charcoal and grease smeared on all his clothes and on his white horse, and his bow and arrow hidden in the long sleeves of his cloak. Outside Lhasa he tied his horse near the river, walked into the city and found Langdarma and some of his ministers in front of the Jokhang. Prostrating himself before Langdarma, Lhalung Paldor loosed an arrow from his bow straight at the King's heart and killed him. In the confusion that followed, Lhalung Paldor escaped to the river, mounted his horse and forced it to swim to the other bank to wash the charcoal away. Then, turning his cloak, and with his horse white again, he galloped to Yerpa and hid in his cave. Although search parties set out in different directions no one could find a man on a black horse wearing a black cloak and hat. At Yerpa a herdsman suspected the hermit but said, 'I would not put salt in the food which is for many people', and kept quiet. Yet a rumour that Lhalung Paldor had killed the King soon spread, so the hermit left his cave and took refuge in eastern Tibet. His image was to be seen in many monasteries and there was also one in his cave at Yerpa. After Langdarma's death the nobility became supporters of Buddhism and founded many monasteries which lasted until the Chinese destroyed them recently.

We often went to Yerpa, a most holy place to which Lhasa people made pilgrimages in summertime. Once the Tsarong, Taring and Dorje families, accompanied by Heinrich Harrer, visited the caves, which are very difficult to get into. One could see the grave of a nun who had fallen from the rocks near the cave and had been killed. Jigme and Harrer went up easily but climbing even to the entrance of the cave made me cry because it was so straight down for thousands of feet and the whistling wind was pulling me off from the little bushes I was holding on to. But at last Jigme came to my rescue.

Tibetans consider India as a sacred country of learned people who are more compassionate than we are because the

Lord Buddha did not step on the land of Tibet. Tibetans are more warrior-like. Hinduism and Buddhism are very close to each other. Lord Buddha, being the son of a Hindu king, took many teachings from Hinduism, and his own teachings now form a part of Hinduism. The biggest difference is that Hindus believe in an ego and Buddhists do not. Also, we have never had either a caste system like the Indians nor social snobbery such as some European countries have. Tibetans were classified by their intelligence and old families were respected for being descended from great and holy people. We consider that kind, intelligent people are those who have gained merit in previous incarnations; and our animals are supposed to be loved and respected because they, too, are going through the circle of reincarnation and must be regarded as our equals. But some Tibetans were not kind to animals – some traders especially ill-treated their pack-animals.

In Tibet our monastic dances were all connected with religion, and we believed that while watching these we gained blessings as well as enjoying the skill of the monk-dancers. The plays performed by lay drama groups – based on the lives of the Religious Kings and Chiefs of Tibet – taught people a lot about history and religion and were so familiar that any Tibetan could catch the stage of the story whenever he joined the audience. The dialogue was sung and each actor had his own tune, which he sang alone, or as a duet, or as part of a chorus. Many people took a great interest in this classical music and were very knowledgable about it. The plays were performed during autumn, when the crops were in, and some of them went on from sunrise till sunset, for four days. The audience brought their food with them and sweets to pass to each other.

Tibetans always greatly enjoyed autumn. When the planet Rishi appeared for two weeks the water was considered to be good for health, so many people swam in the river and some even camped on the banks and bathed at night under the twinkling stars.

Since my childhood the weather has changed a lot and

during recent years we never got heavy snow in Lhasa, but we always played a traditional game to celebrate the first snowfall. We would send a parcel of fresh snow, cleverly disguised, to a friend, with small particles of food and a letter requesting an auspicious party, and if the parcel was accepted the friend had to give a day's party, serving dishes of all the foods sent with the letter. But if the messenger who brought the parcel was caught and the snow detected, members of the family could beat the man with a leg of mutton and rub paste all over his head and body. Then the day's party had to be given by the sender of the parcel. This was a game of the snow-land and it was considered auspicious for the prosperity of the country to play it with happiness.

Once Surkhang *Shap-pē* told Kashopa *Tsi-pon* that he was going to send him a snow parcel next morning, before ten o'clock, and he promised to give the Kashopa family a good party if he failed to do so. Kashopa warned his family and servants to be on the alert and they had a leg of mutton and big bowl of paste ready for the messenger. Next day everybody at Kashopa House was watching out very carefully. Early in the morning Surkhang sent his personal servant, with an arrow in his hand, towards the house and he appeared at quite a distance, looking, and drawing back sometimes. Kashopa's people gave all their attention to catching him as soon as he came forward; but in the meantime some monks came to see Kashopa on business. Being monks, Kashopa gave them his attention, though he was so anxious about the snow parcel that he was to get within the hour. As usual, the monks held a long conversation; then they left him, after presenting a scarf and a packet of money. Kashopa had tried to refuse the money but the monks insisted on his accepting it, quoting the Tibetan proverb 'Though the flower is small, it is acceptable when offered to God.' The moment the monks left, Surkhang's servant came forth with a letter from his master, asking Kashopa to examine the packet he had accepted from the monks. When Koshopa did so, he found that it contained the snow and food. He then felt a great embarrassment and had to give the Surkhang family a very good party.

While His Holiness was studying hard and growing up everybody in the country relaxed and the officials and their ladies played mahjong for high stakes. The Reting Regent was on the best possible terms with the *Kashag*, the Dalai Lama's family and all the monasteries. His own monastery, Sera, gave him full political support and he could have remained in power until His Holiness took over the administration himself. But in 1940 he decided to resign, because he wanted to lead a contemplative life, which could not be done with all his responsibilities as Regent.

When Reting told the *Kashag* and his friends that he was going to resign everybody felt surprised. He was popular with the ordinary people because he had brought good luck to the country and the *Kashag* ministers and the High Lamas of the monasteries came to beg him earnestly not to resign. But he told Jigme and them all that he wanted to meditate, because the State Astrologer had shown that he would die young if he did not devote himself to the religious life. He added that he was going to hand over his power to a person who was even better than himself—Taktra Rinpoche, a quiet man, over seventy years old, who was little known to us all. Spiritually he was good, and very learned in religion, but he had no experience of government work. He had not been Reting's tutor, but the relationship between the two was the same as if he had been and Reting felt a great respect and affection for him. He thought he could influence Taktra Rinpoche, if necessary. So he made what proved to be the big mistake of not letting the *Tsongdu* choose his successor.

In 1933 Tsering Yangzom (Tsarong's second eldest daughter by Tseten Dolkar) had gone with her sisters to Mount Hermon School in Darjeeling and while there she met Jigme Dorje, the eldest son of Raja and Rani Dorje of Bhutan. He was a most brilliant young man and Tsering Yangzom was tall and very pretty, with a charming nature—religious and charitable. Soon the two decided to marry and in 1942 Jigme Dorje's parents asked Jigme and me to organise the traditional engagement ceremony. Rani Dorje was Jigme's aunt, with whom he had stayed during his schooldays in India.

Tsarong got permission from the government to give his daughter away to be a Bhutanese subject and he and Pema Dolkar asked me to take the bridal party to India, since neither of them was too well. It made me very happy to do this. The party consisted of Tsarong's representative, six official servants, a maid for the bride, two servants for me, a mule-driver for the twenty pack mules and a syce for our many riding animals.

The journey was fixed for autumn, so that we would be in India during winter – the best time for Tibetans. Tsarong wanted us to enjoy the trip and it was planned to take exactly a month from Lhasa to Kalimpong. Tsering Yangzom asked her half-sister Tseyang, my eldest daughter, to accompany her. Tseyang had come back from Mount Hermon School in 1939 because she missed home so much and could not study; every time she wrote to us she drew a crying girl. But now, being a little older, she wished to return to India to do more study.

After the home-departure ceremony Tsarong and Pema Dolkar left for Chusul by yak-hide boat and the bridal party rode to Seshika, near Chusul, where we all met. Seshika was a small estate, in a beautiful valley, belonging to Tsarong's sister who had been married to the Chief of Poyul. Being autumn, a number of nomads were camping close by, so we had plenty of dairy food. We spent a most enjoyable week there and the two girls giggled right through the days. Tsarong stayed on after we left, as he had some investigation to do to help the retainers about their debts.

This trip reminded me of my first journey down to Darjeeling as a child. When we crossed the Nathala pass, it was breathtakingly beautiful looking down to Gangtok. The Sikkim State had arranged our accommodation and that evening many Ministers of State came to meet us. Next day we left our ponies behind and drove to Gangtok, where we were state guests. After three days we continued to Kalimpong and by order of the government our narrow road was cleared of all traffic. Sir Basil Gould, the Political Officer for Sikkim, was waiting to receive us at the rest-house and many friends came to see us, including Annie, Vera and Vicky MacDonald. The Second

World War was on, so Kalimpong was filled with American and British soldiers and officers.

Next morning the wedding procession drove to Bhutan House. Many Bhutanese with drums and trumpets, dressed in richly coloured brocade and wearing red shawls over their shoulders, were dancing away in front of the bride's car, in which Tseyang and I accompanied Tsering Yangzom. A Nepalese wedding band also played beside the car. To my surprise I saw Surkhang *Shap-pē* and Kunphela amongst the crowds who were watching. The whole Dorje family was waiting by the staircase at Bhutan House with scarves and after the usual ceremonies in the prayer-room we joined the many guests in the huge, beautifully decorated Tibetan tents which were pitched in the garden. At the reception we finished over a hundred bottles of sherry.

For seven days the celebrations continued. Friends were called to lunch and dinner at the house and some Indian friends were invited to another hall for vegetarian meals. Three thousand poor villagers were given lunch in the garden and our servants from Lhasa received gifts and special entertainment for more than a week.

When our party dispersed in Kalimpong I kept four servants for my return journey. Then Jigme Dorje, his bride and myself went down to Calcutta to shop – but during the war the Calcutta shops had almost nothing. I bought only five hundred loads of tea and a hundred loads of leather for boot-making, but I got quite a good profit on these. I stayed on alone to buy the leather and one day Calcutta was bombed. That evening I met Kunphela, who advised me to return to Kalimpong because if more bombs were dropped the road might become difficult. I also received two telegrams from Jigme saying, 'Why are you staying in Calcutta? Return immediately.' So, since Kunphela was a clever man, I decided to go back and sent my servant to buy a ticket; as he could not get one I went to the station myself and got one after some struggle. I left two servants in Calcutta to send up the goods and after a few days in Kalimpong returned to Lhasa.

In Tibet, all imported goods became very expensive during the Second World War, but much cloth was sent from India to China through Tibet and our traders fetched a good profit on this.

By 1939 many people in Lhasa had wireless sets, so the world news was heard daily. All over Tibet, until peace was declared, religious rites were performed regularly for the war to subside.

12 The Fall of the Ex-Regent Reting

IN 1946 WE had the great expense of giving an official party.
It was the duty of high officials, from the fourth rank upwards,
to give a five-day party once in their career for all their lay-
colleagues, but counting preparations and clearing up afterwards the whole thing lasted for twelve days or more. The
expense was big because the price of food had risen about
ten times since my father-in-law and Chapase gave a joint
party in 1931. Jigme's partner as host was Ngapo Ngawang
Jigme.

During these parties three meals of the choicest food were
served daily to at least a hundred men, thirty women, thirty
children and a hundred servants. Two government-official
friends, who enlisted many helpers, were requested to
organise the whole thing and on an auspicious day the party
committee met to discuss how many servants, cooks and
chang-girls to employ and how much food and extra
furniture would be required. There was a list of those willing
to lend mats, carpets and crockery, and those who would
sell flour, eggs, meat, butter and other foods. The committee
then appointed a storekeeper and hired servants, including

tea-cooks from the monasteries, as monks are the best tea-cooks. Exceptionally reliable servants were borrowed from their usual employers and rooms were arranged for the *Shap-pēs* and their ladies, for senior officials, junior officials, children and servants. An orchestra was engaged to provide music for singing and dancing, as the whole house was expected to have a happy atmosphere throughout the party.

Three days before the party began several servants, dressed in their finest livery and riding good horses, well saddled, delivered the invitations with folded scarves placed on papers requesting the gentlemen and ladies of the house, with their children, to attend the party for two days or so. They were asked to come as early as possible and if they were intimate friends or relatives they would be invited to stay. The servants reported how many had accepted the invitation and returned every morning to these homes to give a reminder; some people hesitated to come unless they got a repeat-invitation early each day. Ladies had to attend these parties in their full costume and, when the party began, stewards, junior officials and a few senior officials waited at the gate to receive the honourable guests. Each receptionist took the guests onward in relays and the last conducted them to a room where their host came to the door to greet them and was offered a scarf which he returned.

The *Shap-pēs* attended their offices early before riding together to the party. All the officials received them at the gate, while flags were hoisted on the house, religious horns were blown, incense was burnt and artists drew auspicious decorations with white chalk on the ground of the courtyard. When the *Shap-pēs* had ceremoniously taken their high seats in the hall—in order of seniority—they were offered tea, rice and *chang*, of which they accepted very little. Their servants then helped them to remove their ceremonial robes and they went to another room where three or four square tables had been prepared. Here they were served tea in old Chinese cups or jade cups with silver stands. Each table was used by eight people at meal-times, or by four people for playing dominoes, mahjong, cards and various other indoor games. Some officials and their ladies enjoyed playing mahjong for high stakes more than they enjoyed the food – which was sad.

Every day the guests were served a breakfast of twelve small dishes and four big dishes consisting of mutton chops, boiled eggs, sweet cheese, dried meat, cold boiled meat, sausages and fried stuffed lungs and vegetables. As usual the main dish was *tsampa* – the staple food for Tibetans of all classes.

For lunch the main dish was egg-noodles, with sixteen small dishes of delicacies and four big dishes. After lunch *chang* was served to laymen and tea to the monks, followed by tea and cakes for all during the afternoon. The monks watched the lay people drinking with big smiles; no monk drank openly, but there were some very naughty monk-officials.

Dinner – the most elaborate meal – started with sixteen small dishes, followed by eight courses served alternately from plates and cups, followed by four big cups of vegetables and imported sea-foods, and finally there was a huge bowl of soup, laid on the centre of the table with rice and *mo-mo* (dumplings stuffed with meat). In between meals different sweets were served at intervals. The children were given an early dinner and went home before sunset with their nannies.

The breakfast menu was Tibetan, the lunch and dinner menus were partly Chinese and we ate with chopsticks or spoons. The organisers supervised the service and occasionally urged the guests to enjoy the food, removing their hats with great courtesy while addressing the senior men and their ladies, but keeping them on while politely addressing the juniors. After dinner, *chang* and foreign drinks were served by *chang*-girls dressed in their best clothes. When everybody was a bit tipsy the men visited the ladies in their room and persuaded them to drink even more, and open flirtations were watched by the servants and those who took no drink. The sober people quietly slipped away when the party got too rowdy. It was fun to watch the end of these parties; some people could not get up because their legs were benumbed from squatting through the long feast. Everyone tried to see the most important guest depart and the kerosene lamp went with him like a moving planet, leaving the rest of us in a dim room with only a few candles. Our servants very kindly looked after us: otherwise we might have stumbled over the steps in the dark at this moment. Even the horses got excited and you could hear them neighing. Good-byes were exchanged hastily and next morning everybody apologised to everybody else for their behaviour – but the same thing happened each night until the party was over.

A special room or tent was set aside for the *Shap-pēs*, who used it to hold important consultations or to do their individual official tasks. Some *Shap-pēs* received a messenger sent to their parties with a letter from His Holiness the Dalai Lama.

On the last day meals were served a little earlier and there was a 'Happy Ending' ceremony. The *Shap-pēs* returned to their high seats, in full uniform, auspicious tea and rice were served, the host's representative gave a scarf to each guest and this time the scarf had to be put around the nexk. Much incense was burned in the courtyard while everyone threw pinches of *tsampa* flour in the air and said '*So! So!*' three times, calling for victory for the gods. While raising the hand holding the fourth pinch of flour we called '*Lha Gyalo!*' – meaning 'Victory to the Gods!' Then the party organisers gave the departing guests a courteous send-off.

It always seemed that a lot of food was going to waste, because some of the guests were too shy to eat much, but after such parties I used to feel happy to see the left-overs being given to the waiting beggars and poor people.

A few months later we had another big expense when my eldest daughter, Tseyang, was married to Jigme's youngest brother, Rigzin Namgyal. Mother-in-law was forty-nine when Rigzen Namgyal was born and his parents – especially his mother – always worried about seeing him married before they died. He went to a Tibetan school in Lhasa and then to St. Joseph's, Darjeeling – at the expense of the Sikkim State – and afterwards he studied Tibetan with me. As the Tarings already

(Previous page) The procession of His Holiness the Dalai Lama leaving the Potala Palace for Norbu Lingka. Photo: Major George Sherriff.

Jigme and myself with our two daughters, Ngowang and Yangdol.

Taring House, Lhasa. Photo: Dadul Namgyal Tsarong.

had two married sons, with many children, they thought it would be suitable for Rigzin to leave Taring and join one of the many noble families who had requested him to marry a daughter. But he hated to leave Taring and said that if his father did not wish him to stay he could ask Sikkim State for a job and leave Tibet. However, he and his mother loved each other so much that they would never have liked to be separated, so I suggested that he should marry Tseyang and this idea made everybody very happy.

Namgyal is an exceptionally nice man – tall, much like his father in features, hard-working and intelligent. After his marriage he worked for twelve years in Lhasa as a secretary to the *Kashag*. To me he is just like my own son, because I have known him so well since his childhood.

When the wedding was over I brought our two daughters and Tsarong's daughter, Tsering Dolma, and his younger son, Phuntsok Gyantsan (two of Tseten Dolkar's children), to school in Darjeeling. The journey took about three weeks from Lhasa to Gangtok, travelling twenty-five miles per day. The Sikkim State lent us a car to drive from Gangtok to Kalimpong, where I had the children's clothes made.

Before returning to Tibet I went with Rani Dorje to Calcutta and Bombay. Calcutta was in trouble; shops were being looted and cars burnt. However, with the help of a friend of Rani Dorje's we got to Howrah Station and then to Bombay, where a Nepalese trader had arranged accommodation for us in a huge eight-storied Hindu hotel. We were trying to do things economically but this was a hopeless place with huge bedrooms, and no bathrooms, and only communal lavatories. It was not very dirty, yet after one look we left it and moved to a small, comfortable hotel. Rani Dorje was interested in buying some diamonds and I also did a little trading because we now had to pay the girls' school fees in rupees. I bought diamonds and cultured pearls from Jain jewel merchants and later sold them to a jewel merchant in Lhasa for not much profit.

While we were in Bombay, Mr. Shakabpa and some of his

friends came to stay in our hotel. Mahatma Gandhi also arrived in the city and next morning there was a big mob outside the hotel, which was near the Navy headquarters. Thinking Mahatma Gandhi might be in the crowd and I asked Rani Dorje to come outside with me so that we might pay our respects to him. We went out, and found that a mutiny had started. From the windows of the Navy headquarters sailors were throwing stools, hockey-sticks and everything they could get hold of; we ran back to the hotel and were told that the Indian sailors were revolting against their British officers. Soon the street was filled with armoured cars, the newspapers said that a hundred ships were leaving England and· curfew orders were issued. It was difficult to leave Bombay but Mr. Shakabpa got our tickets and we all returned to Calcutta together. My two servants told me that whatever happened they would be responsible for our boxes of diamonds and pearls.

The situation had improved in Calcutta. There I bought cigarettes and cloth to send to Yunan, but we got only a little profit. The two faithful servants who went to China with these goods did their best and were not to be blamed.

During this period Jigme and I often visited Shuksep Jetsun Lochen Rinpoche, of whom my sister, Norbu Yudon, was also a disciple. Lochen Rinpoche was a saintly hermit, the reincarnation of Machik Lapdon, a deity of the Nyingmapa seat of Padmasambawa. She had been born in India in about 1820 at Tsopadma (Rawalsar, in the district of Mandi) of a Nepalse mother and Tibetan father. From the age of six she preached, with a *thang-ka*, by singing of religion in a wonderfully melodious voice and whoever heard her found their hearts coming closer to religion. As a child she had a little goat to ride and when in her youth she went along the streets of Lhasa with her *thang-ka*, preaching from door to door, she caught the hearts of many Lhasa girls who became nuns and followed her. She was known as 'Ani Lochen'. My mother, as a girl, often heard her singing and preaching. At the age of about forty Ani Lochen promised her mother that she would always stay in the mountains and meditate; later she found a place near Lhasa called Shuksep, where there was a cave in which Gyalwa Longchen Rabjampa had meditated. This great lama was a follower of Padmasambawa's teaching and many holy lamas walked from eastern Tibet till their feet became sore, carrying their food and bedding on their backs, just to see this cave and pray. Many nuns also came and there was a little nunnery nearby for about eighty women. People regularly visited Ani Lochen, for her cave was near Lhasa and she had many worshippers – lamas, monks, officials and owmen. Sometimes nuns would leave their nunnery to marry, but Ani Lochen always said, 'Never mind – even if they have been nuns for only a week they will be different forever afterwards.' When she was well over a hundred Reting Regent visited her; she was going to be brought down from her cave to see him at the little nunnery, but he asked her not to come down and instead he climed up.

Once, when we had gone to Shuksep to take Ani Lochen's blessings and listen to her teaching, I asked her to pray that I would eventually be able to live in the mountains and lead a religious life. She said it would never be possible for me to do this, but explained that the true religious life consists in watching your mind, as mind controls all our sensory powers. She said, 'There is no need to isolate yourself. If you know, all places are paradise. There are truly religious people, well purified, among all people everywhere. If you practice the teaching of the Lord Buddha in your daily life it is not necessary to go into the mountains. Be kind to all living beings, then I am sure you will achieve what you wish.'

Lochen Rinpoche was often visited by my nephew, Wangdula (Norbu Yudon's elder son), and his beautiful wife, Chodonla, whose brother was married to Lungshar's granddaughter. This religious young couple were very fond of each other and had four lovely babies. Lochen Rinpoche explained the doctrine of karma by telling them about a woman who came to a river and left her two elder children on the bank while she carried the youngest across on her back. The older children were then drowned and the poor mother could do nothing to save them. Lochen Rinpoche said, 'This is the karma of the past, which spares no one.' At the time Wangdula and his wife took this as the usual preaching of a holy hermit and never thought that their karma would be much the same.

In 1941 Wangdula became the *Dzongpon* of Dzonga in west Tibet. A year later an epidemic of dysentery broke out in the town and many children died, so Wangdula took his family to Kyirong Dzong, a very beautiful place close to Nepal. In spite of this precaution the four children got the terrible dysentery. Harrer and Aufschnaiter were then in Kyirong and were asked to help, but as they had no suitable medicine they advised Wangdula to take the children immediately to Kathmandu, where they could get the right treatment. Unluckily, it was impossible to do this and the two boys and two girls – all under seven – died one after the other within a week. Poor Wagdula and Chodonla suffered greatly. Chodonla did not hear for some time that her mother – who was only in her late forties – had also died, in Lhasa, during that week.

Wangdula then resigned as *Dzongpon* and went back to Lhasa where Chodonla soon gave birth to another daughter, which consoled them very much. Ani Lochen's teaching helped them to take their tragedy well and they were quite content with their new-born daughter.

There were many nunneries in Tibet, but to have such a saint as Ani Lochen was rare. The State nunnery was Samding Monastery, about seventy miles from Lhasa, whose Abbess was Dorje Phagmo, the 'Thunderbolt Sow'. Samding had another big monastery called Nanying, in Gyantse, and a number of estates to meet its expenses. The thirteenth Dalai Lama, during his flight to India, stayed at Samding for a few days. The monastery was built on a small hill, overlooking the beautiful lake of Yamdok.

Dorje Phagmo got her name two and a half centuries ago, when the Dzungar Tartars invaded central Tibet, looting villages and monasteries. At the gate of Samding their leader, who had heard that there was treasure hidden in this monastery, asked to be let in. The Abbess refused him admission, so he ordered his men to break the gates. When this had been done the Tartars found the courtyard filled with a large herd of pigs, headed by a huge sow, and the sight disgusted them so much that they turned away immediately. As soon as they were out of sight the pigs again became humans and the huge sow was made Lady Abbess, because by her magic powers she had preserved the monastery and its lamas. Since then, the Dorje Phagmo has been venerated by all Tibetans and is reincarnated in each Abbess of Samding. She is accorded privileges shared only by the Dalai Lama and Panchen Lama.

In 1947 there was a great deal of anxiety in Lhasa about the situation concerning the ex-Regent Reting and the Regent Taktra. When Taktra became Regent his treasurer, Chakzo Chemo, got a lot of power, through being easily able to influence his master; he was not a knowledgeable man and had no experience of such responsibility. he knew his time of power would be short and wanted to make the most of it for himself. He did all the administrative work and disliked Taktra taking advice from Reting, who was also resented by Taktra's other attendants. This made Reting sad. His own attendants then began to plot against Taktra and his vengeful private secretary — a clever lama named Nyungne Rinpoche, who could paint beautifully and do fine carpentry — made a bomb parcel in March 1947, and sent it to Taktra's private secretary's office saying that it came from the Governor of Chamdo. When the parcel was opened the hand-grenade exploded but did no harm. Reting was suspected and after investigating the matter thoroughly the government sent a search-party to his Lhasa office; but they discovered that he was at his monastery. Nyungne Rinpoche then felt guilty and had regrets, so he ran to the house of Numa (Jigme's brother-in-law), got into the lavatory and shot himself.

After this Taktra asked the *Kashag* to sent troops to bring Reting to Lhasa and two *Shap-pēs*, Surkhang and Lhalu, went to Reting Monastery with fifty or sixty soldiers. They told us later that when prostrating to Reting they feared he might shoot them as their heads were bent to take his blessings. But no—he received them courteously. Then one captain prostrated, caught hold of a leg of the ex-Regent and begged him to come to Lhasa. Reting agreed and that very night left his monastery. Some soldiers stayed in Reting and looted the ex-Regent's palace; there was quite a lot of shooting and about twenty soldiers and monks were killed. My sister Norbu Yudon was in Reting at the time; her daughter, Tsewang, had married the ex-Regent's brother and they were all there on a visit. They were nearly killed, but managed to escape in the night, crossing the river in hide coracles and losing everything they had taken with them.

From the roof of Taring House we saw the sad sight of Reting being taken to the Potala, on 18 April, by Lhalu and Surkhang *Shap-pē*. He was brought past Sera Monastery, where he could have been rescued by the monks had they been smart enough; they could easily have held him in the monastery while negotiating with the government on his behalf, but they seemed to be taken unawares and did nothing. The next day the whole monastery was in protest and monks and soldiers were exchanging shots. After about twelve days the monks were subdued, when seventy or eighty of them had been killed.

Meanwhile, investigations were going on up in the Potala and Reting was being interrogated. Enough documents were found to prove that Nyungne Rinpoche had been leading the ex-Regent's followers in an attempt to overthrow the Regent. Eventually, Reting's followers admitted that they had sent the explosive parcel. It was also proved that Reting had often begged his attendants not to make such schemes, but they would not obey him. Those who had been conspiring were sentenced to life imprisonment or exile from Lhasa—depending on how guilty they were. I heard that Reting was very sad and apologised for the upsets caused by his followers' wickedness and the ingratitude and weakness of Taktra, in whom he had had so much trust. All this time the houses of his relatives and friends were sealed by the government. Sealing meant that the family could live in only one or two rooms, while all the others were locked – with a government seal on each lock – and watched by police. The house might be confiscated at the end of an inquiry, or unsealed and returned to the owner. A meeting of the *Dungtsi* (the head committee of the *Tsongdu*) discussed sealing our house, because Jigme had been so friendly with Reting, but as Jigme had never taken any interest in politics or been involved in any quarrels between individuals everybody realised that he could not possibly be suspected of plotting against Taktra. Later, it was found that Reting's relatives were also completely innocent and their houses were unsealed, though one of his nephews – a *Dzasa*, aged about twenty-four – was imprisoned for four years. Nothing was proved against him, yet he was only released when His Holiness took over the administration and granted a general amnesty to prisoners.

Three weeks after his arrest we heard that Reting had been found dead in the Potala. Some said that he had felt so sorrowful he willed himself to die, but because he died suddenly the *Tsongdu* appointed a doctor and several officials to examine the body; Tsarong and Shatase were among the officials and Tsarong later told me that they found no injury except some blue marks on the bottom. In Tibet we had no post-mortems, so it was impossible to find out whether a person had been poisoned or not. Reting's body was cremated and all the people of Lhasa mourned him. I heard that the Dalai Lama's father had begged for him to be released, but before anything could be done he died. His Holiness was then aged thirteen and was very sad to hear of the death of the Regent who had done his duty so well in the search for the new Dalai Lama.

Later that year, Jigme's parents went to Shigatse to see the new house that Chime and his wife had built. Chime was always exceptionally kind to his wife, his children and his parents; whenever his mother and father were ill he nursed them skilfully. Father-in-law used to keep in good health, on the whole, though sometimes he had trouble with his leg and many times his nose bled, often to the extent of a basinful. Everybody felt very frightened during these nose-bleeds, yet always he got over them and he used to say that he felt better afterwards. But soon after reaching Shigatse he had another nose-bleed – and this time he died, at the age of seventy-two, to the great grief of the whole family. His body was cremated at Shigatse and we built a small golden tomb for his ashes.

Before Mother-in-law returned to Lhasa Jigme and I went to India to be with our children during the school holidays. We also visited many of the sacred places of India and Nepal, to pray for Father-in-law. In Nepal we were State guests and as we both speak Nepali were greatly enjoyed our pilgrimage, though we were terribly saddened by the news of Mahatma Gandhi's assassination. All Tibetans had a great reverence for him, as we said that he was a reincarnation of Padmasambawa.

I noticed a lot of changes since my last visit to Nepal, in 1925. There were new big buildings – including hotels and schools – that had come up after the bad earthquake of 1928, and we met many English-speaking Nepalis, though previously no one spoke English, not even the Nepalese representatives in Lhasa. In 1925 the Ranas were in full power and though Tsarong spoke much of the Yampo Chogyal (the Tibetan name for the Nepalese King) he had no chance to meet him. But in 1948 the Rana's power was weakening and when I again visited Nepal, in 1950, with His Holiness's mother, the Yampo Chogyal had taken over and the Gyayum was received by him and his queen. Yet in spite of these big changes the sacred Buddhist places were always serene.

13   China Threatens Tibet

In the late 1940s we heard rumours that the Chinese Communists were coming, but we thought it might take them years to arrive because they had said on the radio that they would first get Formosa. Everybody was worried and many indications showed that something unlucky would take place. In 1949 we saw comet with a long tail and all the aged people said that the same comet had appeared when the Chinese invaded Tibet in 1910. There were also predictions in books that a bad interruption would come to shadow the great religion of the Lord Buddha. As the rumours became stronger the government performed many rites to avert such interruptions and made it clear to other countries that the relationship between Tibet and China had always been that of 'priest and patron'. We explained that Tibet had never been part of China and that there was no need to 'liberate us from foreign imperialists' as no foreign power controlled our country. Our government then appointed delegations to visit Britain, the U.S.A., India and Nepal to ask for help against the Chinese, but all these nations requested us not to send our delegations because they could not help us – and at this Tibet's heart was broken. A petition was also sent to the United Nations, who shelved it.

India then advised us to open negotiations with China, on

the basis of the 1914 Simla treaty, and *Tsi-pon* Shakabpa and *Tsechag* Thubten Gyalpo were selected, by the same ballot system used to elect a Regent, to lead a delegation to Peking. Jigme was appointed to be their English interpreter and in 1950 they went to India, on the way to Hong Kong, but in Delhi were told by the Chinese that their Ambassador to India was coming soon and that they should wait to open negotiations with him. In that September Jigme asked me to join him in Delhi, where the members of our delegation were guests of the Indian government.

On my way to Delhi I stayed at Kalimpong, where my sister, Norbu Yudon, was then having a difficult time with her son, Wangdula. Earlier that year his wife, Chodonla, had become pregnant again and soon afterwards he was appointed *Dzongpon* of Phari. He was a very good father, who used to change nappies and help Chodonla in the night when the babies gave trouble. At this time he was twenty-eight and his wife about three years younger; they had married young because their mothers were great friends who had promised each other to have their son and daughter married as soon as the children grew up. In order to get proper treatment for Chodonla's confinement Wangdula took her to the small British hospital attached to the B.T.A. at Yatung, but in spite of good care she died, after giving birth to another daughter.

Again poor Wangdula suffered terribly. With his baby he returned to Phari, took leave of his job and came down to join his mother, who was having a holiday in Kalimpong. There he became quite mad and lost control of his conscience. He went into the town and started to break things in shops and hit people, so the police got hold of him and he was going to be imprisoned. My poor sister, with the help of the MacDonalds and Tsering Yangzom – Jigme Dorje's wife – got him back from the police and he was put in hospital for a day or two. He then promised his mother to behave well, but they had to watch him all the time. When I came to Kalimpong he was still not right. He told me one day that he was performing rites for his late wife and children, and I noticed that he had opened three tins of cream cracker biscuits, and had a basin full of sweets and several glasses full of water. After a while he threw all these through the window and said that he had finished his rites and that the food must be given to the devils. For some time he went on in the same way.

Norbu Yudon bravely faced this difficulty and after a few months Wangdula improved. By 1953 he was so much better that he remarried in Shigatse, where he was serving the government, and had another child. I never met his second wife.

In 1951 Norbu Yudon's second son, Dorwangla, was killed in Lhasa when he and his wife were returning to his wife's home, Kungsangtse House, after dark. Dorwangla was a tall, handsome, brilliant young man and his wife, Yishy Dolma, was a daughter of the Commander-in-Chief, Kungsangtse *Dzasa*. As they were walking along the street they met a group of people who had been dancing and may have been drunk. Dorwangla shone a torch and somebody shouted 'Behave!' and fired a pistol at him. Then the group dispersed and the culprit could not be caught. Dorwangla was able to run as far as the gate of Kunsangse House, where he collapsed and was carried inside. The bullet had hit him in the stomach and he died after fourteen hours, leaving his wife with a baby daughter.

I did not know what would happen then to Norbu Yudon, but she told me that by the kindness of Ani Lochen she could realise the karma she had to go through. I was very happy to see her having such a good understanding.

When the negotiations started with the Chinese in Delhi there was no question of our agreeing on anything, as the chief Chinese point was that Tibet should be recognised as a part of China. Mr. Shakabpa had already explained to Mr. Nehru that for everybody's sake it was important that Tibet should remain an independent buffer state. But at the time Mr. Nehru did not seem able to realise that this was true.

While we were still in India the Chinese unexpectedly invaded and captured the important province of Chamdo, in eastern Tibet. At the time an official party was being held in Lhasa and though the Governor of Chamdo – Ani Champala's son – tried to hold wireless consultations with the central government replies were not sent promptly because of the party, so Chamdo was lost. The Chamdo officials, who were in such great danger at the time, were very angry about this. Ngawang Jigme, the Governor, and Robert Ford, the English wireless operator, were then taken as prisoners to China.

At once the old Taktra Regent resigned and everybody begged His Holiness to take full responsibility for the government of Tibet – which he did, on 17 November 1950, at the age of fifteen. He then shifted his goverment to the border town of Yatung and sent *Dzasa* Khemey and Tsulten Tendar or Peking, via India, for further negotiations. In Peking they were joined by Khenchung Thubten Lekmon and Rimshi Sampho-sey, who had travelled overland from Lhasa, and also by Ngawang Jigme. In May 1951, these officials were forced to sign the Seventeen Point Agreement without consulting His Holiness or the government. As we could get no help from the U.N. or any country we were compelled to accept this agreement and after five months in Yatung His Holiness returned sadly, with his government, to Lhasa.

At the time of the Dalai Lama's departure from Lhasa most of the Tibetan noble families had followed him, bringing a lot of their belongings with them. Some stayed at the border and some came to Kalimpong. Rigzin Namgyal and his wife brought out their two babies and many of our precious belongings, as Jigme and I were already in India. Mother-in-law and Chime Dorje's family came as far as Sikkim. If His Holiness had continued on into India all the Tibetans were ready to follow him, but when he returned to Lhasa we too went home, taking our belongings. Prince Peter and Princess Irene of Greece, and Mr. Marco Pallis, strongly advised us to remain in India and Jigme hesitated about going back. But I said to him, 'How can we stay away when everybody is returning? We shall never be able to remain apart from our relatives – especially Mother-in-law.' I felt that whatever happened we must go back and share in the difficulties of our relatives and friends. Only to seek our own happiness would not have been fair and I just could not abandon all the faces of our dear ones.

His Holiness stayed at Taring Monastery on his way back to Lhasa. Taring Rinpoche had recently died, to everyone's sorrow, and the monks were searching for his reincarnation. Eventually they found a peasant boy in southern Tibet, but we do not know what has become of him now.

Tsarong had met His Holiness at Yatung and he said afterwards, 'I could not help shedding tears – he is so young, but taking such great responsibility.' Tsarong was as loyal to the fourteenth Dalai Lama as he had been to the thirteenth; he used to say, 'How lucky we are to have such a lovely-looking Dalai Lama – had he been a short, ugly-looking person, what to do? We have to love him!'

The Chinese representative, General Chang Ching Wu, travelled to Lhasa via India just ahead of His Holiness, accompanied by a doctor, an interpreter and a few companions. When His Holiness arrived in Lhasa the General was full of complaints. He was not satisfied with the reception that had been given to him, nor with his accommodation at Trimon House.

At that time there were not many Chinese in Lhasa, apart from the General's group, but within less than a year 10,000 Chinese soldiers, both men and women, had come to the city. They rented or requisitioned the houses of many nobles and had orders to ignore insults from Tibetans. When they arrived our people spat and clapped – Tibetans clap when driving out scapegoats – and the children tried to throw stones at them. The monks were worse: Jigme and I saw them knotting the ends of their shawls and hitting the Chinese who were riding by – but who took no notice, because the policy was that the troops should seem tolerant.

All these extra thousands caused a terrible food shortage; the Chinese could bring no food with them, because of the difficult road, and daily the prices went up. Despite this, the

Chinese started to entertain Tibetan officials, monks and traders. I had thought that Communists worked and ate the same, but we saw lots of differences. The generals had soldier-servants, and were allowed to bring their wives with them, and they got their food from a special kitchen which had to prepare *mo-mo* for three meals a day and four delicacies, to be served with rice, every day. But the ordinary soldiers were going around collecting *tsampa* in cotton stockings, and were given only two meals a day – *mo-mo*, or sometimes *tsampa* with one vegetable dish – and water and Chinese tea once a day. Fuel was so scarce that people burned horns and bones, which filled Lhasa with a most unbearable smell. The Chinese wanted a large loan from the government, which did its best to meet this demand by borrowing from the monasteries and from private individuals. Many songs, resenting the Chinese, were sung in the streets.

Everybody felt very frightened during this period, as we had heard that the Communists were good to start with but later became like a wet hide hat, which gets tighter and tighter as it dries. Yet our government and people had no alternative but to stick to the Seventeen Point Agreement and deal alone with the Chinese as best they could.

Before the Chinese came we Tibetans were happy people, leading comfortable lives. Tibet was not a rich country, but we all had enough to eat and wear and a supply of grain was kept aside by the Government in case of a bad crop. Religion was ever in the thoughts of all Tibetans. You could see a peasant praying while he was driving his donkey, a trader praying while he was doing business, an official praying first thing in the morning, or whenever he got spare time. There were many mistakes in our way of life, but the people were at ease and contented.

This good atmosphere changed as soon as the Communists came. We called them *Tenda Gyamar*, meaning 'Red Chinese Enemies of Religion', and most of our people were sad to have them in Tibet. At first their soldiers werre well disciplined and had the policy to be humble; they said they had come to serve us and would go home when we could stand on our own feet. They gave money to the monks during *Monlam*, and to individual monasteries. They respected His Holiness wherever he went, by sending soldiers and a military band to join our Army. But this did not last long. Constantly we heard news – particularly from Kham – that the Chinese were saying, 'Buddhism is a deceiver of the people. Monks and lamas are wearing their religion as a mask to help them to exploit the people.' Every word of this broke the hearts of Tibetans.

Gradually things got worse. To indoctrinate the people, the study of political science was organised in city schools and various associations were formed. Everybody's movements were watched and the happiness of our atmosphere was changed to fear and suspicion. Yet our government offices remained intact to the end and our little Army never joined the Chinese Army.

The Chinese arrived with about two hundred useful Tibetan interpreters from the province of Ba, which had long been under China. But the Chinese leaders wanted all their soldiers to know Tibetan, so in 1952 an Army school was organised. For a school building the invaders requistioned the Dungchi Trokhang, the summer house of the lay-officials by the riverside. (It had been built to save putting up tents, during official parties, in the gardens of the officials' own homes.) Eight hundred Chinese Army students slept on the floor, on grass, and it was not possible to use the house again for parties. The Chinese asked the Government to lend them four learned scholars, ten ordinary men and five women teachers for the hundreds of girl-soldiers. Everybody felt reluctant to help the Chinese, yet we had to get on with them as well as possible so the government appointed monk scholars from the big mona-steries, ten junior officials and five lady teachers – the officials' wives who were known to be good at teaching. I was one of the ladies appointed, but at first I refused to help, thinking of what had happened to my father and brother when they were suspected of being pro-Chinese. Then one day a Chinese representative came to me with a letter of appointment from the *Kashag* and there was nothing but to give in. I said I would be coming soon but I did not go for about a week, until the Chinese Professor Liu and his wife called one day to see me. He had studied in Yale University, and his wife, Professor Yu, was also a lecturer in English. They were in charge of the school and both seemed pleasant. They said they had been waiting for me and that I must attend at once because they had already started work, with the other teachers, on compiling the necessary text-books; so I joined the school at the beginning of spring, 1952.

The Dungchi Trokhang was about fifteen minutes' walk from Taring House. The other teachers told me they had been asked to give their history, from childhood to the present, and on arrival at the school I thought I, too, would be asked, but it seemed that they had finished this enquiry. Professor Liu led the meetings to discuss preparing the textbooks. These meetings were attended by Tsawa Tritrul and several monk scholars from Drepung and Sera. The ladies were Samling Tsering Pelden, Thangme Kunchok, Tsogo Deyang, Changchen Yungden and myself. The monk scholars produced readers by a new method and we decided to teach sound first, without showing the letters. The teachers had to write useful sentences in colloquial style and put honorfic terms in brackets. The scholars then checked the sentences and it was found very difficult to put them in colloquial language as we write and talk quite differently. However, the textbooks were made at last, with their Chinese translations.

Though the Tibetan language is simple, the use of honorific terms really makes it two completely different languages. For instance:

	common	honorific
Head	= *Go*	= *U*
Hand	= *Lakpa*	= *Chak*
Mouth	= *Kha*	= *Shal*
House	= *Khangpa*	= *Simshak*
Tea	= *Cha*	= *Solcha*

After anyone's name it is polite to add 'la' for the honorific – Pema, Pemala; Wangdu, Wangdula; Tashi, Tashila. It is good to speak in honorific terms to everybody – there is no limit. Still, there are special honorific words for very high persons and these do not suit people who are much inferior, like your own retainers – then they only sound sarcastic. But retainers could be addressed as 'Dondupla', 'Tashila' and so on. Parents do not use honorific terms to their small children, but when children are grown up and married it sounds nice to use such terms in conversation with them.

The Chinese organised the classes very efficiently. Teaching began at 8 a.m. and ended at 5 p.m., five days a week, with an hour's break at midday. All classes were held in the open air and during early spring it was cold, yet the students had to sit on the bare ground. Most of them picked up Tibetan fast, learning a hundred words a day and at the end of every month they had to do a test, reading and writing a hundred sentences. As soon as the students knew enough to make themselves understood they were replaced by others, but those who were very clever were kept on to study fully and many of them became official interpreters instead of the men form Ba, who did not have a good Tibetan education.

When the teacher appeared at the beginning of each class, the monitor made the students stand to attention and say 'Chiling' ('Salute') before they sat down. During the ten-minute breaks between classes they brought me a mug of hot water, to which I added little packets of coffee, sugar and milk-powder. My students were girls of sixteen to eighteen who used to say, 'You look like my mother.' Some of them had not seen their parents for three or four years and the first batch, especially, had a lonely time as the motorable roads from Chamdo to Lhasa and from Sining to Lhasa were only made within the next two years.

I taught my students sincerely, patiently repeating the sentences many times, which the girls appreciated. It gave me a funny feeling to be always amongst the Chinese; we were so frightened of them, yet now we were teaching them. But I carefully remembered that they were human beings and should not be hated. Poor little things, what could they do? They also were very frightened.

Once, before the Chinese came, we asked one of our Taring Estate soldiers, who had met Communist troops, what the Red Chinese looked like and he had replied that they looked like ordinary Chinese, except that their eyes were red. This sounds funny in Tibetan and for a time it was a joke among ourselves.

After classes the teachers had to hold meetings to discuss the best method of teaching and every Saturday we were given political science lectures by Chinese officers who also lectured to the other Tibetans working in various Chinese organisations. My students strongly advised me to study Communism, explaining that if I had to give opinions at meetings I must know the rules of their politics – otherwise all I said would go against them and I would get into trouble.

Sometimes we teachers were made to tell about the history of Tibet and about our traditional customs; these things the Chinese knew already, but they wanted to test our attitudes. We were also asked to point out the mistakes of the Chinese soldiers, so that they could be corrected, and we then said that some of the soldiers were killing animals for food without any compassion, which hurt Tibetans very much. (They were just fooling with the animals and not putting them to death quickly.) We also asked the Chinese not to burn horns and bones by the Jokhang and not to do morning drill where the lamas and monks were praying. These points were noted down, but we never saw them implemented. Every evening we were compelled to learn Chinese, and we could choose to learn other subjects. My fellow-teachers asked me to teach them English and arithmetic; they wanted to know English to read names on maps, which they could never do in Chinese, and as this was the teachers' own wish I taught them. The school also had classes for Hindi and Nepali. Two Tibetan Muslims, who have now settled in Pakistan, taught Hindi. A young Tibetan-Nepalese man taught Nepali; he is now living in Nepal. Then we found that the Chinese did not like anybody to know other foreign languages, though at the beginning they had said 'every language is good.' They considered English-speaking people pro-American or pro-British and they thought we hated the Communists. Professor Liu and his wife, who had studied in America, were sent back to China after spending about a year in Lhasa. They were nice people, but the Communists did not trust them.

It was most difficult to deal with the Chinese as they were so full of suspicion. General Tang Kuan San often came to the school. He was a short, sly-looking person – the teachers nicknamed him *Ani* (Nun) – and he would give an odd laugh and say, 'When I have time I will talk to the techers.' General Chang Ching Wu also had an unkind look. All the senior officers were very proud and I used to feel uncomfortable when we had to mix with them at meetings and parties. Yet there were some pleasant-looking junior officers and the common Chinese were ordinary human beings who could become your good friends. Our people are so hospitable that it was easy for the nice ones among the Chinese to make friends with us. They liked our little enjoyments and some of them were nearly becoming Tibetans; but they were very much scared of each other and were frequently transferred against their wishes.

The Chinese built serveral hospitals in Lhasa, one for the Tibetan public, the others for their own people and soldiers. As a favour, certain Tibetans would be admitted to the Army hospitals, which were much better than the public hospital, though the public hospital was very useful. The Chinese doctors, both men and women, were all in the their twenties.

Tibetan medical treatment followed the teaching of the Lord of Medicine, Sangemenla, and his big medical book gives a most skilful, scientific way of treatment. Tibetan doctors had to memorise this whole book, which describes the nature of illnesses and prescribes medicines, but the practice of surgery was poor, although the book gives detailed instructions. Cataract operations were often performed, but not very well. A great variety of herbal medicines were used; many herbs grow in Tibet and quantities of dried herbs and spices were imported from India. The pomegranate was used for indigestion and any kind of stomach trouble. The private doctors made medicines in their homes and never accepted a penny from poor people but gave them the same treatment as the rich. We have a saying, 'As kind as a doctor'.

Good Tibetan doctors could tell a patient's character, and give information about the health of his dear ones, by feeling the wrist nerves; they talked of female or male nerves. The urine of a patient was inspected first thing in the morning, and beaten with fine sticks, and the bubbles and the smell were observed. If the urine were milky the person was said to be suffering from gonorrhoea and if red he was running a temperature. Nerves were burnt to stop pain; even mental patients got this treatment. There were two methods – to heat an iron and apply it to the nerve, or to mix herbs and garlic, light the mixture over the painful place and let it burn through the skin until it reached the nerve. This was a very violent treatment, yet many people took it for headaches and indigestion. Blood-letting was the cure for high blood pressure. Again thee were two methods – to poke the veins and drip the blood, or to light paper in a little pot about the size of a breakfast cup, which was attéched, over a small opening made with a knife, to the place where most pain was felt. The doctor then kept tapping the pot and when it was removed, after some time, it was full of blood jelly. I saw this done on my mother's back. Hot steam baths, with medicines added, were given for paralysis, rheumatism, arthritis and venereal diseases. Tuberculosis was beyond treatment, but there were good medicines for nervousness; special kinds of vitamin pills were made to strengthen body and mind. Some pills were made by steaming precious stones and most people performed rites so that the medical treatment would be successful.

In recent years, Tibetan doctors imported vaccines from India and penicillin injections for veneral disease, but there were many people who had faith in Tibetan medicine only.

Our doctors made their medicines up in packages, which were accompanied by descriptions of the pains, and full directions for doses. Dingja once told us about a man who took his medicine, got angry when it didn't do much good and said he might as well eat the directions.

We had two medical colleges in Lhasa—Chokpori and Mentsikhang, both sponsore by the government. The Mentsikhang students collected medicinal herbs in the mountains and went to Yerpa every autumn, during the religious Yerpa Tsechu Festival. Many Lhasa people visited this very holy place, which was most pleasant, being full of peace. Once Jigme and I went to the festival with our two daughters, then aged five and seven, and we climbed the mountain to the medical students' camp. When we were coming down we could see our two dear daughters, and some servants, waiting for us with lunch on a green hill far below. I often think now of that time.

14 Fear in Lhasa

EVER SINCE THEIR arrival in Lhasa the Chinese had been against the two *Lonchens*, Lukhangwa and Losang Tashi, who had been appointed Ministers by the Dalai Lama in November 1950, and had bravely protested against the Chinese bringing Lhasa to the verge of famine. In 1952 His Holiness was compelled to ask them to resign; the *Kashag* advised him to do so, to improve relations with the Chinese.

The Chinese bullied us a lot for not giving them good supplies of food and fodder, yet delicious meals were served whenever they held a meeting. Sometimes the ladies were invited to these meals and we were all frightened and hated to go, but as the Chinese had been able to get rid of our two Ministers so easily we thought it best to agree to all their suggestions. Everybody felt terribly unhappy, yet while it was at all possible we wished to stay in our own country.

By the end of 1952 the Chinese had organised new schools for Tibetan children, 'patriotic' associations, cultural groups, a political consultative office and a newspaper office. During that winter, a party was given, under the supervision of General Chang Ching Wu's wife, to all the officials' ladies, and it was suggested that they should form a Patriotic Women's Association to support the nation's activities. Everybody looked at everybody else and the *Shap-pēs'* wives had to speak. They said, 'It would be very nice to have an association like this. But first we must consult the *Kashag*, as we have had no public women's activities before and have no experience.' The generals' wives agreed to our asking the *Kashag* and said that experience could be gained through practice and that they were willing to help us. Two of the *Shap-pēs'* wives – Ngapo Tseten Dolkar (Ngawang Jigme's wife) and Shasur *Lhacham* – were asked to consult the *Kashag*, who reported to the Dalai Lama. Soon His Holiness gave permission for us to organise the Lhasa Patriotic Women's Association (known as the P.W.A.) and I was compelled to join it. (The Patriotic Youth Association (the P.Y.A.) was being started simultaneously, under other Chinese leaders.)

At the preparatory meeting of the P.W.A., held at *Tsi-pon* Shakabpa's summer house, the General's wife announced that a committee must be formed, with one Chairman, six Vice-Chairmen, one Secretary and one Assistant-Secretary. Everybody looked frightened but we had to do what we were told. Tsering Dolma, His Holiness's elder sister, was elected as Chairman. The Vice-Chairmen were the General's wife, Shasur *Lhacham*, Ragashar *Lhacham*, Ngapo *Lhacham* and Tsarong *Lhacham* (my sister, Pema Dolkar). Pema Dolkar told the meeting that her health would not allow her to be a Vice-Chairman and I supported her, explaining that she had gall-stones. The other ladies knew this was true and also supported her, but she was asked to remain on the committee. Yudon Sampo *Shap-pē's* wife was elected to replace her as Vice-Chairman and I was also made Vice-Chairman and General Secretary, with Thangme Kunchoek as my Assistant-Secretary. I tried to avoid this work but all the ladies insisted on my doing it, so a few days later it was announced at a meeting of the Army school that Taring Rinchen Dolma and Thangme Kunchok were being withdrawn from teaching as they had been appointed secretaries to the P.W.A. The students showed to us their reluctance to lose us because they said we both taught well, but they did not dare protest to the Chinese. As teachers, we were paid fifty Chinese dollars a month, which we had all been afraid to accept until the *Kashag* instructed us to do so.

The General's wife suggested that the W.P.A. inauguration should be celebrated at Yuthok House on 8 March, which is the Communist International Women's Day. Everybody agreed and many banners – given by the Dalai Lama, the *Kashag* and the Chinese Army H.Q. – were exhibited on that date. All the women and schoolgirls of Lhasa were invited and about five hundred came. I, as secretary, read out the programme and His Holiness's sister made a speech. The Chinese Army gave a concert in the evening and the *Kashag* and P.Y.A. were represented.

The P.Y.A. was inaugurated on 4 May, which was said to be International Youth Day. All women and young people were made members of these associations, executive offices were set up, daily activities were organised and it was suggested that a hall should be built for each association. The government gave sites and everybody was called to help with the building, but our noble ladies found it very difficult to do manual labour so I told the Chinese that though the younger ones might work, the older ones could not handle spades, having been brought up to do only housework. The Chinese said, 'They may do the work or not as they wish'; but some ladies were so frightened that they came to labour. It was sad to see them at such unfamiliar work, yet we all had to do our share.

Many ladies were reluctant to attend the regular political science lectures. Being the secretaries, Kunchok and I were asked why everybody did not attend and then all members were forced to come.

From the start of the W.P.A. the Chinese never trusted me. In 1953 they asked Ngapo Tseten Dolkar to give a talk on the noble ladies of Tibet and I was asked to talk on the ordinary women. Using an interpreter I spoke for four hours – we had a break half way through – to more than four hundred Chinese women soldiers, including the wives of generals and other officers. I said, 'Tibetan women have always enjoyed equal rights with men, except that no women work in government offices. Yet we are of use to the government, because by caring for the estates we leave our men free to serve the country.

Especially among ordinary families, the wife has to be consulted on all matters – though it is a virtue for women to respect their husbands by getting up when the men come in from a distance, passing them their tea and so on. It is customary for the men of the house to sit above the women, though older women sit above younger men. Tibetan women work in the fields, do most of the dairy jobs, care for animals, blow the bellows of blacksmiths, weave, sew, cook, paint, draw and sometimes go trading or look after shops in towns. They can also shoot and fight and there have been women soldier heroines in our history. The only thing I have not seen is a woman carpenter. They take part in religious ceremonies and some nuns become famous scholars. They have their own social groups of friends who meet very happily for singing and dancing and get quite highly intoxicated when they have special parties. They share in all the social activities of the men, even playing mahjong for high stakes. They act as mediators between disputing friends and bring cases independently to the courts. Never in history have Tibetan women suffered any physical or mental torture, like the women of some other countries – for example, China, with its terrible custom of binding the feet of little girls, with the big toes turned in and the feet pointed and forced into tiny black shoes, so that women could never walk fast. The Muslim women in purdah have to cover their faces all the time, even to this day, and Hindu women had to practise suttee by the wife being burnt alive with her husband's corpse, until this custom was abolished by the British. Instead of suffering such things we Tibetan women are known to be very capable and have always had a most enjoyable life. Men do the hardest work, yet it is believed that without women nothing can be done, as they are considered more intelligent than men. The husband provides the effort and his wife the intelligence; and effort and intelligence combined produce the most fruitful results in every form of work.'

My Chinese audience listened to me with care and sometimes wrote down my remarks. At the end they gave me a hearty clap and thanked me – but I don't think the high officers' wives liked my talk very much. I do not know what Ngapo Tseten Dolkar said in her lecture because we never discussed the matter.

At this time, many nobles' houses were being sold for high prices. Jigme and I were asked to sell or rent Taring House, but we said that having a big family we needed our home. If only we had been clever, but we were real fools – we thought we would be in Tibet all our lives. Having so many relatives we never considered saving ourselves, but felt that whatever happened we must serve His Holiness and stay with our families.

During the *Monlam* festival of 1953 Tsarong presented to the Dalai Lama his whole accumulation of precious jade and coral, gold, silver, ivory, brocade and old china. These gifts were exhibited by being carried uncovered through the streets to the Jokhang, where His Holiness was waiting to receive them, sitting on his throne amongst twenty thousand monks. Tsarong also gave five rupees, and a meal of good tea and rice, to each monk; and to each official he gave money, silk and brocade. At about the same time he presented big sums of money to all his relatives and even divided his five or six houses between his children. Then his heart was content.

In 1954 His Holiness was invited on a long visit to China and we all felt uneasy at the thought of his being away from Tibet for a year. But the Chinese assured us that this visit would help the Dalai Lama by widening his knowledge, as he was to see the whole of China representatives of the monasteries and about a hundred officials were also invited. Eventually it was agreed that His Holiness should go, with a big party, and Jigme was asked to accompany him as his photographer. Tsering Dolma, the chairman of the W.P.A., and Ngapo Tseten Dolkar were also going, and I, too, was anxious to see China. So after Tsering Dolma had spoken to the General's wife, begging her to grant me leave from my work at the W.P.A., I was given permission to travel. Rigzin Namgyal and Tseyang were in Lhasa to look after Mother-in-law.

In 1952 our elder daughter, Ngodup Wangmo, had left

school and a year later she married Sampo *Dapon*, a pleasant, handsome man who was the eldest son of Samdup Phodhang *Shap-pē*, of the house of the seventh Dalai Lama. But by 1954 she had stopped getting on well with her husband, which was very sad. She was already pregnant and wanted to come with us to China: when we agreed to this she felt much happier. All the officials had to take their own tents and arrange their own transport and Jigme, Ngodup Wangmo and myself had two small tents, five servants, two muleteers and supplies of *tsampa*, dried meat, butter, tea, rice, flour, sugar and tinned foods from India.

His Holiness's party left Lhasa accompanied by the Chinese Commissioner and before crossing the Kyichu River they paused for a reception in a huge tent by the riverside. The whole of Lhasa, dressed in their best, had come to see the Dalai Lama off, and in the tent were representatives of the government, of all the great monasteries, and of some Chinese and Tibetan regiments, whose bands provided the music. On the banks monks waved religious banners and hundreds of people burnt incense and hoisted flags to wish His Holiness a safe journey and a happy return. Some had gone on to the mountains to burn incense because the higher you go the more luck is to be had. (The surrounding mountains of Lhasa are supposed to be very auspicious and have eight lucky signs. 'Lhasa' means 'Gods' Place'.)

There was no bridge over the river so everybody crossed in yak-hide boats, tied together. The crossing took about twenty minutes and the Dalai Lama and some of his closest attendants were in the same boat, with a red umbrella over His Holiness. Jigme was in another boat, taking photographs, and the Lhasa people watching from the bank did their best to cheer up but still they were very sad to see His Holiness go.

Being late summer it was very lovely on the road, going past fields of barley, wheat and beans. At each stopping place the peasants and the local monks came to meet His Holiness with great respect and every show of homage they could give. We were all riding, as the Chinese had not yet finished the motor-road, and whenever Ngodup Wangmo and I met His Holiness we dismounted, prostrated and let him pass. It was such a consolation to meet him, because he would always give us a wonderful smile and tell us not to prostrate; and sometimes, when we were very near, he would ask if we found the journey difficult.

On the third day we arrived at a beautiful place, all very green, and His Holiness's camp was ready as usual. (Two lots of attendants had two sets of equipment for use on alternate days, so the Dalai Lama's camp was always arranged when he arrived at a stopping place.) Up to Tamo, in southern Tibet, our government was responsible for the camps of His Holiness and the Chinese General, and on this evening the General complained that his camp did not have a tent wall like the one around His Holiness's yellow cotton tent. So those in charge gave him a wall.

This lovely place belonged to the big Dekhung Monastery, whose highest Incarnate Lama was Tsarong's grandson (Dudul Namgyal's son) then an eight-year-old boy. He came with his monks to receive His Holiness's party and visited us in our tent while the senior monks were arranging everything. (He is a very High Lama, holding the title of *Hutukthu* – the seat above the *Shap-pē*'s. His mother is a neice of Jigme's.) When I remarked that his place was beautiful he said that Yarigang, where he had another monastery, was even more beautiful. I then told him that he should invite his parents and us to his lovely place and he replied, 'The place is nice, *mola* (granny), but we get no good food – the monks give us only black *momo*.' When the monks came to say that he must go it was hard to say good-bye, because he did not like leaving us, and Ngodup Wangmo felt so sad that she cried.

As we went south-east the countryside became still nicer and approaching Medo Gongkar there were more bushes, though the mountains remained quite bare. Farther south it was thickly wooded, with beautiful tall fir and juniper trees, and the people grew *drawo* (buckwheat) and *dhawn* (millet) – from which they made a strong drink – as well as barley and wheat. They also had more cattle than the people of central Tibet and their most famous dairy products were grated yak's cheese (*churship*) and a dried cheese (*churkam*), like chewing-gum, which everybody loved.

The government, the monasteries and the nobility had many estates in this beautiful region, where one could find amongst the trees monkeys, squirrels and various birds, including parrots. The one- or two-storied houses had wooden roofs; in colder regions Tibetan houses had flat stone roofs, but here it is a little warmer than in central Tibet. A number of my relatives came to see us in our camps, and one evening Jigme and I visited a cousin of my father's who every year sent us a huge load of the best dried cheese. After seeing how difficult the road to Lhasa was I appreciated this gift all the more. When we reached Gyamda, where Ngapo *Shap-pē* had his great estate, a reception was given for the whole party and *tsampa* and butter were presented to the many officials who needed extra supplies. Ngapo *Shap-pē* and his wife had gone ahead of us to prepare the reception, but from there on they travelled with His Holiness's party.

The Dalai Lama's mother and elder sister, Ngapo Tseten Dolkar, the General's wife, Ngodup Wangmo and myself were the only women officially in the party, but there was a junior officer who had brought his wife disguised in men's clothes. They were a very nice couple, called Maja, and we became close friends. The wife appeared in her own lady's costume in China.

The Chinese and our high officials were having discussions on the way, but I really did not understand what this meant. The atmosphere was not very happy although the countryside was so beautiful; at Lunang it is much like Switzerland. There we heard the terrible news of the flood that washed away the whole town of Gyantse on 17 July 1954, drowning more than two thousand people, including many of our friends. The Indian Trade Agent, Mr. Pemba, and his wife were amongst our oldest and most dear friends and a year earlier we had begged them to stay in Lhasa to be near us; not knowing that the greatest disaster of Tibet was approaching Mr. Pemba explained that he was retiring soon and needed a job with a bigger pension – so they moved to Gyantse.

In our sadness I remembered what Milarepa sang when he preached to the huntsman. One day a frightened deer dashed past the saint's cave, followed by a ravening hound, and through the power of his loving kindness and compassion Milarepa made them lie down one on either side of him. Then came the fierce and proud huntsman, Kyirawa Gonpo Dorje, who was enraged by the sight of Milarepa and shot an arrow at him, but missed. The saint then sang to the huntsman, whose heart began to turn to *dharma* (religion). When Gonpo Dorje saw what an austere life Milarepa was living great faith arose in him and he wished to practise *dharma*. But after talking with Dorje's family the saint warned him that his present meritorious thought might change and sang:

> Harken, harken, huntsman!
> Tho' the thunder crashes,
> It is but empty sound;
> Tho' the rainbow is richly coloured,
> It will soon fade away.
> The pleasures of this world are like dream visions;
> Tho' one enjoys them, they are sources of sin.
> Tho' all we see may seem to be eternal
> It will soon fall to pieces and disappear.
> Yesterday perhaps one had enough or more:
> All today is gone and nothing left.
> Last year one was alive, this year one dies:
> Good food turns into poison.
> Your sins hurt no one but yourself:
> Among the hundred heads you value most your own:
> In all ten fingers, if one is cut you feel the pain:
> Among all things you value, yourself is valued most –
> The time has come for you to help yourself.
> Life flees fast; soon death
> Will knock up on your door.

It is foolish therefore one's devotion to postpone.
What else can loving kinsmen do
But throw one into sorrow?
To strive for happiness hereafter
Is more important than to seek it now.
The time has come for you to rely upon a *guru*,
The time has come to practise *dharma*.

After twelve days the way became very dangerous, as the Chinese were taking us along the new road then being built for vehicles. This road-making was a great achievement on their part, but during it countless Chinese and Tibetan lives were lost. The Poyul region is so wet that often rain washed away the new road and once a bridge was damaged, but the soldiers repaired it with logs. The mountains were loose and we saw huge rocks rolling down amidst continuous landslides. Many parts of the road were so steep that we had to walk for hours and the mud was about nine inches deep; poor Ngodup Wangmo just managed to get on as I was with her all the time. My boots were looked terrible and made His Holiness's little brother, Ngari Rinpoche, laugh at me. When climbing up this dreadful road a number of mules fell into the river, or over precipices on to rocks, and some burst out their guts. Our worried officials held meetings and asked the Chinese to divert the party to the old trade route. The General replied that his government was responsible for the safety of the Dalai Lama, his family and his two tutors, but that the rest of the officials could go by the other route if they wished. So of course everybody stayed on the motor-road with His Holiness.

Several of my Chinese ex-students from the Lhasa Army school, who were supervising the road-making, came to see me and brought their mosquito nets for us and wished us a happy journey. One stayed on when the others left and said, 'Teacher, please take an interest in learning political science.' He also advised us to sell our house to the Chinese government, give up our estates and join the Chinese, as we would then be much safer in the future.

In spite of the difficult road, we enjoyed this trip from the point of view of travelling. Our white silk tent from England did not let in a drop of water and folded into a neat pack that I carried under my saddle; it held our three camp beds and we used our little boxes as a table. Our cook, Pasang, made lovely curry and rice, and friends came to eat with us every evening. Yet we were always uneasy, being amongst the Chinese. We Tibetans did not know whether or not to be honest with the Chinese for even if one were honest they really trusted nobody. As usual, Jigme and I were suspected of being pro-British or pro-American, because of knowing English and having a standard of living that mixed English ways with Tibetan – for instance, producing knives and forks at meal-times and using a table-cloth. Yet we were nothing else but true Tibetans. Then as now, our hearts were with religion and we were both seeking earnestly for the truth, believing strongly in karma, meditating and praying.

Being late summer we had some heavy rain; but mostly the weather was perfect, with sunshine from blue skies and no wind. In Demo we camped right by a stream where there were bright mauve-pink primulas and yellow buttercups all over the bank. Here the Dalai Lama's old servant, Simyokla, came to the stream, close by our tent, to wash His Holiness's socks and underwear. I helped him, and then offered him tea and sweets. Every day I was attending on His Holiness's mother and his sister, Tsering Dolma,. because Tsering Dolma was taking Tibetan lessons from me.

After twenty-four days, Chinese vehicles met us near Tamo in Poyul. There were new Russian jeeps for His Holiness's group, about thirty jeeps for officials from the fourth rank up and about fifty trucks for junior officials and servants. Keeping one servant with us, we sent the others back to Lhasa with the mules. From here the Chinese arranged our accommodation and fed everybody and their food was good. They prepared meals in three categories and had a big kitchen, a middle kitchen and a small kitchen for the highest. At first Jigme was in the small kitchen and Ngodup Wangmo and I were in the middle kitchen – which made His Holiness's mother and sister very sad, because they felt that we should eat together as a family. Jigme used to say that he would come and eat with us to keep us company, but we persuaded him to have his meals as arranged; we had some nice companions among the junior officials and were quite happy. Later we were squeezed into the small kitchen.

Tamo is in a beautiful valley, full of trees and evergreen shrubs, and a river runs through the centre of the village. The Chinese had built new houses and here His Holiness made a short speech – through an interpreter – to the many Chinese workers of the area, thanking them for building the road, explaining the purpose of his journey, encouraging more hard work and wishing them good luck. It was very sad for us Tibetans to see him holding an enamel mug in his hands as he spoke. I had a nice glass beer-mug that we had brought with us – at least it looked much better and cleaner than the enamel mug. We couldn't give it to him directly, but I asked Dode Rimshi, Jigme's cousin, to present it to one of the attendants. First Dode washed it and held it over burning incense to purify it; I do not know whether His Holiness used it or not, but it was in our spirit to give it to him.

Kundeling *Dzasa* was in charge of the transport, with some Chinese, and when we were leaving Tamo he asked if I would like to travel in a truck or a jeep. I said that we would prefer a jeep but, although Jigme was sent in one, Ngodup Wangmo and I were put in a truck which bumped and bumped until sometimes we were hitting each other like bouncing balls. I felt very sorry for Ngodup Wangmo, because of her pregnancy. Luckily, we were put in Jigme's jeep next day.

In every valley we heard the big sound of Chinese music through microphones and at every stopping place there was a welcome-gate, a banquet and a military guard of honour for His Holiness. After two days we reached Chamdo – a lovely place, with not many trees but something like Scotland, near Perth. Here I visited the Ngapos' room and happened to meet His Holiness, who was also visiting Tseten Dolkar and

Ngawang Jigme. He kindly asked after our health and enquired if we had had a good journey and now had decent accommodation. I took his blessings and told him that everything was all right for us.

At Chamdo Monastery we burnt lamps and prayed, and at the lovely Darge Gompa Monastery the monks gave a reception, attended by thousands of people, for His Holiness. As Ngodup Wangmo and I did not mean to attend we stayed in our jeep; people threw scarves on it, imagining that I was His Holiness's mother, and however much I told them I was not they refused to listen. Soon a monk came to call us in; it was wonderful how they could be so thoughtful when they were so busy. We tried our best to be excused, but the monks would not spare us and we were taken up to the room where Gyalwa Karmapa (the leader of the Karmapa sect) was being entertained. There we were given lunch and a packet of twenty Chinese dollars each, with a scarf. This present was given to all His Holiness's followers.

As the Dalai Lama's party was leaving we found that somebody had locked Gyalwa Karmapa's room door by mistake, in all the excitement, and we could not get out. Below us the monastery courtyard was packed with Khampas, of both sexes and all ages, who were looking up hoping to get a glimpse of the Dalai Lama—so I requested Gyalwa Karmapa to let the people have the satisfaction of seeing his holy face. He was a charming person and looked from every window into the courtyard: the people were very happy and with folded hands they prayed. Then somebody discovered what had happened to us and opened the door.

The small town of Tachienlu is in a sweet, green valley and I liked the atmosphere there because the people were all Tibetans. This was the last Tibetan town, near the ancient original border between Tibet and China. The whole region was very beautiful, with a river running between the hills; the rush of the water hitting against the rocks and making white effervescence reminded me of my happy days in the Chumbi Valley, where the MacDonalds treated me so lovingly. Jigme and I went to the small market and bought delicious Chinese *tenshin* (cakes).

From Drichu on we were in an area where the Tibetans had been under China for twenty years, but this had caused no change in their way of life since the faith of our people is too strong to be shaken. In many places here His Holiness stayed a day or two to give blessings and sermons, and whenever people waited for him by the road he stopped his car and blessed them.

15 My First Visit to China

Not far beyond Tachienlu there was a big suspension bridge called Luthing Chawo and Jigme was asked not to photograph it. On the other side of the river we were in China proper and crossed the famous, huge pass of Arleng Hren, where the scenery reminded me of the Himalayan foothills. The weather was perfect, the soil seemed rich and living was cheap in that area. We saw Chinese villages scattered on the mountains and the people looked completely different from us, with their blue padded trousers and coats and black turbans. Even the way of carrying loads was different; we carry them on our backs, the Chinese carry them on sticks across their shoulders, with half the load hanging on each side. Our peasants sit in the lotus position and eat *tsampa* with their hands and vegetables with spoons out of wooden bowls. The Chinese squat on the ground with their knees up, or sit on stools at tables, and eat with wooden chopsticks from flat porcelain dishes. In Tibet the majority did not use chopsticks but we nobles copied the Chinese by using them, just as we copied the Europeans by using forks and knives.

Beyond the great pass we were in Szechuan province and we stopped at Lang-Tretse, where our lay-officials all washed their long hair. They had brought with them a man hairdresser, named Gyurme, because Tibetan lay-officials had to have their hair plaited and put up in a special way. It was then left up for ten or fifteen days. Ordinary laymen plaited their hair themselves and sometimes tied their two pigtails across the tops of their heads. All monks had shaven heads, except those of the Sakyapa sect.

From Chengtu, His Holiness's party flew on to Sian with all the high officials, including Jigme; two days later the rest of us followed on by road. While we were waiting at Chengtu, Ngodup Wangmo (Peggy) and I visited the zoo with some other Tibetans and the Chinese officer who had been left behind to guide our party. Ngodup Wangmo wanted to have an ice-cream, so we went to a restaurant and had one which was not good. Back at the rest-house a Tibetan official talked to Ngodup Wangmo about her husband until she cried – that also upset her and she got ill. Chinese doctors were called and expected a miscarriage. They wanted us to remain at Chengtu but we wished not to be left on our own and insisted on leaving; so after consulting a local Chinese woman doctor they agreed that it would be quite safe. We were told we were to have one of the best jeeps but next morning we found all the good jeeps occupied by junior officials and only a poor jeep, with no cushions, was left for us. I explained that my daughter was very ill but those who had already got into the good jeeps just looked at each other and would not get out. I felt sad, yet could do nothing. We were taken to a wide space where the Chinese checked up on our vehicles, and soon a white ambulance came with two doctors who enquired after the sick person. (One doctor spoke good English and the other spoke a little.) Ngodup Wangmo was then put in the ambulance and I was allowed to go with her. We travelled for a week by the new road to Pouchi and though it was extremely hot the drive was interesting. We stayed at old villages and at each rest-house our Chinese guide, who spoke quite good Tibetan, brought a local lady doctor to see us, and two women were sent to help me nurse Ngodup Wangmo, who was getting better every day. Most of the village women over forty had bound feet and their houses and furniture reminded me of Pearl Buck's novel *The Good Earth*.

Sometimes we had to cross rivers in steam-boats and once a bridge was covered by the river. The local people advised us to wait so we watched the water going down and could see the railings of the bridge appearing gradually. As we waited the door of the lovely ambulance was open and the cool breeze was really good. There was singing, dancing and shouting everywhere since young officials and servants were in the party. Sometimes we saw very peculiar villages of cave-like huts, with little windows, carved out of the mountains. The people who lived in them did not look comfortable; otherwise the country was rich. The Chinese were making the new railroad from Pouchi to Sian, with numbers of tunnels; their construction work was wonderful. At Sian we stayed for a week at the beautiful guest-house. As soon as we got there the two kind doctors returned to Chengtu; Ngodup Wangmo was then right out of danger and we felt most grateful to the doctors. During this week we were taken to see a movie picture about Pope Alexander VI; the talk was in Chinese and the picture was really just anti-religious propaganda. There were many Russian technicians in the town and part of the hotel dining-room was partitioned off for us.

We went to Peking by a spotlessly clean night train. The journey lasted about twelve hours and in every carriage there were noisy loudspeakers giving music and announcements; as our people were not used to so much noise they put clothes in the loud-speakers to lessen it. Hot water and Chinese tea were often served.

At Peking we joined Jigme in a small, cosy guest-house; the three of us felt so happy to be together again. The lay-officials were being helped by Jigme to plait their hair and the Sakya Lama, who also has long hair, came to Jigme too. Jigme was able to plait his own hair.

Peking is an ancient city situated much like Lhasa, on a flat plain with hills around. It is very clean, but the climate is extreme, winter being far colder than in Lhasa, with lots of snow, and summer terribly hot – though there are no mosquitoes; autumn and spring are really pleasant. We saw many lovely wood or stone palaces there, wonderfully carved. There were also many Buddhist temples and monasteries, with hundreds of images of the Lord Buddha and his disciples, though few monks could be seen and the religious buildings were becoming more or less museums.

New buildings were coming up everywhere, with the traditional roofs and external decorations but completely modernised inside. There were also beautiful universities, big cotton and steel factories and the lovely Peking Hospital and National Radio Station. The old shops were dying out but one could buy for a few dollars beautiful Chinese vases, golden images, tapestries and jade cups – how I wished that I could carry them back to Lhasa! Though China is known for cotton one had to get coupons to purchase cotton clothes. There were picture-houses and theatres, but nobody was allowed to keep a radio that would give them the world news.

Both the Dalai Lama's and the Panchen Lama's permanent representatives at Peking lived in old summer residences of the Emperor's relatives – all centrally heated, with well-fitted sanitation – but when we first arrived the two High Lamas stayed in separate houses and only went to their representatives' places for *Losar*. The Panchen Lama was accompanied by his mother and a dumb brother and had about two hundred in his party.

The Peking government organised us very thoroughly. Each High Lama and *Shap-pē* was given a car with a driver; all the officials from the fourth rank up had one car between four, and the junior officials and servants were taken everywhere in buses. The arrangement of the three kitchens was always observed. Officials and servants were given pocket-money, according to rank, and when winter approached new warm clothes were made for everyone. A daily programme was fixed and we were taken to see factories and ancient places. Only those officials with important work had to attend meetings; the others spent their time shopping and resting. We Tibetans enjoyed shopping outside Tibet and taking things home for presents or for sale, and in Peking the servants wanted to take advantage of the free transport to do trade when they got back to Lhasa.

Every evening we were entertained by plays or dancing. Some of our officials liked the classical plays very much and the acrobatic plays were wonderful. Surkang *Shap-pē* loved dancing, so Jigme and I often joined him. The main recreation for the youth of Peking was dancing; every Saturday evening all the students and workmen came to dance at the Great Peking Hotel and many others. The bands were from various organisations and coupons were given to the people by these organisations, so there was no admission fee. Everybody came in their daily dress so these dances really did not look like balls and it seemed as though it were a duty to attend them.

Our officials liked the Chinese beer and grape wine and, though we were fed well, some of us used to go to restaurants to eat the famous Chinese dishes of roast duck, or noodles, or a cooking-pot of soup with the raw materials for a meal served beside it. Jigme and I often went to a Honan restaurant, for delicious sweet-sour fish, and we also went to little local restaurants in the streets where the food was good but cheap. We Tibetans are very enjoying people and when given an opportunity we try to get the best out of it, so Jigme and I enjoyed ourselves greatly though having been to English schools we were watched continuously. The atmosphere of suspicion was always there and every Tibetan was watched closely; in the guest-houses nice young waiters had to report on each one of us. This was the first of my three visits to China and it was the best, because everybody was still hoping that relations would improve.

I saw nurseries for workers' children and visited homes for retired factory-workers; these poor old people were not happy — they had no peace. Even the oldest had to register under the organisation of the city and go to meetings to give their opinions. If they failed to say that they were happy under the leadership of the great Mao Tse-tung they would have their brain washed more strictly until the authorities were satisfied. All the people did not have the same standard of living; the rickshaw drivers, cart drivers, house builders and so on were quite poor. The whole city was divided into groups and at their meetings criticism of each other was the chief activity. They could not trust each other – that is Communism.

All over China there are public bathing-houses with small resting rooms where you can call for tea. Men or women give you the bath and they have a way of scrubbing as in Turkish baths. Our people loved going for these baths, especially in the cold winter.

Whenever there were receptions for His Holiness, all the officials were invited. The Dalai Lama had met the Panchen Lama at Sian and always the two High Lamas were entertained together. I noticed that they were getting on very well; the Dalai Lama was the only person with whom the Panchen Lama would talk and smile. The Panchen Lama was an exceptionally tall and handsome young man, then aged seventeen, and was very stern-looking, but the Dalai Lama has a nice smile and was friendly and relaxed with everyone.

Once the Peking P.W.A. gave a big banquet for us Tibetan ladies, which was attended by the wife of Prime Minister Chou En-Lai and many other Chinese ladies – who all seemed pleasant. During that year the Chinese were busy framing a constitution for the Chinese Peoples' National Assembly and they were also having talks with us about setting up the Preparatory Committe for the Autonomous Region of Tibet. All our officials who were concerned looked worried and tired.

On our arrival in Peking, Ngodup Wangmo had joined the National Minorities' School, to learn Chinese, because she still had to wait about six months for her baby. I also studied the spoken language, as there was not much else to do, but I never even tried to learn the script. Both Jigme and I soon knew enough Chinese to go shopping without an interpreter. Every day I went to the house where His Holiness was staying to give Tsering Dolma her Tibetan lesson, and often I lunched there.

On 1 October China celebrated the fifth anniversary of the Peoples' Revolution and we all saw Mao Tse-tung waving to the crowds as he left the Heavenly Gate. Then preparations were made for the northern tour of the Dalai Lama and the Panchen Lama. Jigme accompanied His Holiness's party but I only went with them as far as Tientsin and then returned because Ngodup Wangmo was getting bigger and bigger.

The international port of Tientsin was quite cold in October. Jigme and I, with all the officials of the Dalai Lama's and Panchen Lama's parties, stayed at a guest-house where the rising-bell was a xylophone that I enjoyed. One evening there was a banquet in a lovely club which used to be British and had swimming pools and sports grounds. The Dalai Lama and the Panchen Lama watched the swimming and tried to play bowls. When we were taken to the dance-hall, which had lovely springy boards, I was asked to dance by the Chinese officer who was the party's chief guide. While we were dancing he suddenly laughed and said, 'Dalai Lama!' Looking round, I saw both Their Holinesses, the Dalai Lama and the Panchen Lama, standing by the gate. They just glanced at the dancing, but our monk-officials were sad and shocked and asked the Chinese not to bring Their Holinesses to dancing places. I do not think the two High Lamas went to see any more dances.

When His Holiness's party continued its tour I returned to Peking and found Ngodup Wangmo with terrible mumps. Her face was so swollen that I could hardly recognise her but she soon got better, after being treated by our Tibetan doctor. Ngapo Tseten Dolkar and Lhagyari Palyangla were also pregnant and had remained at the Great Peking Hotel. Ngodup Wangmo and I then moved to the Dalai Lama's office and were given a nice room with good heating, where it would be easy to dry nappies after the baby came.

When I asked the National Committee to allow me to take Ngodup Wangmo for check-ups to the Peking Hospital, where the treatment was excellent, they said we must go to the Peoples' Hospital, as only *Shap-pēs'* wives and the wives of high Chinese officials were admitted to the Peking Hospital. But they assured me that the treatment was the same and only accommodation and food were different.

When Ngodup Wangmo's pains started I took her to the Peoples' Hospital at dawn and I, too, was admitted to the delivery room, in a white jacket and cap. The capable lady doctor spoke fluent American-English; poor Ngodup Wangmo was screaming at her and once she nearly kicked off the nurse's spectacles. Between pains she laughed at me and said, 'Mother you look like a Muslim in Lhasa!' After about six hours' labour a lovely son was born, just like his father.

Ngodup Wangmo was treated most kindly and shared a room with a Christian Chinese woman who left, with her son, before Ngodup Wangmo did. When the father came to take them away Ngodup Wangmo envied this family and felt terribly sad. She was discharged after a week.

When His Holiness's party came back to Peking in February preparations were made for our return home and I asked the National Committee to give me a guide, as I wished to visit Shanghai and Hangchow. They kindly provided a Tibetan Bapa named Dawala. Though Ngodup Wangmo was again in hospital, with a breast abcess, I was able to leave Peking because Jigme was back. For ten days he took care of the baby, who had a little skin-trouble when I was leaving but on my return was looking splendid; Jigme had given him his daily bath because we could not trust the Chinese nanny I had hired to give a bath properly. We asked His Holiness to name the child and he was called Tenzin Wangdu. Tenzin is the Dalai Lama's first name and for a boy he always gives a part of his own name.

Bapa Dawala and I first went to Shanghai and during the train journey had long talks. I have Bapa blood in myself — because of my mother's descent from the family of the tenth Dalai Lama, which came from Lithang in Ba — so I asked Dawa many questions about life in Ba, which has been under

Chinese rule for a long time. Dawa said that before the Communists came there were many Christian missionaries there, who were friendly and useful, particularly in giving medical help, but no Bapa was ever converted. The Bapas were strongly united amongst themselves as Tibetans and Buddhists, and would not intermarry with the Chinese. They were very clean (unlike most Tibetan peasants) and exceptionally fond of horses. They ate and drank well, but never accumulated wealth. If thieves occasionally appeared in the community everybody worked together to drive them out, so the people in general lived happy, peaceful lives. Tibetans from the east – Bapas and Khampas – are brave, handsome, tall, loyal and religious. Of course, we people of Ü-Tsang are just as good in many ways, but not so brave.

At Shanghai we were put in the eighteen-storey Shanghai Hotel for two days and I was shown the museum, the aquarium, some schools, the huge skeleton of a whale and two well-kept workers' day-crèches. I was given dinner by the Women's Association at the twenty-three-storey National Hotel.

At Hangchow – which is in most beautiful country, near a lake, with green hills all around – we were taken to a small factory, where pictures were woven by hand; they had done Mao Tse-tung, Stalin and the Panchen Lama. Our officials had objected to them weaving the Dalai Lama, but they had woven a lovely picture of the Potala.

When it was time for us to go home Ngodup Wangmo got several letters from her husband in Lhasa, asking her to return with the baby; but she wanted to stay in Peking until Tenzin Wangdu was a little bigger and she had finished studying Chinese. It was very sad leaving her and our small grandson, but luckily she had many Tibetan friends in Peking. The Chinese thought Ngodup Wangmo beautiful and used to call me 'the mother of the pretty Tibetan girl'.

On our return journey we went with His Holiness's party from Peking to Hankow by rail and from Hankow to Chungking by boat. At Hankow Tsering Dolma left us to go home via India, and Ngapo Tseten Dolkar and I were invited to a farewell party for her. I had to take six or seven small glasses of grape spirit, to be polite to everybody, and after that I began to feel terrible and my head was going round and round. I did not know what to do so I hid myself under a bed in Tsering Dolma's room. Then His Holiness's little brother noticed something under the bed and poked me with his foot and said, 'What is this?' He thought it was very funny when he recognised me. Since we were leaving by boat that night somebody drove me back to the guest-house where Jigme was anxiously waiting, wondering what had gone wrong with me. Yet in spite of feeling like this I insisted on going out to a store to buy baby vests, which Ngapo Tseten Dolkar needed badly – even though the store seemed to be going round and round I managed to get the right size.

In Chungking we got the news of the bad earthquake in Tachienlu; it was terrible to think of that nice little place looking very sad.

On our way through eastern Tibet His Holiness visited many monasteries and gave sermons at each important town. Everywhere the people showed him much faith and love and were so happy that they threw themselves towards him. When he visited the great monastery of Tashi Kyil thousands came from far away to greet him and our buses were used to stop the crowds overrunning each other; one or two may have got killed by trampling. At heart the Chinese did not like this devotion to His Holiness. As he couldn't get to all the places he deputed a few other High Lamas to represent him. He visited his birthplace and met many of his relatives, to whom he gave presents.

The new motor-road to Lhasa had been completed and the journey that had taken twenty-four days a year earlier could now be done in a week. But the way was still very dangerous and at Thangme we heard that the nearby bridge might soon be washed away. We drove on quickly for hours, right up to the river, and saw the terrible water looking absolutely black; one could not hear anything else above the terrific noise of water falling down and pushing boulder against boulder. This was in the late afternoon. His Holiness, with his family and some officials, crossed the bridge on foot, Jigme and I followed them and everybody watched as a number of trucks, His Holiness's jeep and several others crossed. Then, when Kunde-ling's jeep was crossing, bang went the bridge – but the driver reversed quickly enough to get back to the bank safely. Our jeep, with all our coats, and the servants' trucks were left on the other side. It was getting late and everybody squeezed into the jeeps that had got across; we were put in the Ngapos' jeep – and their baby was there too. The road was so bad that at another place we had to stop again for hours. By then it was dark and raining hard and everybody was very worried; even at two o'clock in the night His Holiness was still on the road. At about four o'clock we reached Lunang, where officials from Lhasa were waiting with kerosene lamps to meet His Holiness. Nobody had any blankets, but we heard that His Holiness's religious shawl, which he must always have, had been tied to a rope and thrown across the river from the far side. Blankets were borrowed from here and there – the Chinese soldiers at Lunang lent us some – but it was very cold for everybody. By the time we arrived in Lhasa, two days later, all the remaining vehicles had caught up with us.

The people of Lhasa rejoiced greatly at the return of His Holiness, as they had feared he might not be allowed to come home. He had promised them that he would be back in a year and it was their confidence in his word that had kept them going during his absence.

During my journey I often thought the whole of China was so rich and beautiful they needed not Tibet at all. But they saw that it was most important to take our country, from the military point of view – which the great nations did not see, at their distance, and so they made no attempt to help the Tibetans to keep Tibet. I suppose this is also karma.

16   Our Struggles against the Chinese

AFTER HIS HOLINESS's return from China, in May 1955, the Chinese in Lhasa were busy arranging for the inauguration of the Preparatory Committee for the Autonomous Region of Tibet. Our government was carrying on the same as usual, but the offices started by the Chinese – to reorganise communications, finance, education, agriculture and medicine – were going to be directly under the P.C.A.R.T. The Chinese deputy Prime Minister, representatives of various Autonomous Regions of the New China and many press men were coming to the inauguration ceremony, and the P.W.A. and P.Y.A. were told to make sets of all the Tibetan regional costumes. The Chinese Liaison Office arranged accommodation and within three months a huge guest-house, a bathing-house and a Lhasa Municipal Hall were built. This hall stood right in front of the Potala and was a two-storied modern building with a corrugated iron roof. About twelve hundred people could sit on chairs below the big platform and another three hundred in the gallery.

The inauguration of the P.C.A.R.T. was a big show, attended by representatives from all over Tibet. The Lhasa Hall was decorated with many flags and the most important officials at a long table in the centre of the platform. A Chinese Army band played and as usual Communist songs were sung. I was invited to the gallery, as one of the observers from the P.W.A., and speeches were made by the Dalai Lama, the Panchen Lama, the Sakya Lama, other important lamas, Marshal Chen Yi, members of the P.C.A.R.T. and Tsarong, as a famous man of Tibet. It was obvious from the speeches that the land reform activities of the Chinese were still not popular with the majority of our people. Nobody openly criticised the Chinese, but everybody except the Panchen Lama said politely that we would not like Communist-type reforms. The Panchen Lama's speech, welcoming the reforms, was understood to have been given according to the wishes of the Chinese.

When Tsarong came on to the platform everybody was eager to hear what he would say; even the Chinese were nudging each other. He simply said, 'We Tibetans have always resisted invaders and have never given away our country to anyone.' Then he walked off the platform and we all looked at each other and smiled, but neither side showed any resentment and the meeting went on quite smoothly. At a big reception afterwards Marshal Chen Yi gave presents of broadcloth, serge and silk to all our high officials. Later on, the organisers were accused of having been too extravagant in the preparation of this show.

After the inauguration we waited anxiously to see whether or not our own government was going to be abolished. But it was simply ignored by the Chinese, while the P.C.A.R.T. ran a completely separate governing committee, of which His Holiness was compelled to be chairman. The Panchen Lama was Vice-Chairman and Ngawang Jigme was General Secretary.

In his autobiography the Dalai Lama has described the situation at this time: 'Twenty of the members of the P.C.A.R.T. committee, although they were Tibetans, were representing the Chamdo Liberation Committee and the committee set up in the Panchen Lama's Western district. These were both purely Chinese creations. Their representatives owed their positions mainly to Chinese support, and in return they had to support any Chinese proposition; though the Chamdo representatives did behave more reasonably than the Panchen Lama's. With this solid block of controlled votes, in addition

His Holiness the 14th Dalai Lama.

His Holiness the 14th Dalai Lama, before his recognition, with his mother, father and brother, Gyalo Dhondup.

His Holiness the Dalai Lama and his dog with Jigme and myself at Dharamsala in 1966.

My niece, Tsering Yangzom (widow of the late Prime Minister of Bhutan) and myself with some Tibetan orphans at Happy Valley, Mussoorie, India.

to those of the five Chinese members, the Committee was powerless — a mere façade of Tibetan representation behind which all the effective power was exercised by the Chinese. In fact, basic policy was decided by another body . . . which had no Tibetan members. We were allowed to discuss the minor points, but we could never make any major changes. Although I was nominally chairman, there was nothing much to do. Sometimes it was almost laughable to see how the proceedings were controlled and regulated, so that plans already completed in the other Chinese committee received a pointless and empty discussion and then were passed. But often I felt embarrassed at these meetings. I saw that the Chinese had only made me chairman in order to give an added appearance of Tibetan authority to their schemes.'

Marshal Chin Yi and his party had to go home soon, to attend the second meeting of the Chinese National Assembly, and as Tsering Dolma was one of the ten Tibetans chosen to attend she asked me to accompany her as her secretary. I was then busy doing up Taring House and our guest-house, but it was my duty to help His Holiness's sister so I left all the work for Jigme and returned to China. We flew with Chen Yi's party from Yanpachen Airport, five hours' drive from Lhasa, and the flight to Sining, in three small aeroplanes, took three hours. Oxygen masks were provided but we Tibetans did not need them, though some of the Chinese felt the height very much.

At Sining we found lots of changes. New bathing-houses and a big four-storied guest-house had been built; two years earlier, there were only old houses. We flew on to Lanchow — a very dry area — and motored out for a few hours to visit a lovely Buddhist place where there was a small temple. We climbed a pretty hill to a peaceful hermitage and saw a big stone which barren women carry three times around the temple on their backs.

Marshal Chen Yi and his wife seemed nice — the wife spoke Russian and a little English — but I never like to be with Chang Ching Wu and General Tang Kau hua. They said nothing in particular to upset me, but they always looked the unfriendly type and it was difficult for me to accompany them: yet it was my duty to go.

From Lanchow we went on by train to Peking, where we were put up at the Peking Hotel and given a packet of coupons for meals. During my first visit to China I had noticed that there was much respect for Russian technicians, who were called 'the unselfish friends from Russia'. This time they were still being treated specially and we could see what quick service they got in the dining-hall.

Tsering Dolma attended the Assembly meeting every day and had to give a broadcast speech and meet the radio news people. I was busy preparing her speeches and did not attend the Assembly, but in the evenings I accompanied her to concerts, theatres and variety shows. We were entertained to lunch at Marshal Chen Yi's house, which was enormous and lovely, with its own cinema hall. From the drawing-room a chauffeur drove us across the huge compound to the dining-room. There is no doubt about Chinese food being the best in the world.

Tsering Dolma invited the Tibetan children who were studying at the Peking National Minorities' School to lunch at our hotel. There were about twenty of them, from both noble and poor families, and when they complained that their school food was getting worse Tsering Dolma promised to speak to the National Committee on their behalf.

After a month in Peking Tsering Dolma and her maid-servant left by air for Sining, but as there were only two seats I had to wait a week for the next plane so I toured Peking again. The wonderful old palaces were all empty and were explained as being the consequences of exploitation by the Emperors. Still, they are the beauty of the country.

In Sining, Tsering Dolma and I visited lovely nomads' grazing places and some monasteries, including Kumbum where His Holiness's elder brother had been an Incarnate Lama. There were few monks left, but we met His Holiness's pock-marked monk uncle, who gave us lunch in a typical

Amdo house, sitting on mats, and was very kind. We heard later that he had died under torture.

From Sining we drove for a week, back to Lhasa, and everywhere saw new buildings; there was not a town without a Chinese restaurant and little shops where one could buy soap, candles and enamel mugs. On the bitterly cold plateau there were some very poor Chinese, dressed in thin rags, road-making. They were fed only on *mo-mo* and hot water and were said to be Kuomintang officials undergoing punishment. There were no good rest-houses but usually we were given a hut or some sort of shelter. Only once I had to sleep out on the grass – which was not comfortable as the wind blows hard across the plains.

At this period the ladies were coming less and less to our W.P.A. meetings. Kuchok and I were questioned about this, so I organised a course of religious teaching to bring them. The subject was the explanation of *Geting* – a wonderful series of letters from Phagpa Ludup to a King by the name of Decho Gangpo – which is written in such very high Tibetan that every sentence has to be explained. The course lasted more than two months and the ladies came very nicely. Our teacher was a young, learned Khampa Lama, Tulku Kyenrab Hoser, and I sent the office car to fetch him thrice a week. At first the driver went as I directed; but after some time, whenever I told him to fetch our teacher he made an excuse, saying that he had to go here or there or that the car had gone wrong. So we bought petrol and asked the Tulku to ride his own motor-bike, which he did, and so we were able to continue our good course of religious training. The Chinese never actually stopped us but they instigated some young girls to complain that I was organising religious teaching instead of a course of political science. One of my nephews said, 'What on earth are you doing? Religious training at a Communist office – you are brave indeed!' I told him that as we were all Buddhists I saw no reason why I should not organise religious training; but after only one religious course the Chinese insisted on our having political science lectures. The ladies were not at all keen on coming to these, but by then they were very frightened, so many came reluctantly.

According to our own government's policy, and by order of the *Kashag*, many Tibetans were working with the Chinese. Yet nobody trusted them, because we all knew that eventually they would attack our religion and those of us who possessed anything.

In August 1956, the present Chogyal of Sikkim came to Lhasa as President of the Mahabodhi Society of India to invite His Holiness to India to take part in the Buddha Jayanti – the 2,500th anniversary of the birth of the Lord Buddha. The Chogyal was a guest of the government but we had the pleasure of entertaining him at our house for a whole day. By then the Khampas had already revolted against the Chinese, who were asking all the Tibetan officials and their ladies to give opinions about the situation. Nobody knew what to say and the atmosphere in Lhasa was terrible. First the Chinese did not want His Holiness to go to India but when the Panchen Lama was also invited they agreed to both High Lamas going. Everybody felt happy about this journey – not like when His Holiness was invited to China.

Hundreds of Tibetans went to India on this pilgrimage in November 1956, and quite a number stayed there, though the majority came back. Jigme accompanied His Holiness's party and Namgyal, Tsewang, Ngodup Wangmo and Tenzing Dondup also went, so I had to stay at home to look after Mother-in-law. Jigme wrote to say that he had been unable to do much of the pilgrimage because His Holiness's brother, Losang Samten, had had to have an appendicitis operation and spend a month in Bombay, with Jigme as his companion and interpreter.

Then Mother-in-law became very ill and would not see the Chinese doctors, so we called the Sikkimese doctor of the Indian Consul-General and she gradually got quite well again. Luckily Chime Dorje was in Lhasa and helped me very lovingly to nurse his mother.

Most of the Tibetan pilgrims had gone to India in trucks or

cars, by the new Chinese motor-road, and the journey that used to take us twenty-four days now took only three; but many people were killed in accidents on the passes and I worried a lot about everybody, especially Jigme. However, he got back safely, with His Holiness's party, in March 1957.

Soon after, Pema Dolkar became seriously ill. A nice Chinese lady doctor gave her injections but seemed quite hopeless about her case, unless she had an operation, and at sixty-five they thought her a bit old for this. She had never been healthy, right through her life, but Tsarong was always very good to her; he loved her so much and always paid great respect to her. Especially in her later years, when she had so much agony and needed a lot of nursing, he devoted himself to her and used to search to see if any stone had been passed, supervise her diet, keep her chart, take her temperature and say, 'I only know the nature of her illness.' (He was also very good when any of the children were ill and would bathe and feed them.) He brought potted plants to her room to brighten it, gave her the best kinds of ornaments and every morning brought her her bed-tea, which had been prepared by the maid-servant. Since he himself always got up at three o'clock he had finished the day's work of an ordinary man by breakfast time.

Despite her poor health Pema Dolkar often went into trance and was visited by various spirits; only Tsarong knew who these spirits were. He also knew whether or not her attacks of illness were accompanied by a spirit, and if he felt that she was going to be possessed he would send everybody else out of the room and stay to talk to it. Sometimes it would be a good spirit who had come to seek help; but whether a good spirit or a bad spirit, Pema Dolkar would get much pain and feel sick for the rest of the day after the few minutes' trance. Sometimes Tsarong would tie a thread around both her fourth fingers – very tightly without any sympathy – and keep it on until the spirit begged to be released. He was able to stop some of the bad spirits from attacking her by making them take an oath; it is said that even bad spirits do respect their oath.

Tsarong had a small estate at Chusul, thirty miles from

Lhasa, and whenever anybody was coming from there, to work or do business in the city, the spirit of the Chusul deity would enter Pema Dolkar without the knowledge of the person who was on the way. Tsarong would then try to fulfil the wishes of the man from Chusul – otherwise the spirit would make Pema Dolkar very ill. This spirit was supposed to belong to a steward of Chusul who had died long ago and whose family were still running the estate. We say that if there is too much attachment to your family, or to any place or object, your soul finds it difficult to take a reincarnation after death and remains roaming for a long time wherever the living family is attached. Our religion teaches us to practise non-attachment to everything.

I remember once in Darjeeling, in 1924, Pema Dolkar came in trance at Mr. Ladenla's house – and that time it looked like one of the State-protecting deities, who sometimes enter bodies other than the State Oracles. By the action as she went into trance we could see that it was not an ordinary spirit; State deities are so strong that they make the body shiver very much. Tsarong said it was Gyalchen and told the servants to bring a good scarf. He then shut the door and never told us what talk he had with this spirit. Afterwards Pema Dolkar was in great pain for the rest of the day.

At the time of Pema Dolkar's illness in 1957, the P.W.A. was preparing a delegation of Tibetan women to attend the All-China Women's Conference. Ngapo Tseten Dolkar was pregnant for the twelfth time and Surkhang Dekyi had just returned from visiting China with her husband, so I was asked to lead the delegation. I refused, because both Mother-in-law and Pema Dolkar were unwell, so the W.P.A. sent a telegram to Tsering Dolma, who was still in India, and she also urged me to go. Again I refused, but when they said it would only take a month and if necessary I could come back by air in a day, I decided to go. Nobody in the family liked this – Jigme didn't want me to travel so soon after his return from India and Mother-in-law was always sad during my long journeys. But I could not escape from this work and our Tibetan ladies were glad that I was going because they knew I would always speak out, even if it did not please the Chinese.

About twelve of us were appointed to the W.P.A. delegation; our Chinese colleague, Shue Turin, and the Chinese secretary were to accompany us. Before we left I was asked to prepare my speech for the meeting and it was shown to General Tan Kuangsan, but no corrections were made; yet I somehow knew that they did not like all of it. I could not express their views strongly – neither, of course, could I oppose them directly, unless I wanted to get into bad trouble.

When I went to say good-bye to Pema Dolkar we both felt terribly sad. At the send-off ceremony many women wished us good luck but the only thing I was looking forward to was seeing our younger daughter, Yangdol, who was then studying at the National Minorities' School in Peking. The Chinese had these schools at Peking, Sian and Lanchow, and over five hundred students were sent to them from Lhasa, Shigatse, Gyantse and Chamdo. In 1952, when a group of officials' children – including several of the Ngapos – was sent to Peking, Yangdol had refused to go because she knew the road was not good. That first group was taken by Professors Liu and Yu and suffered greatly. Their pack-mules were drowned when their ship sank in the Yellow River and though no child was drowned they all lost their luggage. Yangdol went with another group of sixty students three years later. The conditions and food had been good at first, but they eventually became very poor so our children rebelled against the school and many of their parents felt troubled. Some children were called back to Tibet, and one of them was a brilliant young man who had learned Chinese thoroughly and joined our Khampa guerrillas to become one of their bravest leaders.

Shue Turin and I shared a closed jeep while the rest of the party travelled in two trucks; they were quite comfortable because they made their beds in the back and lay on them sleeping or singing. We got to Peking in about two weeks. On the way we laughed a lot and made ourselves happy, though at heart I was sad to think that I had left Pema Dolkar ill in bed.

Tunhuang was the most interesting city we visited; it is hot and dry with no trees around. I had heard of the famous caves of a thousand Buddhas, twenty-five miles away, so I asked Shue Turin if we might visit them and she agreed. A guide took us to this very holy, quiet place, in a river-valley between two hills on the edge of a sand desert. About four hundred caves lead from one to another, like rat-holes in a row. The Chinese were restoring the wall-paintings so ladders and workmen were everywhere; yet the place felt serene. It was a pity to see the ancient images and paintings being repainted so badly. Many Tibetan books of Buddhist scriptures, written in gold on black parchment, were piled up carelessly, all mixed. It seemed to me that the whole place was going to become a museum; nobody was there to burn a single bit of incense before the two huge Buddhas in the nearby temple. I and my senior Tibetan colleagues prostrated at the feet of one of the great images, but some of our younger colleagues hesitated and then did not prostrate. The Chinese constitution says that all are free to respect their own religion, yet in China there is not this freedom. None of the Chinese women who were with us objected to my religious ideas, but still the young Tibetan women seemed frightened – they were not really Communists, but had been influenced by the Chinese indoctrination courses.

We arrived in May and in Peking stayed at the modern Peace Hotel, which is said to have been built in forty days. A small van was put at our disposal; the leaders of earlier Tibetan delegations had been given small cars, but now everything was on a more economical basis and we received no luxurious hospitality though the Women's Association gave a banquet for us, at which we were told that our meeting had been postponed for a month because of the heat. We were asked to stay in Peking and see as many factories as possible, but I requested permission for us to tour Manchuria and Inner Mongolia, as a number of us already knew Peking well, and this was granted.

After our arrival in Peking Shue Turin changed completely and was not so sweet to me as she had been. She was not the type to be rude, but she became very quiet and gave me no more friendly smiles. I could not guess why she had changed.

The first thing I did in Peking was to visit our younger daughter, Yangdol, at the National Minorities' School. It made me very happy to see her again.

A few days later we left by train for Manchuria, where we visited Mukden and Harbin, staying in comfortable old hotels. The atmosphere in these cities was quite different from Lhasa. In Manchuria everything looked modern, like Europe, and the people showed no sign of the gaiety we were used to in Tibet.

From Harbin we went by train to Inner Mongolia, where I had to talk to a People's Meeting. I said that by the kindness of the Chinese government we were able to come to Mongolia without much trouble, and I mentioned the time and effort the Mongolians used to spend coming to the Holy City of Lhasa on camels' back across many mountains and plains. Now, I said, one can get to the Holy City in a short time – and since China's constitution grants religious freedom the Tibetans were hoping that in future many more Mongolian pilgrims would come to Lhasa than ever before, taking advantage of the easy communications.

The local Communist leader also spoke, mentioning the present good relations between us brothers and sisters and saying that we must strive together for our common interest, which was flourishing daily under the leadership of Mao Tse-tung.

After attending a sports' meeting we were shown a blanket factory and taken in a big red bus to visit Mongolian shepherds living in tents. They were expecting us and about forty galloping horsemen came to meet us and tried to keep up with the bus. At the camp, where they had already started co-operative farming, we were divided into groups and taken to visit some families who were so poor that they hardly had anything in their tents; yet they were very pleased to see us and gave us lunch of boiled mutton and *phing* (noodles). They had to tell us that they were happier under the Communists, but they all had pictures of the Dalai and Panchen Lamas and there were prayer-beads in the hands of the old people. Their food was stored in horse-carts with lids, so to shift camp they just had to pull down their tents, put them on the carts and go. The grass was long and rich on their pastures, where many sheep and horses were grazing.

The weather was good when we left the camp, but at about three o'clock in the afternoon a terrible storm came with hailstones like glass marbles that cracked the bus windows. Then the bus got stuck and we were left in despair on the plains of Inner Mongolia; I felt so sad that I wrote a letter to Jigme while we were waiting. After about an hour the Mongolian leader of the next small town came in a jeep to fetch us, because he knew our bus would be stuck in the mud after such a storm. The senior members of the party were taken first, then the jeep came back for the rest. We praised the Mongolian leader and thanked him heartily.

At the famous and beautiful Kagyur Temple, which was supposed to have eighty monks, there were only about a dozen left. The head monks had been told to expect us and came in their yellow satin robes to give us a good welcome. (The Mongolians got their religion from us in the sixteenth century, A.D.) The deities' images and the religious books were all intact, yet it was obvious that here, too, religion was going to fade sooner or later. When the lamas told us that they were working on the land most of the time I could only say that since the Chinese constitution respects religion it was important for them to practise Buddhism well, though everybody now has to work for a living.

From Inner Mongolia we went to Yenpen, in Korea, by train and car. At all the towns we were met by representatives of the Women's Association and after a meal at our guest-house (most of the good old hotels had been converted into guest-houses) the local governor lectured us on the town, giving full details of the population, the number of factories and schools and the general progress of the place. I made careful notes because I had to prepare an official report about every place we visited for the W.P.A. in Lhasa. The Chinese secretary and our translator also made notes. Then a banquet was given, at which I, on behalf of the delegation, replied to the Governor's welcome speech. I always said that we were grateful for local hospitality and happy to see such speedy progress in the town by the hard work of the people under the leadership of Mao Tse-tung. I mentioned that we Tibetan women were also making progress and would follow in the footsteps of the Chinese women and work still harder. After that we were taken to see a classical Chinese play, or to a dance at the guest-house hall.

Korea is a nice, warm, sweet place—all green, something like Ireland—and the Koreans greeted us kindly. Their agriculture was a bit more advanced than the Mongolians'; in this region of co-operative farms they seemed quite gay and the old ladies danced in the villages. They had their Communist leaders and told us they were very happy, but I simply could not judge whether this was true or not. During our travels we never discussed Communism amongst ourselves because all the time the Chinese were with us. Sometimes we had to hold meetings to make our reports, but the Communist Party was never discussed as the Chinese felt we had not yet reached the necessary standard of loyalty. Our delegation sang and joked right through the journey and I used to amuse myself with them.

At Yenpen I got a telegram from Jigme saying that Pema Dolkar's condition was serious. We left for Port Arthur by a comfortable night train and I thought I was going to have a restful sleep but it was just the contrary; if I slept I dreamt of Lhasa and soon woke. At Port Arthur station another telegram was handed to me by the ladies who came to meet us at the station and Shue Turin offered to read it. I told her I knew the contents and put it away in my bag: I thought, 'I will do my duty first, then I can have the whole night to myself to think of my dear sister.' I could not hear or see well but I did not disturb the usual routine—except that I refused to dance that evening, saying I was not feeling very well. When we went back to our nice workers' rest-house by the port I asked Shue Turin to read the telegram and she said, 'It is what you thought.'

I felt very sad to have lost my beloved sister while I was away. Later, Jigme told me that he did his very best to serve her right to the end. Her body was taken to Rigya – by truck to the foot of the hill, from where it was carried up by servants. Jigme himself cleaned and decorated the truck and accompanied the funeral to the foot of the hill. He said he did all that I would have done, to repay her kindness to us both.

From Port Arthur we went to Chingtow, where the local cooperative farms had wonderful fields and fruit trees. The workers told us that they felt happy, but none of them looked it and compared with our peasants they had nothing. In the house of a Chinese farmer there is just a plain bed, a table and a few cooking-pots, whereas our peasants had full houses, no matter how rubbishy their possessions might be. They knew they were free to have as many belongings as they could get and even the dogs in their kennels were contented. Sometimes our people felt uneasy, when certain government officials came to inspect land and collect taxes, yet amongst themselves they were always at ease and full of happiness and trust. But in China now the poor people are afraid and feel as though they are sitting on thorns.

We spent fourteen days in Chingtow, where we had to have meetings and make our reports on the whole tour. Many debates took place. I said that the people did not seem to like the cooperative system; in 1954 I had noticed the traders in Peking market being very enthusiastic about their business, but since the market had been turned into modern co-operative shops they showed less enthusiasm. This Shue Turin did not like and then arose quite a lot of argument. I said I thought individual ownership was enjoyed better by everybody and I pointed out that the Communists did not all have the same living standard. Shue Turin replied that different people have to have different standards. There were about thirty different grades of salary for Chinese workers, from government officials to ordinary soldiers. We had already seen the living conditions of the high Chinese officers, whose three luxurious meals were always accompanied by wine or beer. These Communists had their own cars, built their own houses and kept their wives always with them. (The wives often took office jobs and were much respected by the junior officers.) Whatever we wrote in Tibetan was translated into Chinese and we had great difficulties in making this report; the Chinese liked my hard work, but they did not like my ways of thinking.

When we returned to Peking the date of our delayed three-day conference had been fixed. About two thousand delegates came and the hall was magnificent; each table had eight different language phones. Various ambassadors' wives attended and when the delegates sang the national song at the opening it was frightening for us to hear. Part of the wording was 'Arise, those people who do not wish to be slaves any more.'

At this time, there was a great movement of criticism going on in China. Mao Tse-tung had been asking the intelligentsia to give their opinions of the Communist administration, and when they did so they all turned out to be against the régime. They were then called 'Rightist' and one by one were pressed to wash their brains. Four of the delegates to our conference were supposed to belong to the intelligentsia and most of the two hundred or so speeches asked these ladies to repent and reform.

We Tibetans gave our speeches on the second day. My speech reported on our work since the Chinese came and at the end I wished long life to Mao Tse-tung and the Peoples' Government of Great China. The speech of the Tibetan working women's representative had been entirely drafted by our Chinese colleagues and the main stress was on thanking Mao Tse-tung for granting them equal status and equal rights.

After the conference we were photographed with Mao Tse-tung; he just came to a garden for the picture to be taken, greeted the delegates and left. Then our delegation met General Chang Ching Wu, who asked us whether we thought it would be good to have land reforms soon or to delay them. We all felt very frightened, so we said that we would like them now – but we added that the majority of our people did not want them. He said, 'Never mind – the Tibetans didn't seem eager to have reforms at the inauguration of the P.C.A.R.T., so Mao Tse-tung has kindly decided to postpone them for six years and you need not be afraid.'

Before I left Peking, Yangdol and her fiancé, Kalsang Thubten, said that they wanted to return home with me, so the National Committee reluctantly granted me permission to take them back to Lhasa.

This homecoming was very sad, because of Pema Dolkar's death. Tsarong gave most of her ornaments to the wife of their son, Dudal Namgyal; their daughters got some souvenirs from her many accumulated jewels and I got a beautiful gold chain studded with pearls and jade and hung with tooth-picks and ear-picks. This I gave to a Ladakhi monk to be sold when he was doing his metaphysical examination, on which occasion he had to give a big feast to his fellow-monks; it was difficult for monk-scholars to get enough money without help.

Pema Dolkar had kept everything very well, especially Tsarong's clothes. Since he had been serving the government for many years she made all his old yellow satin dresses into wrappers, not to waste the material, and then folded into them his beautiful fur and brocade robes. He gave her a wonderful funeral, on which he spent a lot, sending presents to monasteries all over Tibet. But the most merit would have already been gained, for both of them, by the love and respect they showed each other while living together.

Another very sad event at this time was the death of Tsawa Tritrul – brother of Dingja and Delek Rabten – who had led a sorrowful life. As a High Lama he had often been invited to preach to rich nomads; holy lamas always felt happy to have an opportunity to preach – and their attendants were even more happy to receive gifts. Tsawa Tritrul's attendants became quite well off through receiving many gifts of wool, sheep and butter and trading a lot in the wool. Then Tsawa Tritrul left his monastery to marry – before the death of the thirteenth Dalai Lama – and was degraded. He had two daughters and a son, but his rich attendants left him with nothing and he underwent great hardship. He was very learned and had no pretence or hypocrisy in him; Tsarong used to help him financially when he was trying to earn a living through teaching young officials. In 1953 he was put at the head of the Chinese Army school, where I taught, to check the new textbooks; later he worked for a Chinese-run Lhasa newspaper, checking its Tibetan spelling and grammar – yet he was always in financial difficulties. Then one day in 1957 a beggar, who believed him to be pro-Chinese, gave him a bad beating while he was walking through the street and Tsawa Tritrul, the great scholar, died almost immediately.

17 The Uprising

ON MY RETURN to Lhasa, in August 1957, I heard that the Khampa revolt was getting stronger and stronger. When the Chinese first came to Kham, in eastern Tibet, they pretended to be friendly, but in 1956 they suddenly asked the Khampas to hand over their arms. The Khampas are brave men who love rifles, pistols, revolvers and daggers – not to fight against any nation, but to guard their lives while travelling and to show that bravery which is born in them. They also like good horses and mules and take a great interest in beautiful saddles and saddlemats. They would not give up their arms for anything, so the Chinese instigated some of the retainers to revolt against their masters and beat and humiliate them, putting horse reins in their mouths and riding on their backs. The Chinese also destroyed monasteries and precious books and images, to humiliate the religion of the Lord Buddha, and when the Khampas could no longer tolerate these actions they organised guerrilla warfare and fought all over Kham, under the command of Asuktsang.

The Chinese repeatedly asked our government to let the Tibetan Army join their army to put down the insurgents and when our government refused the Chinese got very angry and used to abuse the *Shap-pēs*. General Tang Kua San would come to the W.P.A. meetings and say, 'The *Shap-pēs* of the Tibetan *Kashag* are worse than you women members.' We had several *Shay-pēs*' wives among us and of course Tsering

In our house in India, 1986.

Jigme and myself with our two granddaughters Kunsang and Tsering Chodon, India, 1986.

The Taring Family, India, 1986: (Back row, left to right) Tenzin Namgyal, Tenzin Wangdu, Tenzin Dhondup, Ngodup Wangmo, Gyala, Tsering Yangzom, Konchok Gyaltsen, Yangchen Dolkar, Tsering Choden and Kunsang. (Middle row) Myself and Tenzin Deki, Jigme, Shelok and Tenzin Norbu. (In front) Lhaki and Tsering Dolkar, Tseten Dorje, Tenzin Namdol, Dorje Tseten and Tenzin Thogme.

Dolma, our Chairman, was always there, but none of us had the power to say anything so we could only keep silent while the General was hitting the table and looking angrily at us. To Surkhang *Lhacham* he would say 'Surkhang *Shap-pēs* is senseless — worse than you!' However, we were consoled by reports coming from all over the place saying that the Khampas were doing well.

Once the W.P.A. was told to visit injured Chinese soldiers at the Lhasa Military Hospital, so Tsering Dolma, Kunchok and myself went together. The soldiers were all boys, from about sixteen to eighteen, and some had lost their eyes, or legs, or arms and many had white hair. We consoled the poor things as we passed by their beds. I really felt very sad to see them having been compelled to go to war; it was not their fault — they were taken away from their parents so young.

In February 1958, Yangdol and Kalsang Thubten got married and we gave them the best possible wedding, as we had done for our elder daughter, Ngodup Wangmo. I then divided all my ornaments between our two daughters.

During the following year the fighting continued and the unhappiness of the Tibetans increased. The Chinese had become so cruel in eastern Tibet that about ten thousand refugees from Kham and Amdo had arrived in Lhasa — which made the food shortage even worse. The fighting then spread to areas near Lhasa and people feared every hour that open warfare would break out in the city itself. We were in such a terrible state of worry that no one even sat down to have a meal properly. Our greatest anxiety was for the safety of His Holiness.

At the end of 1958 His Holiness had to begin his very important and most difficult metaphysical examinations: he had been studying volumes and volumes of books, under many tutors, since becoming Dalai Lama at the age of five. For his examinations he had to spend a month at each of the three great monasteries, debating with many scholars, and Jigme accompanied him to take still and movie-sound pictures of the ceremonies. The high government officials also accompanied him, as usual – leaving their wives and families fearful in Lhasa – and *Kashag* meetings were held at the monasteries. The government had to spend a lot on the traditional feasts, and on the presents of tea and money given to each monk on behalf of His Holiness.

Although Tibet's situation was getting worse daily the examination activities went on successfully and were completed before *Losar*. Then, during the New Year celebrations, we heard that His Holiness had accepted a Chinese invitation to attend a theatre at their Army headquarters after the *Losar* ceremonies. Everbody worried about this, as the Chinese were becoming much more aggressive and had told the commander of His Holiness's bodyguard that the Dalai Lama was to come without his usual escort.

On 8 March – Women's Day – I attended a W.P.A. meeting in the Lhasa Hall, though I had just been ill with a serious stomach complaint. The other committee members also came and there were over a thousand shouting, anti-Chinese women whom we could not control. General Tang Kuan San presided over the meeting; he too was shouting, saying that the Khampas were behaving very badly and that it would be easy for the Chinese to shell and destroy the monasteries in no time if the guerrillas refused to surrender. He looked very fierce and it was terrible to hear his shouting. The Chairman and the Vice-Chairman told me to request the women to keep quiet, so I asked them through the microphone to listen to the General – who was so suspicious that he asked an interpreter what I was saying. When the meeting was over I went straight home, feeling weak and frightened.

Next day I visited Tsarong and told him that the situation was becoming worse every hour. He said that he, too, was much worried; but our talk was short, for when a Khampa lama came to see him I went to my office. This was only my second visit to Tsarong House since Pema Dolkar's death; I used to feel very sad even looking at the place, never mind stepping into it. Poor Tsarong had moved to another wing, as he could not bear to stay in the one that he and Pema Dolkar had shared. I never saw Tsarong again.

At home, Jigme, Mother-in-law and myself felt dreadfully anxious, as we knew that the ordinary people of Lhasa were being driven to open rebellion against the Chinese – though they would have to fight machine-gunners with their bare hands. When I went to the W.P.A. office two days later all my colleagues were there; the Tibetan staff had remained unchanged since the start of the W.P.A., but in accordance with Communist policy the Chinese staff was often changed. At ten o'clock that morning one of the members of the Y.P.A. came running from their next-door office to tell us that everybody in Lhasa was hurrying to Norbu Lingka and to ask if we also were going. He said that the people were mad with worry about His Holiness going to the Chinese Army headquarters that evening and had decided to block the way. Everybody knew that the Chinese had already invited some lamas in eastern Tibet to their theatres and then kidnapped them, so now thousands were around Norbu Lingka, begging His Holiness not to go into such danger. The young man said that he was on his way to join the crowd and my colleagues and I told the Chinese staff that we were going home.

I found Jigme, Mother-in-law and our two daughters discussing the situation; Ngodup Wangmo's husband had already joined his regiment. Soon we heard that a junior monk-official – a member of the Y.P.A. – had been stoned to death by the crowd outside Norbu Lingka because he was suspected of being a Chinese spy. (His younger brother then held a high position in the P.C.A.R.T.) Jigme said that he must go to see what was happening and took his motor-bike but found that he couldn't ride through the crowds. He came back late and told us that His Holiness had promised not to go to the Chinese Theatre so most of the crowd had dispersed, though many were still by the palace gate. Very early next morning Jigme went to a meeting of all the high officials at Norbu Lingka and remained there for two nights. Mother-in-law, the girls and I did not know what to do.

In the meantime, the W.P.A. had collected in front of the Potala and on 12 March I was called there. We ladies of the committee could not lead the Lhasa women because we were all too afraid of the Chinese; worry about the consequences of our actions for our husbands, children, fathers and brothers kept us bound. So this meeting was bravely led by Serong Kunsang—the eldest daughter of Tsarong's brother Kyenrab and the mother of six children—who was like a Tibetan Joan of Arc. Usually she was shy and respected us and would not speak frankly to me, but now she instructed me to go to the Indian Consul-General to ask India to help Tibet—which I did. She was a real heroine. Poor woman, we heard that when she was arrested and interrogated, after the uprising, she said that her actions were all her own responsibility and that no one else should be blamed. She was beaten and lost an eye; she may still be in prison.

The Lhasa women had made many anti-Chinese posters and when I joined them they were lined up around the Barkor shouting slogans—'From today Tibet is independent!' and 'China must quit Tibet!' Our women were more fierce than our men. It was frightening to walk through the Barkor, where Chinese soldiers with machine-guns were watching us from the roofs. All the shops were shut and no one was on the streets except the shouting women.

The Chinese were constantly threatening us through microphones, saying that if all Tibetans did not surrender, Lhasa would be shelled. I was in despair. Two months earlier my daughter, Tseyang, had gone to India with her husband, Rigzin Namgyal, who had been asked by the government to buy new camping tents for His Holiness's official visit to the sacred lake of Chokhorgyal. (This lake is visited by every Dalai Lama when he takes over the government of the country at the age of eighteen.) They had left their four little children, aged five to eleven, with me, though Tseyang had wished to take at least one with her. Unluckily Rigzin Namgyal was not keen on the idea—which has caused them great unhappiness ever since. So now I had my old mother-in-law, four small grandchildren, my two other daughters and their babies to worry about. And Jigme was almost all the time with His Holiness at Norbu Lingka.

On 16 March I myself was summoned to Norbu Lingka – about two miles outside the city – to report to Tsering Dolma on the women's activities. It is heartbreaking to think now of how my grandchildren asked me, '*Mola*, where are you going? What is happening?' – and other very sad questions that I just cannot put on paper. I asked our servant Tashi – a very strong man, aged about forty – to accompany me; I couldn't take more than one servant because the house and family had to be guarded. To protect me from stray bullets I took an old dress of Lochen Rinpoche's that I had exchanged for a new dress some years before. I never guessed that these were my last moments in my own home. When I went to Mother-in-law's room she was in great distress and anxiety; we had all had a terrible week of sorrow and suspense, nobody knowing what to do for the best – whether to stay in Lhasa or try to escape – or what the Chinese were planning to do next. Yangdol had gone to her own home the day before, but Ngodup Wangmo was still at Taring House with her children, and I asked her to look after her *Mola* and all the children while I was out.

Tsering Dolma, too, was in great anxiety; she told me the situation was becoming so bad that His Holiness might have to leave Lhasa for a while. She asked if I would like to accompany her to India, as it now seemed impossible for us to live in our country any more. I knew that the Chinese did not trust me and might soon imprison and torture me. But I said, 'What about my children – and especially my four grandchildren? Their parents have asked me to take care of them – how can I leave them, whatever happens?' Then Jigme joined us and we had a long conversation; but nobody could give anyone else advice – we were all in despair and could not foresee what might happen within the next hour never mind the next day. Many people were coming to see Tsering Dolma, whose husband was Commander of His Holiness's body-guard. When evening came and she saw that I still wished to remain in Lhasa she asked me to leave Norbu Lingka, since no women – except His Holiness's family – were allowed to spend the night there. Many people then warned me not to go home, as shots were being exchanged in the streets, so I said that I would stay at Norbu Lingka without sleeping. Soon after, Jigme's nephew, Ragashar *Dapon*, came in and we talked and talked, trying to decide what to do about the children. Jigme was all the time going out and coming in and many others were doing the same. We were given *mo-mo* in soup for our supper and I said to Jigme that whatever happened the next day I must go home and see the children. But all the news that was being brought in said that the situation was getting more and more intense and everybody expected the shelling to start at any moment.

Next morning I tried to go home but it was too dangerous to cross Lhasa through the shots that were being fired here and there. Again the day passed in terrible suspense. At about four o'clock in the afternoon Tsering Dolma asked me to go to stay at the summer house of His Holiness's family, at Gyatso, about fifteen minutes' walk from Norbu Lingka, and gave me permission to use anything I needed there. I left Norbu Lingka escorted by two of His Holiness's bodyguard, who had been told by Tsering Dolma to protect me. My faithful servant Tashi was also with me.

When we go to Gyatso — where once Tsarong and Pema Dolkar lived — the kind servants gave me a room and I waited, wondering how I could get home. Then, quite late, Jigme came, and we talked the whole night through without one blink of sleep. Jigme told me that if His Holiness left for India he felt it would be his duty to accompany him, as no other official knew English; so he had to stay at Norbu Lingka and he advised me to look after myself. Although this was very sad there was nothing to be done about it, except pray. I gave him my ring and told him to keep it as a souvenir in case we did not meet again. I said that I would go to Drepung Monastery and wait there, hoping to get home soon. Somehow, I had faith in Drepung, the greatest of our monasteries, where my mother was so well cared for in 1912 at the time of our terrible family tragedy.

The dawn came and as soon as the sun was up Jigme went back to Norbu Lingka.

When I said to Tashi that we must try to get home he insisted that it was impossible because of the shooting in the streets. I then told him – but not the Gyatso servants – that we would go to Drepung, which is only about two miles from Norbu Lingka. The servants begged me to stay, saying that it was too dangerous to walk back to Lhasa and that we would both be killed. They assured me that they had enough food to last some time and would look after me well – but I was determined to leave Gyatso, for I still hoped that somehow we might get home. After thanking the servants I left on foot, with Tashi carrying Lochen Rinpoche's old dress.

On the main road we could hear shots and though I was longing desperately to get home I did not have the courage to walk through the firing. Instead we turned towards Drepung and, as we climbed the hill, I saw the temple to which my father had called me to meet him the day before he was assassinated.

At the monastery I went into two of the colleges to look for monk friends. Both had gone to the prayer assembly and while waiting for them I sent Tashi to get me accommodation at the college where women were allowed to stay, but he found that during this critical time no women were being accommodated. I then sent him to Tema, where the only lady State Oracle lived; her husband, Senangse, was my cousin. Senangse gave Tashi a message saying that I would be most welcome at their home and he offered to provide a pony if I needed one.

While I was thinking about going to Tema, Jigme's servant, Norbu, brought me a note telling me to go some five miles further on, to Namka Estate, which belonged to Yangdol and her husband. I asked our two monk friends to accompany me, pretending to be my sons, as I would have to pass one of the many Chinese check-posts. They agreed to come and at the village below Drepung I changed into Lochen Rinpoche's nun's dress and stayed behind some huge rocks while Tashi exchanged my nice new serge dress for a greasy old black tweed *chuba*. I was wearing beautifully embroidered new Tibetan boots that I could not exchange, so I rubbed them with mud. Then I hid my dentures, powdered my hair with *tsampa*, put a dirty cloth over my head and we continued down the hill. On the main road I sent Tashi and Norbu ahead and walked about sixty yards behind them with the monks.

My muddied boots were soon blown clean by the wind and I did not know what to do; yet if I had gone barefooted I would have been terribly obvious, so we just put more mud on them. At about five o'clock we reached the Chinese check-post – one had to pass it, as there was no other way. I rested on a parapet for a few minutes and a Tibetan girl, with a tray of sweets and cigarettes to sell to travellers, looked at me hard. Four Chinese soldiers – standing with tommy-guns in their hands, ready to fire at any time – also looked at me, but I felt confident that Dolma was protecting me and walked slowly past them. Tashi and Norbu were still about sixty yards ahead and none of us was stopped.

Crossing some fields, we asked the way to Namka, which was close to the main road. We got there quite late and the steward and his wife welcomed us and gave us food and put me in the best room. They advised me to move into one of the retainers' houses next day until we saw how the situation was develolping, but I wanted to go a little further, to where I could see Lhasa from a distance. So I decided to move to His Holiness's dairy at Maling, as I knew the man in charge very well, and the steward agreed to lend me a pony.

We all stayed at Namka that night and early next morning the monks returned to Drepung and Norbu to Lhasa. I asked Norbu to try to come to Maling with my elder grandson, my toilet kit, a tin of coffee, some sugar and my two riding-mules; I wanted the mules because I could not walk properly for a whole day and I thought I might have to go further.

Before Tashi and I left Namka the steward's wife told us she had heard of His Holiness's secret flight from Lhasa during that same night that Jigme and I were talking at Gyatso.

It was still early when we got to the small dairy at Maling, ten miles from Lhasa. It had only one hut but I asked the dairyman to let me stay there for a few days and said I would be happy to stay outside as I knew that only he was allowed to sleep in the dairy. He welcomed me warmly and assured me that I would be permitted to sleep inside the hut. Four Khampa fighters were camping outside and their twenty mules were grazing nearby. From here I could see both Norbu Lingka and the Potala.

During the afternoon Norbu returned alone, saying that it was too dangerous to bring any child through Lhasa. He had another note from Jigme, to tell me that he was still in Norbu Lingka but mentioning nothing about His Holiness's flight or his own future plans. I wondered very much then if he meant to follow His Holiness. As Norbu had to get back immediately I just could not keep both mules; on foot he could never get past the check-post before dark and might find himself in great difficulties, so I told him to ride back and asked him to beg the other servants to take good care of mother-in-law and the children and to assure them that I would be home as soon as the trouble had subsided. He left with tears in his eyes.

I talked to the dairyman until after ten o'clock, when I felt so tired that I slept on the floor for about five hours. Then we heard the start of the shelling that we had been dreading so much, first one shell, then more, followed by too many to count. The Khampas, who were sleeping outside the window, immediately woke up and said, 'Now the real fighting has started – we must go.' And off they galloped on their mules. The dairyman was weeping and prostrating to his altar. He cried, 'My Holiness, the devils have started to shell Norbu Lingka!' I consoled him and said I had heard His Holiness had left Lhasa and would be safe – but I knew that Jigme was still at Norbu Lingka and that the whole city was being blasted. I thought that no one could come out of that dreadful shelling alive and I prayed to Dolma to protect everyone.

There was nothing to do but wait and think. After booming like hell the shelling stopped at sunrise. By then I had decided that Tashi and I could not stay at the dairy because we might easily be caught there and put to death. So I told the dairyman that we had no alternative but to go towards India. He begged me to stay, saying that the situation everywhere would be the same and that nothing could be better for us than to wait with him and see what happened. I replied that whatever happened we must go, as the Chinese would soon be searching for me – and then not only Tashi and I, but he himself would be in terrible danger.

I hurriedly wrote notes for Jigme and our daughters using difficult poetical language and mentioning no names in case anyone might get into trouble. I told them that I felt compelled to go, to avoid being captured, but I assured them that if I got through safely the rest of my life would be devoted to seeking the truth and that my prayers and love would be with them for ever. I said that the sun can come out of the clouds and asked them never to lose courage and faith, because by struggling through hardship our karma develops itself. I reminded them that none of us can escape our karma and asked them, if they were still alive, to pray always and consider that this was what our karma had to lead to.

After giving the notes to the dairyman I asked him if he could lend me a horse. He told me to take his own small pony, which I rode while Tashi rode the mule. He cried like a child when I thanked him and said good-bye. I also felt very sad at heart, but I did not cry. My faithful servant Tashi was silent and calm, as usual.

18   My Flight towards India

WHEN TASHI AND I left Maling, at about eight o'clock, all was quiet, but even before we reached the main road the terrible bombardment of Lhasa had started again.

Near the Nethang precipice we saw about twenty Khampas and local men on the high hill above the road. Tashi's mule was going quite fast, but the steps of my little pony were very reluctant so I was a bit behind. We knew that some of the Khampas were very rough and wild and Tashi waited to ask me what he should do when we reached the watching men; I told him to go straight on without hesitation. As he rode forward the Khampas quickly came down from the hill, pulled him off his mule and began to beat him with daggers and sticks. I jumped off my pony, ran towards the Khampas, prostrated to them and begged them not to beat my son. They looked very fierce and said he was cheeky because he had not dismounted, but I told them that if they felt like fighting they should be putting down the Chinese and not attacking us poor villagers. This quietened them and when they noticed that I had no teeth they mistook me for an old peasant woman. Again I prostrated and begged them to let us pass. They asked where we were going and I said we were returning to Chusul, after visiting relatives at Drepung Monastery. They searched our pockets and I was worried when they found my toilet kit, a tin of coffee and a little sugar – things no villager would be carrying – but they were so excited about the shelling, which was now going on like hell, that they paid no attention and just sent us ahead with a horseman escort to be checked by their Chief at his head-quarters in Nethang.

We soon got to the village, because our escort beat our riding animals harshly and my poor little pony had no time to drag his feet. Before reaching the Khampa headquarters there was a small bridge and here our escort again hit my pony, who stumbled and threw me. Luckily I was thrown on the ground, not into the stream, and I only scratched my cheek and hands, but I later found that I had dropped my prayer-beads. At the headquarters – a two-storied villager's house that had been requisitioned – Tashi stayed outside with the animals and I was taken into a big room where six or seven men were sitting on mats. I saluted by removing my hat and as I bent down to tell the senior man that we came from Lhasa he got up and greeted me, saying 'Oh, My Lady, welcome! Please take your seat and talk.' I had never met him before, but when I asked, 'How do you know me?' he said. 'Of course we all know you.' He ordered his men to unlock the Chief's room, took me in there, and gave me tea saying. 'I am Rabge, the paymaster of this army.' I told him that I wanted to see the Chief because my servant and I were fleeing to India. I explained my situation in detail and he said that I could have brought the children had I come a few days earlier, like Surkhang *Shap-pē*'s mother and wife; they had been helped by the Khampas to follow His Holiness's party, which was being escorted by fifty most brave soldiers. 'But never mind,' he added, 'It is wonderful that you yourself have been able to escape. And our Chief is a good man who will certainly give you all the help you need.' When he told me that the Chief had gone to Ramagang Ferry, near Norbu Lingka, I wanted to go back there and asked him to give me an escort; but he advised me not to return to Lhasa when it was so dangerous and promised to help me to see the Chief as soon as he came back. Hearing all his words, I was both glad and sad at the same time.

It was then about ten o'clock in the morning and being

march the weather was still quite cold. Rabge seemed to have a lot of power for he called the headman of Nethang and told him to give me accomdation. The headman said that I could stay at Dolma Lhakhang – a temple I knew, quite far away – but I begged Rabge to let us wait at the headquarters instead; so they gave us a small, bare room downstairs, near the Chief's quarters. On the wall there was a picture of His Holiness, with a scarf on it, and as I was fond of observing indications I said to myself that this meant I would reach India and meet His Holiness again. Then I felt happy.

Tashi went to feed the animals, got hot water and brought me *tsampa*. We waited and waited. The Khampas were very busy; I really did not know what was happening, but the local people were busy too, getting fodder for the Khampas' animals. Several people poked their heads into the little room where Tashi and I were sitting on the floor and when they asked me who I was I told them I was the wife of a junior Army officer. It was a long day and I feared that the Chinese might shell Nethang because it was the Khampa headquarters. Twice Rabge looked in and promised to tell me as soon as the Chief returned – but when night came there was still to sign either of the Chinese or the Chief.

Then, at about nine o'clock in the evening, we heard hundreds of horse-steps and the Chief and his men arrived. I was told they were all wet, after crossing the Kyichu. The Chief sent me a message saying that he had no time to see anyone and that I should be brought immediately – with the three hundred Khampas – to Gongar, where we could meet. I told Rabge that I was worried about Tashi and me being left behind because our animals were poor and the Khampas had very good horses, so he promised to ride slowly beside us.

After riding for five hours under the twinkling stars a Khampa shouted that the Chief would stop at Jangme for a while and the rest were to stop at Jangto; Rabge said he would get accommodation for me there. At the village everyone was ready to receive the Khampas and I was given a small hut, like a cowshed, where I rested for a couple of hours. A villager brought a ladle of tea and poured it into the red enamel mug which had been given to me by the steward's wife at Namka. (My only other possessions were my watch and fountain pen.) I could not sleep; Tashi was outside, looking after our animals.

The cocks were crowing when we all started again; it was still very dark and the Khampas were murmuring prayers or talking to each other. Some asked me who I was so I told them I was the Lady of Taring and the daughter of Tsarong. One asked me where Tsarong *Dzasa* was now; I told him that as far as I knew he was at Shol, below the Potala.

As the sun rose we reached the small town of Chusul, where I was given tea and *tsampa* with the Khampas. I asked Rabge for some fodder for our animals and when they had been fed we continued to Chaksam Ferry, where once Tsarong stopped the Chinese. As we were with the Khampa paymaster we had no difficulty crossing the river; everyone was very polite and they let me into the first boat. Each boat held about twenty men and horses and we were all on the other side within half an hour. Here Chaksam Monastery was above us and a Khampa was shouting to Rabge at the top of his voice, saying that I was to be sent up to the monastery to see the Chief. I climbed up and was given tea but an hour later someone told me to go on to Gongar, as the Chief was after all too busy to see me.

It was a lovely sunny morning as Rabge, Tashi and I rode on, with about sixty Khampas; the rest had dispersed. I wondered all the time about the situation in Lhasa – whether or not Jigme had been killed in that terrible shelling, and if the children, and my very dear mother-in-law, were still alive. There was nothing I could do to help them except pray to Dolma to keep them safe. But I reminded myself that through this cruel aggression of the Chinese I must achieve something spiritual to help Jigme, my children and all who were suffering as we Tibetans were. I thought much about becoming a hermit on the plains of India and said to myself that I had always been a true Buddhist and that advancement towards enlightenment is gained only through pain, not through pleasure. Our scripture says, 'He whose mind is not whetted by lust, he who is not affected by hatred, he who has discarded both good and evil – in such vigilant ones there is no fear!' It is difficult to practise this truly, but having read the scriptures daily helped me to have courage in that hour of despair.

As we rode along the narrow, rocky track, beside the River Kyichu, I could still see the mountains of Lhasa and my heart was there with the children. The Khampas told me that by hiding behind a nearby hill they had been able to shoot at four trucks, full of young Chinese soldiers, and send them falling into the river. The soldiers had surrendered by raising their thumbs, yet they had to be shot without mercy. When a Khampa went to make sure they were all dead he was killed by one who was not dead.

As soon as we had passed the dangerous precipices the Khampas went ahead as fast as their horses could carry them and Tashi and I were left far behind; but Rabge patiently rode along with us. At about three o'clock that afternoon we reached Gongar, where Rabge told me to wait in a village house while he went further on; he assured me that I would be called when the Chief came. Tashi then boiled water, and we had a few potatoes and I drank a mug of weak coffee – I took great care not to use much from my small tin.

While we were waiting, a polite old peasant came to see me. I asked him to sit and he said, 'A black cloud has spread over us.' He told me that when His Holiness was passing, a few days earlier, he had blessed the local people, explained that it was better for him to take flight rather than be arrested by the Chinese and said that he hoped to come back soon. The people believed him but felt very sad. The old man asked my opinion of the situation and I said it was really a miracle how His Holiness had been able to escape so wonderfully, although his palace was surrounded by the Chinese. The man told me he had heard there was a duststorm just as His Holiness left the palace, and he believed the protectors of religion were on guard all the time.

I asked him if there was a road to Pede that avoided Kampa

La, the high pass near Gongar. I had crossed this pass many times and feared to cross it now; at certain places somebody could kill you by throwing you away down the far descending hills and nobody would know anything about it. He told me there was another one, that he always used, and when I asked if he had any mules for sale he said he had one very strong mule which I could see on my way if I stopped a night at his house. I accepted his invitation and offered him one of my potatoes, but he didn't take it. Then I told him about myself and my family and he said, 'All our troubles were caused by these Chinese beggars: what have we done to suffer so much under them?' (Tibetans always called the Chinese 'beggars' behind their backs.) 'I know why your good father and his son were killed.' He shook his head and had much sympathy for me. When I told him how I had left everybody behind in Lhasa he said, 'I do not blame you, *Lhacham*. Come to my house and if you like the mule you can pay me later when His Holiness returns.'

At about six o'clock Rabge called me to the Chief, Changbhu Lhagyal, and as it is our custom not to go empty-handed I brought a scarf that I had managed to borrow. Rabge left me in the kitchen of the headquarters while he went into the room where the Chief was discussing provisions with the *Dzongpon* and instructing his men to go here and there. There were several people in the kitchen but nobody said anything to me as I sat on a dirty, black, greasy hide mat near the door, beside the water-container. All the time my thoughts were with Jigme and the children, but there was no one to tell my heart pains to. While I waited and waited many Khampas and donkey-drivers came in and talked much about the fighting, the Khampas saying that our soldiers were not strong enough to resist the Chinese. Yet they all looked cheeful – talking, laughing, coming in and going out. I kept quite and they just looked at me occasionally. A big pot of *thukpa* (*tsampa* and vegetable soup) was boiled by the Chief's cook, and everybody who came brought out their wooden bowls and took four or five helpings.

I waited for about five hours, somehow having patience. During this time poor Tashi got frightened and came to see me and I told him that I had to wait, because without a letter from Changbhu Lhagyal we could never travel through the country at war. By eleven o'clock the kitchen was becoming quiet, but still Rabge was busy with the Chief. At last the cook said, 'If you want to see the Chief you had better go in now, as most people have left.' I thanked him, entered the room, offered my scarf on the table, saluted and told the Chief that if the Chinese caught me they would certainly throw me into prison and torture me to death.

Changbhu Lhagyal was a nice, gentle man of about thirty-seven. He asked me to sit and congratulated me on my escape, but he was sorry to have to tell me that Taring *Dzasa* was not with His Holiness's party: he had seen the party off, so he knew. He added, I, will gladly give you a letter – from where do you intend to enter India?' I replied 'Bhutan,' and he assured me there were no Chinese on the way but asked, 'Will the Bhutanese let you pass through?' At once Rabge said, 'Yes, they will, because their Prime Minister's wife is Tsarong's daughter and their Queen is Taring *Dzasa*'s cousin.' When I asked for an escort the Chief said that all his men were needed to fight and not one could be spared; he suggested that instead I should join some Khampa lamas with their families, but I refused because they were going too slowly. I begged him to order a villager to guide us and he asked the *Dzongpon* – who was sitting there as if with a *Shap-pē*, all the time bowing his head – to provide a man next morning. Rabge then wrote a letter, requesting all Khampas to help us, and the Chief kindly told me to take care of myself.

It was now midnight and Tashi and I slept for a few hours. I had a woollen rug, given to me by the steward at Namka, but poor Tashi had no bedding yet he never complained. Before dawn he brought some *tsampa*, and hot water for my coffee, and at sunrise we left. Our guide was a nice humble peasant in a white homespun *chuba*, who walked beside me and told me a lot about the region as we travelled. It was a beautiful spring

morning, without wind, and still I could see the faraway hills
of Lhasa. I was fleeing from the Holy City, yet my mind was
haunting it.

This unfamiliar track was very lonely, but not so steep as the
Kampa La road. Lovely brownish shrubs grew on the slopes
and the smell of the azaleas made me very homesick. From the
top of the pass we were happy to see the peaceful lake of
Yamdok; somehow I had imagined that no place could any
longer be at peace. We rode by the lake for miles, meeting no
one but passing one or two villages and seeing many yaks and
sheep grazing contentedly.

That night we stayed at the house of the kind old man who
had a mule for sale. He put us up in the prayer-room, gave us
tsampa to take with us and particularly asked his wife to give
me potatoes, saying, 'The lady seems fond of potatoes,
something that we villagers can give her.' This whole region
around the beautiful lake was wonderfully quiet, with not a
sign of the Chinese anywhere.

The old man insisted on my taking his very strong mule,
which he had bought from a trader for about £50. (Good riding
mules were expensive in Tibet; they all came from Sining, near
the Chinese border, because our own mules were small and
weak.) As I had no money to pay for it he said, 'Leave a receipt
with me – that is the same as leaving gold in the rock. We can
get the money any time.' Now this debt is a burden for me, so
whenever I do a little charitable work I think of the old man
and pray that my earned merits may go to him.

When we left I rode Tashi's mule and Tashi rode the big
mule and my small pony was let loose to follow us. We
travelled by the lake for another fifteen miles and all the time
could see Pede – our next stop – but going round the lake was
not easy. There is a song saying that the eighteen long curves of
the shore approaching Pede are too long to be the life of a man.
On the way we met some Khampas, who paid no attention to
us. All the hills looked brown and the lake was blue and there
were no clouds or wind. We could see Samding Monastery
from afar and near Pede we joined the familiar Kampa La road.

I was now getting frightened of the next stage, so I prayed to Dolma for protection and guidance. Then we were overtaken by an elderly man on a small bay pony and I addressed him politely, asking the way to the local Khampa headquarters. He said it was at Mending House, on an estate leased from the government by the Mending House, on an estate leased from the government by the Mending family, who were not nobility but something like the English yeomanry. We knew this family well and usually stayed there on our journeys, but since the Chief was at Mending I decided to go on to Pede Dekhang, another yeoman estate belonging to people we knew. My heart was beating very fast; yet there was nothing to do but be humble, so we got down from our mules and Tashi led them. On the way we met Mending *Pala*, the head of the Mending house-hold, who at once recognised and saluted me. I was in poor clothes and always had my dentures out near a town, so his eyes filled with tears. He said, 'My Lady, how did you come? What has happened to the rest of your family?' I could not speak a word for some moments, because my throat was blocked. Then I told him how I had become like a fox chased by a hunter, trying to get into every hole, and at last had had to leave Lhasa, after seeing the terrible shelling which left no hope in me of meeting my people again. He advised me to report to the Khampas immediately and settle down for the night. He said, 'Go soon to the headquarters, because the Chief has a short temper and towards evening has nothing else to say, but shoots.' Outside the headquarters a Khampa was standing; I showed him my letter from the Chief at Gongar and told him I would be spending the night at Pede and coming soon to see his Chief. He just nodded his head.

It was then about four o'clock. At Pede Dekhang I was given a small, black, smoky hut and Mending *Pala* brought a pot of tea, a dish of *tsampa*, and grass and grain for our animals. He advised me to see the Chief next morning, when he would be in a better mood. Mending *Pala* told me that his son, an old friend of ours and a disciple of Ani Lochen, was the Chief's secretary, and as we were talking about the terrible shelling in

Lhasa his son came to call me, saying that the Chief, Gojo
Dowa, wanted to see me at once. I felt a little frightened, but
had a feeling that Dolma's protection was there. I gave a
borrowed scarf to Gojo Dowa, humbly saluted him by taking
off my hat and showed him our letter. He welcomed me and
told me to sit. Tea was poured and he said, 'Haven't you
brought your children?' We will certainly give our best service
to all Tibetan officials and their families.' How I wished then
that I had brought even one grandchild, to hand over to my
daughter in India! But fate did not allow this. Gojo Dowa gave
me another letter, asked if I had any food or money and
offered me both. He also where I would be stopping next and
when I said, 'Nangatse and Talung Monastery' he told me that
he, too, would be following this route and wished to meet me
again.

Next morning we set off on the trade road and met many
Khampas and caravans of mules and donkeys. We reached
Nangatse at about ten o'clock and stopped to have breakfast in
a villager's courtyard. After a while Gojo Dowa also arrived
and called me again to ask if I needed any more help and to
wish me a safe journey. On my return to our shelter I saw three
horse-men approaching and excited villagers hurrying to greet
them. I found that one was the Abbot of Talung Monastery,
Jigme's cousin Thubtenla. He recognised me at once and gave
me much respect, which surprised the villagers, who immediately let me into their prayer-room. Thubenla had come to
meet the Khampas; he told me to wait at his monastery, about
fifteen miles away, until he returned next day and sent one of
his own servants with us to show the way.

Talung Monastery looked like a small Potala, for it stood on
a high rocky hill. Thubtenla's room was right at the top and
from his window one could see all over the beautiful countryside, so quiet and peaceful. Next day I prayed at the shrines but
was worried because Thubtenla did not come. When he came
on the following day and urged me to rest longer, I explained
that I was anxious to continue because the Chinese could

appear from either Lhasa or Shigatse. I warned him to be careful, because if they did come the monks would have to flee.

Before I left, Gojo Dowa arrived and called me again, just to ask if I was all right. The monks gave me food, and new boots for Tashi, and Thubtenla lent me six hundred *sangs* (about £6) and packed a saddle-bag with candles, sugar, tea, dried meat and *tsampa*. He insisted on sending one of his young monk-stewards, Jigdrol, and a syce with me to the Bhutanese border. I did not want to take them, though I knew they would be useful, because I was anxious about what might happen to them; but Thubtenla said, 'How can I let you go in such a poor condition, with only one servant?'

During the next week I often told Jigdrol and the syce to go back, but they refused to listen. On the second day after leaving Talung a group of Khampas stopped us and said they had orders to allow no one to go in the direction of His Holiness's flight. We begged and begged, and because Jigdrol was a monk of Talung at last they let us go on.

Next day, we met some of the soldiers of His Holiness's body-guard and they, too, were determined to sent us back. I asked who was their captain and when they said, '*Gyapon* Soté,' I told them that he had been one of my husband's machine-gun students and asked to see him. (He was the young soldier who once nearly killed Ngodup Wangmo.) Soté was very happy to meet me again and told us that he and his men had seen His Holiness safely into India and were now on guard against the Chinese. I asked if Jigme was with His Holiness and he said 'No' — but assured me that he felt Taring *Dzasa*, with his many skills, would be safe. He added that they were especially glad to see me because they feared I might have stayed at Gyatso, which had by now been shelled to ashes. Soté gave me another letter, in case I should meet with more obstacles, and I gave each of the soldiers a piece of Ani Lochen's dress to protect them from bullets. I knew one of the old soldiers very well because he was particularly good at taking care of cups and crockery at Lhasa parties. Soon after our meeting these soldiers fought a big battle at Lhuntse Dzong and killed many Chinese. Only two of our men were killed; the rest escaped to India through Bhutan.

At some villages on our way they said that a Chinese aeroplane had passed over, probably looking for His Holiness. Everybody was terribly sad, because our country was now overshadowed by such bad clouds.

After travelling for six days, and crossing about nine high mountain passes, we reached Lhodak, a small village with the famous nine-storied temple that Milarepa was ordered to build by his teacher Marpa. Before Marpa would give him the teaching Milarepa had to undo his building work again and again until his back became sore from carrying stones – because he had been a very sinful person. I was deeply happy to see this temple, since I had read so many of Milarepa's poems and thought so much about his teaching. I spent an hour praying and then we continued to the village of Longdong, near the foot of the Monla Kachung, an eighteen-thousand-foot high glacier pass near the Bhutanese border. Normally this difficult pass was used only in summer and early autumn, but it was our shortest route to Bhutan.

We stayed in a hut for the night and a poor woman came and gave me three lovely eggs. She said she came originally from Lhasa and knew our family. The villagers told me that I was very unlucky; had I come two days earlier I could have joined the party of the High Lama, Gyalwa Karmapa, who was travelling with about eighty companions and had a hundred yaks to carry luggage and trample a way through the thick snow that was completely blocking the pass. We were warned about the dangerous cracks in the snow – some thirty or forty feet deep – which one could easily drop into by mistake. The villagers said that loaded yaks often dropped into them and nothing could be done to rescue them or their loads until summer. Then men would be lowered on ropes into the cracks and the frozen carcase – which was eaten – and the valuable loads of salt or rice were drawn up. We heard that the weather had been good when Karmapa crossed, but now another blizzard had covered the track and everybody said it would be impossible to cross without many yaks to clear a way. Yet I was determined to cross, whatever happened; it would have been too dangerous to try any other route, with the Chinese all over the place, and since Karmapa's party had crossed so recently I had more hope of succeeding.

I offered one hundred *sangs* to any man who would guide us and a villager at once volunteered to come, because the usual payment was only about twenty *sangs*. Here I again asked Jigdrol and his friend to return to Talung, as I was so worried about them, but they said that Thubtenla had asked them to see me right into Bhutan.

At about two next morning we left Longdong, our kind guide walking beside my mule. It was bitterly cold and we crossed several streams of solid ice. I just could not walk to warm my feet because the climb was so steep and the track so rough.

At sunrise we reached the foot of the Monla Kachang and stopped to rest. All of us were now frozen through, so Tashi and Jigdrol picked dried sticks and made a fire. The sky was absolutely blue, with not a spot of cloud, and looking down towards Longdong the brownish hills had many shrubs. On our left was the great snow mountain, with its pass that is 4,000 feet higher than the highest mountain in Europe, and not a sign of the track up – yet we had to climb it without making mistakes and falling into those horrible cracks. We were all very much afraid that here the Chinese might overtake us. But I felt thankful for the great help that had been given me on the way and for being safe up to this spot.

While we were sitting by the fire we heard bells and saw six yaks and two men coming down from the pass. When we asked them how the way was they said it was so terribly dangerous that they had had to come down very slowly. I begged them to use their yaks to help us to cross, but they said that having just been over, to give service to Karmapa, the yaks were exhausted and they themselves were longing to get home. I offered them one hundred *sangs* if they would help us to see the summit and after much persuasion one of them agreed to come, but the other took the yaks down.

When we started this frightful climb there was no track to be seen. Sometimes I stumbled into new snow that went above my knees, and once I fell into such a deep drift that I had to be pulled out by the others. I soon felt it would be impossible for me ever to get to the top, though being a Tibetan I suffered no discomfort from the altitude. The weather was perfect and luckily there was no wind; a blizzard would have been fatal. Tashi and Jigdrol pulled and dragged the mules and our guide dragged me up, while the yak-driver went ahead, prodding the deep snow with a stick to find the rough track. It was like being in a cup, and the white snow on every side hit our eyes. It took six hours to get to the top and I prayed every minute and felt very grateful that we were getting so much protection. During those hours I thought constantly of Jigme and the children.

At last we were on the summit and I shall never forget how beautiful it was there, overlooking Bhutan. All around us for many miles was nothing but pure snow. Away in the far distance were hills with less snow and thick forests; but we could see no way to go down.

Here I told Jigdrol and the syce that the time had come for them to leave me and return to Tibet; so they went back with the yak-driver.

On the summit I felt much relief, because we were now in Bhutan – but even more sadness, since we had left our own country behind us.

19 Delay in Bhutan

GOING DOWN FROM the summit Tashi looked after the mules—we had had to leave my poor little pony behind at Talung—and our guide took my hand while we walked through the spotless snow, sometimes falling into drifts, but hoping for the best. The guide said that we must spend the night in a cave he knew of, as it had begun to snow heavily and we could never find a house before dark. At sunset we reached the cave; it was large, but one could not stand upright in it so the mules had to stay outside in the deep snow. Tashi gave me my rug and I lay on it while he and the guide went to fetch sticks from far away. A fire was made in the cave and between the smoke and the snow-glare of the day our eyes were red and watering and very sore. The night was extremely cold and passed slowly. I sat up and prayed hard for the safe return home of Jigdrol and the syce. (Soon after, Thubtenla and Jigdrol fled from Tibet together and I was very glad they had not been separated through helping me). Poor Tashi had nothing extra to wear; we usually wore the saddle-blankets but now the animals had to be kept covered. My feet were completely numb and Tashi's boot-soles were cracking, but at least we three were inside the cave. It made me very sad to see the poor mules outside, covered with snow and suffering.

Before sunrise we left the cave and our guide went home, after advising us to keep to the left all the time. Tashi gave me a stick to help me walk and went ahead with the mules, looking back often to see that I was all right. I can never repay the kindness of this faithful servant, who spoke nothing on the road except to say, 'What can have happened to *Kungo*?' because he was always worrying over Jigme. He had left his wife and children behind, but he never said a word about them. It is my karma that I was able to bring such a loyal friend with me.

As we came down, soil and trees gradually replaced the snow and at about three o'clock we saw some mules grazing in the forest and a few empty huts. I said to Tashi that we might have to spend the night there because I was getting very tired. As we rested two men drove yaks up the track and told us they were on their way back to Longdong, after escorting Gyalwa Karmapa over the pass. When we asked how far the Bhutanese military barracks were they said only about three miles away, at Tsampa, and told us that the grazing mules belonged to Karmapa who was camping near the barracks.

So Tashi and I continued down, through a valley full of little trees, with patches of snow between them, until we saw the small, two-storied house where the frontier guards lived in summer and autumn, when the pass was open. We found that the caretaker was a Tibetan and some of Karmapa's servants were sitting around a nice fire. The many tents of the great lama's camp could be seen on the other side of the river and I asked when Karmapa himself would be going down, but the servants said that first Bhutanese soldiers were coming up to discuss the situation.

Gyalwa Karmapa is the head of the Karmapa sect, which is a sub-sect of Kagyupa, and since the Sikkimese and Bhutanese are Kagyupa they respect him greatly. He comes from a Khampa family and ranks next to the Dalai Lama and equal to the Sakya Lama. He and his followers have now built a monastery in Sikkim and he visits Bhutan regularly.

I begged the caretaker to give us a corner to sleep in but he explained that he had no authority to do so. He said, 'The soliders will arrive at any moment and you can ask them!' My long boots and the ends of my clothes were soaking wet, so I took off my boots and tried to dry them by the fire. Tashi kindly boiled water and I had taken such good care of my precious tin of coffee that I was still able to have a little taste of it.

Before it was dark twenty Bhutanese foot-soldiers came, with their captain on a mule. He went straight upstairs but I followed him to ask permission to sleep in the barracks. When I told him that I was the aunt of his Prime Minister's wife he agreed to my staying in the little hall, but insisted that I must go back to Tibet next day because the Bhutanese government was not at present admitting Tibetans for fear of Bhutan also getting into trouble with China. He said that he and his men had been sent to guard the frontier and to request Karmapa to return to Tibet, so I explained that as the Chinese were killing many important Tibetans and thousands of others we could never return. When he replied that he had to obey orders and send us all back I told him that I would choose to be shot by the Bhutanese rather than tortured by the Chinese. I said, 'We Tsarongs gave our daughter to Bhutan and when I came here I had no doubt you would help.' After much talk he said he had to see Karmapa, so I sat in a corner in the dark hall with a number of Karmapa's servants while Tashi went out to attend to our mules. He had been told there was poisonous grass in the forest so he was afraid to let them graze and we used some of Thubtenla's money to buy rice for them.

I felt very much worried, but was absolutely determined to remain in Bhutan, even if we were to be shot. The servants were noisy, going in and out, but after hearing who I was they were quite polite, which was some consolation. Tashi wanted to light a candle, but I told him I preferred staying in the dark. At about ten o'clock more servants arrived and I overheard them talking about Karmapa having been asked to return to Tibet. One of them said, 'In peacetime our Gyalwa was often invited to Bhutan yet now, at this critical time of our difficulty, they wish us to leave. But Karmapa has decided to go down tomorrow, whether given permission or not.' At this I became even more anxious, and could not sleep all night.

At dawn I again went to the captain, and asked permission to go down with Karmapa's party. He said, 'The Gyalwa is determined to go and I don't think we can stop him. But I asked his secretary about you and he told me that though you are the Lady of Taring you are not in their party, so I must send you back.' I then begged him so hard that he finally relented and said that if Karmapa agreed to my joining his party I could go down. Having thanked him, I told Tashi to saddle our mules, get ready to leave and wait by the river.

At Karmapa's camp all the tents were packed. Karmapa was sitting on the ground, but instead of going direct to him I went to his secretary who said how wonderful it was that I had been able to come all by myself with only one servant; the Tsarong and Taring families have great faith in Karmapa and we often met his party in Peking. He enquired after Jigme and I told my sad story of leaving Lhasa after seeing the horrible shelling. Karmapa's party had left their monastery as soon as they heard of the Dalai Lama's flight.

When I was taken to Karmapa I prostrated three times and received his blessings; he was as calm and friendly as usual. With a nice smile he said he was glad to see me and he, too, at once asked about Jigme. I told him everything and he was very sorry and agreed to my joining his party. We left a few minutes later and I walked beside Karmapa's horse so nobody tried to stop me. Although the soldiers had been compelled to convey their government's order to Karmapa they really worshipped him and would never have considered using force against him; as we passed they were all there on the road, burning incense and prostrating. I was so grateful not to have been delayed another day as I would then have been held up for a month at least.

Our way was so steep that we had to go down very slowly and carefully; in many places there was no track and we were just scrambling over natural rock. All the riding-animals were led by servants, since it was impossible to go on horseback. Sometimes the ponies and mules had to jump boulders two or three feet high and they often tumbled but we carried on as best we could. We walked for fourteen hours the first day and for sixteen hours the second day; as I had lost twenty pounds since leaving Lhasa I found it not too difficult to walk. For the first three or four hours of the descent we could see snow here and there in the shade of the thick forest on either side and sometimes we met very high, strong waterfalls. Karmapa was extremely kind; whenever he stopped I was called and given tea. At the end of the first day it became so dark that we could hardly see the track, but we had to keep going until we reached the village of Nangsig.

Next evening about ten o'clock we got to Shabje Thang (meaning 'Plain of Footprints'), where it is said that Padmasmabhawa left many footprints on rocks. As we approached the village, crowds of Bhutanese were coming up to greet Karmapa with big fires in their hands. They had put oily rags on sticks and at first these huge lights helped us a lot on the rough road, but eventually I was no longer near the Gyalwa and could see nothing. We heard monastic trumpets being blown and everybody hurried ahead. When Tashi and I got to the village, long after the rest, we did not know where to go, so we called at the house of the late headman's widow who kindly showed me into a dirty little room where she said I could stay, as her prayer-room was full of Karmapa's servants. The Bhutanese have a sweet-smelling oily wood, which they burn instead of candles or lamps, and I was given a stick of this to light my room. Tashi said that he would sleep outside, by our mules, and after saying my prayers I went to sleep.

Next morning I saw that we were in a beautiful place, surrounded by pine-covered hills. My hostess's house had quite a big living-room where the whole family slept around the hearth. The structure was good, because Bhutan has abundant wood, but the furniture was poor; in the prayer-room there was just a black chest, a wooden altar and a few images.

Beside this house was a nice little temple, where Karmapa

stayed for a week. Many Bhutanese came to see him and when I went to pay homage he asked if I needed anything but I said, 'No.'

My dirty, black room contained about twenty sacks of rice on which I sat, near a small window. Every day Tashi brought my *tsampa* and a mug of tea in the morning, rice at midday and whatever was left over in the evening. (Karmapa had sent us a small bag of rice and we still had some dried meat and Tibetan tea.) From the temple, where there were many religious books, I borrowed a beautiful work called *The Will of Kunsang Lama* which made me very happy. It taught all about life and how every living being has to suffer. This teaching was based on the Four Truths – the existence of sorrow, the cause of sorrow, the cessation of sorrow and the way which leads to the cessation of sorrow. I was again reminded that one cannot escape one's sorrows – 'Whatsoever is originated will be dissolved. All worry about self is vain.'

I read and read; the days were long, but my wonderful hostess came to see me often. She was poor in possessions, yet rich in spirit. She consoled me by saying that, as I was the aunt of the Prime Minister's wife, I should not worry since only patience was needed. She assured me that if Karmapa's party left she would put me in the prayer-room, but I told her that I was content where I was. She had a married son and two pretty married daughters, who often came to see her. They have a nice way of living in the east of Bhutan, with a very happy family life.

After a week I heard that Karmapa had received an invitation from the King's aunt, who was his disciple, to visit one of her palaces; then he was to be allowed to proceed to India. I tried to leave with him, but the soldiers stopped me, saying that I must remain at Shabje Thang and might yet be sent back to Tibet. I did not pay much attention to their threat and was content to stay in this village because it was such a nice place, with plenty of books to read, and we had enough food and fodder. Every day Tashi went into the forest and collected good grass for our mules.

Before Karmapa left I asked him to request the King's aunt – or anyone who could help – to let me pass through to India, which he promised to do and said he was sorry I could not accompany his party. Three days later he sent me a letter, saying that the King's aunt had no authority to let me through, and I appreciated this kind letter very much.

After eight days in the filthy little room I was given the prayer-room – which was also filthy, but Tashi swept it well. There was no mat, so during the day I sat on my precious rug. From the windows the country looked beautiful, with a little waterfall nearby where I used to go to wash every morning. After finishing *The Will of Kunsang Lama* I borrowed Milarepa's poems and these, too, were full of good teaching which helped me a lot. One of them tells us that our meetings and partings are inevitable and this made me realise the Truth that people cannot be together for ever. So I consoled myself for another month, although my thoughts were mostly with Jigme and the children.

We Tibetans consider Milarepa everything that a great saint should be. He was born in A.D. 1052, near Kirong on the Tibetan – Nepalese frontier. His father was a wealthy merchant who died when Milarepa was small, leaving the boy – named Thopaga, meaning 'Delightful to Hear' – and his mother in the care of an uncle and aunt. Instead of caring for them, this couple plundered all their possessions, made them work like slaves, gave them the poorest food and kept them in rags so that they became numb. They often beat Thopaga and both he and his mother suffered so much that at last she forced him to learn magic spells, and with them he was able to take revenge by destroying his uncle and aunt and bringing much disaster on their village. Later he went to seek the Truth and met Marpa, the Great Translator, who would not give him the teachings until he had abolished his sins by the terrible physical pain he suffered for six or eight months, while building the temple at Lhodak.

During the weeks that I waited at Shabje Thang I gained much understanding of religion through finding so many precious books and having time to concentrate on them. I appreciated what a great opportunity this was to realise the teaching of the Lord Buddha, through the grief that I was enduring. Now I could see for myself that all things are impermanent. I thought of our beautiful possessions and of how hard we had tried to accumulate wealth. Yet when the time came, according to our karma, for us to part with everything – even our children – it happened just like that. Now the pain was making me think much and I understood that one must come to the state where one is meant to be. Although children are born to us they each have their own karma and must bear it alone. I feel that parents are like fruit trees, from which the fruit is separated when it ripens.

I had a very quick temper when I was young, but was able to improve through the goodness of my sister-in-law, Rigzin Choden, who advised me that one's temper must be controlled and that this could be achieved through prayer and practice. Then, when I married Jigme, everybody in his family was so good-natured that I had no cause to get into tempers; and he himself has no bad temper, which also helped. In later years, I closely studied the Lord Buddha's teachings, which say that there is no better virtue than controlling one's temper and that a bad temper can destroy in a second all the earned merit of a life-time.

At Shabje Thang I experienced the reality of the Lord Buddha's teaching that only love can conquer hatred, that goodwill towards all being is the essence of religion and that we must trust in the Truth – which is best as it is, though it may be bitter and we may not be able to understand it. I saw that Self is a transient vision and that the way to real happiness is the path of unselfishness. I found that my own suffering could be lessened by thinking of the sufferings of others.

I made many notes from the books I was reading and some of the villagers reported to their headman that, 'The couple in the house of Tongsa *Tsonpon* [the name of my host] are not a couple, but the woman is mysterious – the whole day putting down something in a book. And it seems she is much superior to the man.' So the headman of Shabje Thang came to see me.

He was quite polite – but he had to do his duty. I asked him to sit and he sat on the floor, too, while Tashi stood. He asked me to show my papers, looked at them and said, 'Are these all your own writing?' When I answered, 'Yes,' he pretended to be amazed and explained that he would have to take them away to show to the higher authorities. He called for a lump of sealing-wax, sealed them up in my presence and said they would be returned soon. Before leaving he said that during this critical time it was his duty to be strict to all who came into Bhutan and he took my permission to search Tashi. Tashi undid his belt and showed the empty purse which was round his waist. Nothing was what poor Tashi had, so the headman left with much courtesy. My papers were returned to me several days later, still sealed.

While we were at Shabje Thang my hostess, Ama Dorje, and her sister were building a new house. The Bhutanese have a very nice system; neighbours give labour service to each other, going into the forest to get wood for building and then all helping to put the house together. Only food is provided for these workers but sometimes they are entertained to a party and then everybody stays late, dancing, singing and drinking by the fire. At these parties Tashi and I were always given food along with the guests. I was unable to manage their very greasy curry and rice but Tashi enjoyed himself, with greasy lips. He had an enormous appetite. I used to ask, 'Tashi, how can you digest such food?' He would say nothing, but smile a bit.

At last I wrote to Their Majesties and to the Prime Minister but my letters were returned with a message saying that no mail was being allowed through. Then we saw many soldiers going up to the frontier and coming down, and we heard that hundreds of refugees were at Tsampa and that the government had not yet decided whether to admit them or not. One day a letter from Thubtenla was handed to me, by one of the soldiers, and it said that he had come to Tsampa with some of his monks and that Jigme had been seen in the south, fleeing. This I just could not believe.

Soon thousands of refugees had accumulated at Tsampa; they were starving, but still had no permission to come down.

The Bhutanese soldiers were afraid of the Khampas making their own way down and, though the villagers had full sympathy for us, they were terrified of being looted if the Khampas did come. Poor things, these villagers were not rich at all and it was pathetic to see them hiding their little treasures, like aluminium bowls and copper plates. The monk in charge of the temple was also hiding the precious religious books under rocks. I guaranteed that the Khampas would not loot, even if they forced their way down, but nobody would believe me – and I don't blame them. Eventually the Khampas very nearly did make their own way down and were only controlled by the influence of the Sakya Lama and some of our high officials. Then suddenly, before it was too late, permission was given for all the refugees to come down.

I at once sent a Bhutanese messenger to Kalimpong to ask my niece, Tsering Yangzom, and Rani Dorje (Jigme's aunt) to help me to get to India quickly. I was very weak, and daily getting weaker, because I had been so ill just before leaving Lhasa, though I had forgotten my illness in the terrible worry. About two weeks later a Bhutanese official came to Ama Dorje's house to tell me that the government would take care of me and very soon I would get good news. I could hardly believe him but after two days, to my great joy, I received a letter in English from the Prime Minister, Jigme Dorje:

> My dear Mary La,
>   I hear you are in Bhutanese territory. I am so sorry that you have had to bear a lot of hardship. I will be up there to greet you in a few days' time. I shall bring you down with me. I am sending you some *tsampa*, sugar and tea – very little, because I am in a hurry and my pack mules have not arrived. Do not worry. I hope to be there in three days' time.
>   Yours, Jigme Dorje.

I was very happy, yet now I wished more than ever that I had been able to bring just one of Tseyang's children who could soon have been handed over to Jigme Dorje. Tashi must also have been feeling very happy though as usual he remained calm and quiet.

We settled down to wait for Jigme Dorje but next morning a soldier came with two mules and a message asking me to ride down to Bumthang. It was sad leaving Ama Dorje and her family. We thanked them heartily and gave them the remainder of our Tibetan tea and dried meat. Later, I used to send Ama Dorje parcels from India whenever I could, but in 1966 a letter came from one of her daughters saying that she had died. She was a truly wonderful person and I felt that I had lost a real friend.

When Tashi and the Bhutanese soldier left Shabje Thang I went to the temple to pray; but I soon overtook them because a good mule, well-saddled, had been sent up for me.

20   Our Life as Exiles

THE WEATHER WAS perfect as the soldier, Tashi and I rode down the beautiful valley, which became wider and wider every mile. After a few hours we suddenly saw in the distance many horsemen coming down a steep hill ahead. 'This is the Prime Minister's party,' said the soldier, and as they drew nearer Jigme Dorje waved his hat at me. We greeted each other with great joy and sat on saddle-mats for about half an hour, talking. He told me that he had heard that Jigme and Tsarong were somewhere on the Assam border, and his wife, Tsering Yangzom (Tsarong's daughter), was very much worried and wanted to go to look for her father. He said that Tseyang was also terribly worried, and added that His Majesty the King had given him permission to look after me, and had asked him to go and offer every assistance to our Commander-in-Chief, Kungsangtse *Dzasa*, and Kunsangtse *Tsipon*, the Commander-in-Chief's brother-in-law, who were friends of the King's father. He asked me to wait for him at the small town of Bumthang and look after the Kunsangtses when he sent them down. His large mule-caravan was carrying food for the refugees and he himself was going up to greet them and tell them that they could go through to India, where a camp was being set up for them at Misamari.

Bumthang is in a wide and lovely valley; I stayed at the comfortable rest house and my food was sent from the house of Dasho Ugen, the King's brother-in-law. After five days the refugees began to pour down; most of them were poor peasants from regions near the border but among them were the Kunsangtses, the Sakya Lama and his family, Dorje Phagmo, the Abbess of Samding Monastery and others for whom accommodation had been arranged by order of the Prime Minister. When I met the Kunsangtses they were looking so haggard and sad that I could not speak for some moments. They, too, had left their families – wives, children and grandchildren – behind. The Commander-in-Chief told me that he had heard from someone reliable that Jigme was fleeing and that I should be meeting him soon. *Tsi-pon* Shakabpa's daughter and her children also came down; she had carried her baby on her back over that huge pass. Their estate was two days' ride from Lhasa and her husband – who had been in Norbu Lingka during the shelling – had afterwards crossed the river, collected his mother, younger brother, wife and children and fled. I thought he was really a hero.

When Jigme Dorje returned from Tsampa he advised me to see the King's aunt, Her Highness Ashi Chodon, who would be coming to Bumthang next day. As he had been educated in Darjeeling he could not read Tibetan much, though it was his own language, so he asked me to translate a letter that the refugees had received from the Chinese at Longdong. (They had arrived at Longdong very soon after I left.) It requested those Tibetans who had entered Bhutan to return home, pointed out that they would suffer a lot through becoming slaves of the Bhutanese and promised that if they came back, with a scarf tied on a stick, they would be forgiven their mistake and not punished. Nobody went back.

Next day Her Highness Ashi Chodon, accompanied by about ten servants, arrived riding a beautiful mule with a lovely brocade saddle-mat. Within an hour she sent me a tray of tea and iced cakes and on the following day received me in a very nice room where she was sitting on the shiny wooden floor on a thin mat. (The Bhutanese nobility have clean, simple houses.) She was deeply sorry about the Chinese usurping our country and apologised for all the hardship I had endured at the frontier. She told me to get anything I needed from her and after my return to the rest-house she sent new shoes, socks and underwear. Jigme Dorje said that he got a scolding from Her Highness for leaving me in such poor clothes. 'But,' he added, 'I couldn't very well give you my clothes.'

A wireless station had been set up in a bamboo hut at Bumthang and next day Jigme Dorje came quickly into my room, shouting 'Mary La, Jigme has arrived safely in Mussoorie!' I just got up and put my arms around him. I realised that this was the result of the prayer for Jigme's protection that I had said every day during our long years together – and also of the prayers of our beloved children. Jigme Dorje and I then sat on the floor, while Tashi remained standing; he was so happy that his eyes were full of tears, though as usual he said nothing. I could not cry.

Jigme Dorje and I talked for some time and in spite of having had such wonderful news I was saddened to hear that no one knew what had happened to Tsarong. The rumour that he had left Lhasa with Jigme now proved to be untrue.

I sent a wireless message to Jigme, telling what an indescribable relief it was to have heard of his escape, and how full of joy I felt, and saying that I also was safe and well. A few hours later Jigme Dorje brought me a letter that Jigme had sent him from Mussoorie, asking him to look out for me and saying that he feared I might have been left behind or killed. When I saw his handwriting it gave me the same feeling of happiness as seeing his own face. Yet the teaching of Milarepa had moved me so much that I was still thinking of the final parting that must come sooner or later and I knew that Jigme too would have the same feelings. I said to myself that after meeting him once again, with his blessing and my own effort I should seek truth in solitude on the plains.

When I saw so many refugees bringing their children with them, often on their backs, it pained my heart to think of our children left behind. Yet the circumstances may have been different and there was nothing to do but think of our own karma. I found later that the majority of the refugees had had to separate from their families.

During the ten days we spent at Bumthang streams of refugees passed through on their way to Misamari. It was heartbreaking to see them — old and young, monks and nuns, peasants, nomads and small traders, all carrying whatever new possessions they had been able to bring over that high pass on their backs. Some were looking very sick and tired, but some were cheerful. At Bumthang our two mules were fed with the Prime Minister's animals and when we left, on 8 May 1959, they were looking much better.

For fifteen days I rode towards Kalimpong, together with the Kunsangtses, the Sakya Lama's party, Dorje Phagmo, and Shakabpa's daughter and her family. Jigme Dorje sent a guide with us, and two soldiers to carry the Shakabpa babies. Every evening we met the Sakya Lama, his beautiful wife and their three lovely little sons. The local people always came to pay homage to the Lama and brought him rice and eggs, which he shared with us. He had a Murphy radio set with him and each evening I was asked to listen to the English news and translate it. He also had a set of injections with him and when he gave people penicillin injections I helped him to boil the needles.

Now that I was safely through I worried all the more about those left behind. So many changes of thought came to me — sometimes I hoped that through some mediator we might go back soon; at other times I felt, 'How can we live with the Chinese? Unless we get our independence we can never go back.'

From Shabje Thang I had sent a messenger to Kalimpong and near Tongsa Dzong I met him on his return journey. We had left the main track to pay homage to Karmapa, who was staying nearby, and on our way back we met him at the junction — a minute later we would have missed him. He was carrying a big box on his back and I remember that it was drizzling a bit as I dismounted and took the letters he had for me from Tseyang, Namgyal, Tsering Yangzom, Rani Dorje and Dudul Namgyal. When I read these letters I felt so sad that I could not speak for a while. Tsering Yangzom had sent me bed-sheets, towels, knickers, socks, shoes, soap, tea, coffee, sugar, biscuits, fish, condensed milk, soup and oats. And for Tashi she had sent an outfit of clothes. To me, the towels and soap were the best things; I went straight to the river and had a luxurious bath. Yet every time my situation improved I missed my children more.

Up to Thimbu we spent the nights either in bamboo huts or in tents, but at Tongsa Dzong we stayed in a small rest-house overhanging the river; it was so small that I let the ten men sleep in the room and I slept on the verandah, using my new bed-sheets to shield myself. Through the cracks in the verandah wall I could see the water of the river bubbling and jumping only a few feet away.

In Bhutan villages are few, the tracks are very steep and many leeches cling to both people and animals. The mountains have great waterfalls and are covered by pine-trees and beautiful red and white rhododendrons. We often saw deer. There were some good rest-houses and whenever we came to an estate the nobility treated us well. We crossed many small passes and finally a high, lonely one called Tala. At the small frontier village of Jaigong we met a local Bhutanese official who told me that Tseyang and Tsering Yangzom were waiting to meet me at the rest-house.

When we met at last they both tried their best not to show sadness – and I just managed to greet them with a smile. There I left my friends and went on into India with my daughter and niece. Before leaving Jaigong I handed our two mules over to the Prime Minister's syce, to be kept with Jigme Dorje's riding animals; I knew that he would always be kind to them. Many of the refugees sold their mules and ponies to the Bhutanese for high prices but, though our mules were valuable, I just could not bear to sell them because we owed them so much. I can never forget the hardship they suffered – their flanks heaving and pouring sweat as we climbed the high mountains, then our long night in the snow with no food, then their poor mouths and eyes bitten by leeches in the forests of Bhutan. Tashi hardly rode his mule and I always walked on the worst bits of track, but I had to ride most of the way because my legs could not carry me fast enough. Even now, those two mules are always remembered in my prayers.

At the little town of Harshimar, Tsering Yangzom had a Chinese engineer friend, who had lived for years in India and was then employed by the Bhutanese government, and we stayed the night at his house where I told the girls my story in detail. The feeling I had was very strange – I just could not cry. Later, I learned that before we met Tseyang nearly became mad with worry about her children; but when she heard that Jigme and I had reached the border safely she felt so thankful that she made up her mind not to worry any more. She never did complain about the fate of her children who were left in my care. Poor Tseyang – she keeps her sorrows in her heart.

We went to Siliguri by train and then drove up to Kalimpong. There I spent a month at Tsering Yangzom's most beautiful house, meeting many friends, resting, praying, and wandering in the garden – but I felt sad because Jigme did not come immediately to see me. As usual, he was busy giving help to His Holiness; yet he wrote often and told me exactly what he was doing at Mussoorie where he had been put in charge of all the food rations for the whole party with His Holiness. There were very few who spoke English and he had to stay there until things were organised.

As soon as we got to Kalimpong, Tashi told me that he must go back to Tibet because whatever happened he couldn't stay away from his wife and seven children. I begged him to remain in India and promised to look after him like my own son, but was only able to hold him back for a month. Before he left he gave me his gold earring and asked me to sell it and use the money to help the refugees. Later on, his brother came to India and told me that Tashi got safely back to Lhasa, having stopped in Dopta on the way, to see his mother – who died soon afterwards. We have heard no more news of him.

While I was in Kalimpong news was brought to Tsering Yangzom that Tsarong had died, on 14 May 1959, in a Lhasa prison. When the Chinese stopped shelling Lhasa they arrested him and many other officials at the Potala, and imprisoned him and gave him hard work to do—which he was not afraid of because he loved working. One of his fellow-prisoners was Dromo Geshe Rinpoche, a High Lama who was eventually able to get to India—through the efforts of his many devoted followers—because he was the son of a Sikkimese nobleman. Dromo Geshe Rinpoche told me that in the prison he used to serve Tsarong with his morning drink of hot water and Tsarong always advised him to work hard. The prison food was terrible, yet everybody had to do a full day's labour. One day the Chinese ordered Tsarong's servants to humiliate him next morning, but when morning came he did not turn up to work as usual—so another high official went to wake him and found the old hero dead in his bed. His body was then handed over to his sister, Tsering Dolma.

We felt very sad when we heard this news. Tsarong always seemed able to make each of his children feel that they were his special pet and my daughter Tsering Yangzom was heart-broken but she was very brave.

On 13 June Jigme took some leave and came to Kalimpong and we spent a month together. He looked strange with his hair cut short; he handed me a bunch of his long hair which I still have. When I asked him why he had cut his hair, since he used to be so against the idea, he explained that it was too difficult to look after long hair in the heat of India. (Though he knew how to plait his own hair I usually did it up in Lhasa and it was very troublesome.) His hearing had been affected by the appalling sound of the shells falling all around him at Norbu Lingka and we both felt that he had been protected because he is such a selfless person and would give up his life for His Holiness and the people of Tibet; he really and truly cared more for the cause than for his own family. If I had not realised the purity of his devotion I would have got very fed up with him for always putting His Holiness before his own wife and children. He told me that when he reached India he was terribly worried about his mother and the children, but then he prayed, and believed that the Truth would also protect them, in some way.

During his flight Jigme had a much worse time than I had, though he told me I had lost a great deal of weight since we parted. After leaving me at Gyatso he had returned to Norbu Lingka for a couple of days, to help give the impression that His Holiness was still there. When the shelling started he got the official ciné-camera from one of His Holiness's personal attendants and took many pictures, but unfortunately the camera was given to a junior official whom he never met again. He saw His Holiness's stable being shelled, the ponies in great agony with their guts out and the poor ducks killed on the small lake. He also saw many people being injured and tried to console them, but when there was no more hope of resisting he decided to run away and exchanged his fur hat for an ordinary soldier's balaclava and got a rifle from a junior officer who did not know how to handle it. His only other possessions, when he fled, were a camera, some films, a pair of binoculars and a revolver. As he left Norbu Lingka by the north gate the shelling was going on terribly. Just before leaving Norbu Lingka he met Pasang Dondup, who had been a shepherd on Taring Estate before joining the Army. Jigme asked him if he would like to accompany him on the flight and Pasang said, 'Yes,' and got permission from his captain. He walked fifty feet behind Jigme and to avoid being tortured by the Chinese they made a pact that if either of them was hit by a shell the injured one should be shot dead. Shells were whizzing through the air without stopping and bullets cracking continually, yet they had to risk crossing the big marsh, about three hundred yards wide, near Norbu Lingka. The crossing was very difficult; as Jigme was wearing half-length boots the mud got into them. At the other side they climbed a thirteen-thousand-foot mountain pass; from the top Jigme looked through his binoculars and saw the Potala being hit, Kundeling Monastery in flames and our own house badly damaged by shells. He knew that Mother-in-law and the children were there, yet could do nothing but pray.

He and Pasang went east towards Gyama and one night met Khampas who suspected Jigme of being a Chinese spy, because he had a camera and his official's hair-style was undone. They confiscated his camera and binoculars, took him into a tent and discussed how he should be put to death; some said he should be tied in a sack and suffocated. He was put to many excruciating tests in the dark, to find out whether he was frightened or not, and he felt this torture was a bad one. He explained that he was Taring *Dzasa*, who had been left in Norbu Lingka by His Holiness to take photographs as proof of the shelling. He said, 'Please shoot me instead of torturing me, and hand my films to His Holiness without fail.' Eventually they believed him, gave him back his camera and binoculars and let him go.

During the next six days he and Pasang walked on and on with almost no food. They met many people fleeing and saw machine-guns being fired on the refugees from low-flying aeroplanes. Pasang has told me since that Jigme's hands started to swell from malnutrition and one day he was terribly in tears from weakness and grief. At last they came to an estate belonging to the Namgyal Datsang Monastery and took refuge there for the night. Jigme immediately fell asleep on the floor and when the head monk examined his face by torch-light he said to Pasang, 'This is the Prince of Taring,' and shed many tears. Next morning the monks gave Jigme food, clothing and a blanket to take with him. He advised them to go to India, having no attachment to anything, only carrying what they could.

When Jigme got to Samye, the Khampa Chief, Alo Dowa, gave him a nice riding pony and two escorts and Jigme presented Alo Dowa with his binoculars. The Chinese had dug themselves into a nearby mountain but Jigme and Pasang quickly passed it in the night. Further on, they stayed with Samchok, a fourth-rank lay official wo had become one of the guerrilla leaders. Then they met Kundeling, the administrative head of Kundeling Monastery, and with him followed His Holiness's route to India; at the border they were met by Indian officers who were much surprised by Jigme's fluent Hindi and English. His Holiness had left a special request that if Jigme and

Kundeling arrived they should be allowed to travel at once by train to Mussoorie. Jigme said that when he again met His Holiness he could not help shedding tears.

I soon told Jigme that I was planning to leave for the plains, to seek the Truth and lead a religious life; I explained that I had been thinking about this ever since leaving Lhasa, when I remembered clearly my mother's words often telling me that I could become devout. Jigme understood me very well but advised me to think more before making such a decision. He said he had no objection to my going – he was only worried about my not being able to stand the hardship, as we had been brought up so very delicately. He reminded me of Lochen Rinpoche's teaching, that anyone can lead a religious life anywhere by watching their own mind, and he said he felt I could achieve my aims by giving service to others. I thought and thought over this matter for many days, and had not yet made up my mind when Jigme returned to Mussoorie.

At that time there were some Chinese Communist agents in Kalimpong, including Hutsung, who used to be in the Lhasa P.Y.A. office and spoke good Tibetan. He met me one day in the market and we smiled at each other and he asked 'Did you have difficulties on the way?' I said, 'No, not much.' We never talked again, though we often met and smiled.

Soon after Jigme's departure, Samchok told me that the young officials and many other refugees then staying in Kalimpong would like me to teach them English, as they were finding it difficult to get along in India without either English or Hindi. The refugees who claimed to be self-supporting were allowed to stay in Kalimpong, but most refugees had to go to the camp at Misamari. They found it very hard to adjust to the heat there and suffered terribly; also the sanitation was far from adequate. The Indian government and voluntary agencies gave enormous help in the form of food, medicine and clothing. But many died of the heat, their children surviving them in deplorable conditions.

I agreed to help as soon as a classroom could be found, and before long I was teaching about twenty students, from 7 a.m.

to 1 p.m., in a poor underground storeroom we rented for about £1 a month from an Indian merchant. Daily the students increased – they were aged from ten to nearly fifty and His Holiness gave me Rs. 1,000 to buy stationery, expressing his appreciation of the school. After four months I had more than a hundred happy students and I was happy, too, because my class was doing so well. By this time I had realised that I could best achieve my religious aim by helping the other refugees.

The Dalai Lama was deeply distressed at the deaths of both young and old and felt his first priority was to open schools, nurseries and homes for the increasing number of orphans. His elder sister, Tsering Dolma, started the first orphanage in Dharamsala in 1960. At the end of 1959 His Holiness ordered me to come to Mussoorie where he was about to open a school for three hundred children. I wrote to explain that I just could not come until I had found another teacher for my enthusiastic students. Luckily, Major Cann, a retired Army officer who had been giving private tuition to Tibetans in Kalimpong, soon offered to take my class and it was agreed that he would teach for a month while I acted as his interpreter. He was a good teacher, but very strict; he would hit anyone who did not remember what he had been taught and the students disliked his strictness. But I reminded them of how we were beaten at school in our own country and, by the time I left Kalimpong on 25 January 1960, the students loved Major Cann.

Tseyang's husband, Rigzin Namgyal, accompanied me on the train to Lucknow; he paid no heed when I told him I could go alone and he insisted on buying first class tickets, though I wanted to travel third class. He has always looked after the comfort of Jigme and myself and he treats us as though we were his parents, waiting on Jigme like a servant and even taking off his shoes. At Lucknow Jigme met me and we travelled to Mussorie, by train, for two days and a night. We stayed in a quiet well-furnished room in Kildare House, which was to be the temporary school building. This old two-storied house – in a beautiful place called Happy Valley, a few miles from the town of Mussoorie – belonged to an Indian Army officer, who I believe thought it was haunted. Later, the Indian government bought it for our refugee school and Jigme and I lived there in one room partitioned by a curtain. Pasang was also at Kildare House when I arrived and he has remained there as our cook ever since. He is very good-natured and one of the happiest of men, always singing and jumping.

Next morning I went to pay homage to the Dalai Lama at nearby Birla House, which belonged to the wealthy Birla family and had been lent to the Indian government for a year to accommodate His Holiness before he moved to his present home in Dharamsala. I was very happy to see again the Dalai Lama, his mother and his sister, Tsering Dolma. His Holiness did not look at all aged or worn by his terrible experiences. He asked me to help Jigme organise the school and when I went to the *Kashag* office for instructions I was told that after three days I must go to Lucknow for a teachers' training course, with four other Tibetans.

In Lucknow we met Dr. Wealthy Fisher, the American lady-missionary who was organising the course. She said that she had met Tibetans before, in Calcutta in 1925, and their names were Commander-in-Chief Tsarong and Princess Mary of Tibet. When I told her that I was 'Princess Mary' she showed me a book she had written in which Tsarong and I had signed our names in Tibetan. In another of her books she has mentioned that she and her husband, the late Bishop Fisher, advised Tsarong to send me to America for further study, but he refused to consider the idea, saying that I must return to Tibet.

During the month we spent in Lucknow we compiled a textbook to teach Tibetan to Tibetan adults by the latest methods. It was rather a hard life, for I was much bitten by mosquitoes and missed my tea very much because we only had tea once in the afternoon.

On our return to Mussoorie fifty young men were selected from the camp at Misamari, and from among the soldiers and monks at Mussoorie, to be our first pupils. Kundeling, Jigme and I organised everything, Lhadingsey was our store-keeper and the school was inaugurated by His Holiness on 3 March 1960. Our students, aged eighteen to twenty-five, were in rags and had no toilet facilities; we fed them, but could not give them enough. They were all the time hungry, yet they never complained. Various individuals and international charitable organisations helped at first, and gradually the government of India took charge of the school, which has now become a recognised High School with Jigme as Principal. A year later the young men dispersed, twenty of the most promising going to Denmark for vocational education and the rest becoming teachers of Tibetan among our people. They were replaced by boys and girls, and now there are about six hundred students at Mussoorie. Jigme is also Education Director of the Tibetan government-in-exile. The Indian government has given us seven big residential schools in India and a number of day schools at resettlement places, yet there are more than ten thousand Tibetan children who cannot be educated and this greatly worries His Holiness.

In 1960, the Gyayum, His Holiness's mother, had to go to London for medical treatment and I was asked to accompany her. During my stay in England I met Lady Alexandra Metcalfe, of the Save the Children Fund, and after our talk she started the Simla homes for Tibetan children. After some months in Britain the Gyayum and I flew back to India via Switzerland, the United States, Japan and Hong Kong.

On my return to Mussoorie I was invited to Tokyo by Tokwan Tada, a Japanese professor who had spend twelve years in Sera Monastery and wanted me to help him to compile a Tibetan-Japanese dictionary. I declined this invitation, as I was determined to work for our children, so Tsering Dolma, Tsarong's sixth daughter, went instead and spent six years in Tokyo. She is now back in India, working as the secretary at Tibet House in Delhi, which was recently opened as a Tibetan museum and a salesroom for our refugees' handicrafts.

In August 1962, His Holiness told me that he was considering starting homes for our children – with twenty-five children, under house-parents, in each home – because so many little boys and girls had been given into his care and were living in transit camps under appalling conditions and day after day many died. He wanted them brought up in Tibetan ways and educated for their new life – especially he wanted the orphans cared for kindly. He had discussed the matter with the Indian government, who had agreed to give help if we ourselves could run the homes to their satisfaction, and he asked me to organise a few pilot homes in Mussoorie. I pointed out that Jigme badly needed my assistance in running the school, where we already had six hundred children, but since His Holiness wished me to do this work faith was my support and obedience my only guide.

I then sent out a circular letter to organisations in many countries, rented three houses and carefully chose three educated Tibetan couples as house-parents. Help came at once from all over the world: from Swiss Aid to Tibetans, the Ockenden Venture, the Tibetan Refugee Aid Society of Canada, the American Emergency Committee, German Aid to Tibetans, the SOS Village of Austria, the Japanese Red Cross, the Tibet Society and Relief Fund of The United Kingdom and Dutch Aid to Tibetans. Thus the Tibetan Homes Foundation was established in 1962. The first seventy-five children were selected. When they arrived I wept – they were so under-nourished, with bloated tummies, various skin diseases and severe eye infections.

After some time the government of India inspected and approved of these pilot homes and gave a grant for fifteen homes to be established. We now have twenty-five, some sponsored by foreign charitable organisations, and all our children are happy, healthy and contented. Every day, morning and evening, they pray for the well-being of their benefactors.

I feel very grateful now for having had the chance to learn English when I was young; it has been most helpful throughout my life and was the keystone of the success of my marriage with Jigme. It is wonderful that we have been able to use English rightly, without changing our religion and attitudes. It has been like a bridge over many rivers and has enabled us to make friends throughout the world. Most important of all, without speaking English we could not have helped our refugees and I am very glad that we now have the opportunity of taking care of hundreds of orphans, in place of our own two daughters.

About two years after the uprising a Sikkimese truck-driver — who had been living in Taring House at the time of the trouble — was repatriated to Sikkim, having been imprisoned for some time. From him we heard that Mother-in-law and the children had a terrible fright when the house was shelled. Our drawing-room was hit and the altar broken into pieces. Everybody hid in the dark cellar, where we used to keep our spare furniture, and after two days, when the shelling stopped, they were all taken to a prison — except Mother-in-law and the babies. Tsarong House happened to be the prison and over two hundred people were shut up in the hall, with no room to sit down. Poor Ngodup Wangmo almost went out of her mind with worry about her little baby and cried so much that someone took pity on her and let her return to Taring House. We don't know what has happened to her since. At the time of the uprising Yangdol, our younger daughter, had a baby girl who was only three months old. Yangdol's husband, Kalsang Thubten, came to India with His Holiness's party, leaving his wife and baby behind. Now he misses them — and his mother — so much, and has so many worries about them, that he is suffering from serious mental trouble. I can never forget the last time I saw Yangdol and her lovely little baby in the courtyard of Taring House; I remember every day the last kisses I gave them both. Now Yangdol is said to be working under great hardship in a torn tent.

In 1960 we heard that Mother-in-law had died in Lhasa, after enduring great hardship. The Chinese took her out from her cosy rooms at Taring House and made her live in a mean house without even one servant; none of her grandchildren was in a position to help as they wished to do and we were told that while trying to look after herself she had a fall which caused her death.

Six of Tsarong's ten children have been left behind. Those in

India are Dudul Namgyal, his son by Pema Dolkar, Tsering Yangzom and Tsering Dolma, his eldest and second youngest daughters by Tseten Dolkar, and Tseyang, my eldest daughter. His son by Tseten Dolkar had just left school at the time of the uprising and we hear that he is still in a Chinese prison in Lhasa. An official who escaped in 1964 told me that Norbu Yudon, my only surviving sister, was imprisoned for a year after the uprising. This official said that he and she were in the same prison, where they were given very mean food and made to do manual work. I have heard no more news of her.

Most of my eighteen nephews and nieces and my fifty-two grandnephews and nieces have been left behind in difficulty. Ani Lochen died in 1950, at the age of a hundred and thirty, and her reincarnation was born to Jigme's brother, Chime Dorje, in 1955. He was a fine little boy, who remembered his prayers and many of his disciples, and he had just been recognised by the Dalai Lama as the true reincarnation when the uprising took place.

Our very dear friend, General Dingja, represented the Tibetan government in Peking from 1957 – 1959. During his absence his wife, Tsarong's sister, died, and when he returned to Lhasa after the uprising to find his wife dead, many of his friends and relatives gone into exile, many killed by torture, many in prison and his beloved country so changed he got such a dreadful shock that he also died of heart failure. Poor Dingja! It is very sad to think of the most humorous, happy man in Tibet experiencing such terrible things.

The Duchess of Lhalu, a good friend to all of us, died in Lhasa a few years after the uprising. The Chinese had taken all her possessions but she was treated most kindly by the Lhasa beggars, to pay back her great kindness to them. She was a wonderful lady. Her servants managed to send her ashes to Dharamsala, requesting the tutors of the Dalai Lama to pray for her.

We get little news from Tibet now and always it is heart breaking. So many of our friends in Lhasa committed suicide, to avoid being tortured, by throwing themselves into the Kyichu that the Chinese had to guard the river banks.

Nobody knows exactly what is going on in Tibet present, but we have heard that the Chinese plan to let the Holy City of Lhasa become a ghost city. They are building new houses and roads on the outskirts but the old buildings are not allowed to be white-washed or repaired and the hoisting of prayer-flags on the roofs is forbidden. Our own dear home is being used by the Chinese as the foreign registration office and our servants' quarter has been made into a prison for Tibetan women.

Tseyang and Rigzin Namgyal have become one of the saddest couples, as a result of the tragedy that befell them like being struck by a thunderbolt. Tseyang, a beautiful young woman, has completely lost her health. For a year she tried her best to teach our children in Mussoorie, but this hard work was too much for her so she is now with the Tibetan Unit of All-India Radio. She has a sweet nature and is loved dearly by her sisters. Once she nearly lost her belief because she felt that though she had always tried to be good she had received no mercy; but she is intelligent and now understands that her suffering is only a part of the great suffering of all living beings. I hope very much that as she and Rigzin Namgyal grow older they will study the realities of life more deeply, as Jigme and I are doing. As soon as they truly understand the doctrine of Cause and Effect I have confidence that they will achieve joy and peace.

In 1964 poor Jigme Dorje, the Prime Minister of Bhutan, was assassinated, and Tsering Yangzom suffered terribly; yet she is always cheerful and most helpful to the refugees. In Mussoorie she teaches the children affectionately and makes the older ones work, paying them to encourage the idea of earning and being independent. She knits garments on a machine for the old Tibetans and to Jigme and myself she is the karma daughter. She is still in her early forties and everyone admires her, yet when she remarried it was to a penniless refugee — Samchok, who is a few years older than she but was not married before.

About eighty thousand Tibetans have come into exile in India, Nepal, Sikkim and Bhutan; the majority were retainers on government, monastic or noble estates fairly near the border. When the Chinese reached these areas, immediately after the Dalai Lama's flight, everyone who owned even a tiny bit of land was called a landlord and cruelly tortured. Many refugees left because they did not want their children to be indoctrinated and most of them have to work hard on road construction in the Indian Himalayas, as they can't do anything else to earn a living. Yet they are happy to be in a free country, where you can practise your own religion and share what you have with your family. By the wonderful help of the government of India and other great nations of the world some of our children are already in a position to help their poor parents.

Some of the retainers even now help their masters, by giving them money, as they say they want to repay past kindness. Tashi's brother, who is doing quite well in India, always brings us fruit and eggs when he comes to Mussoorie. The Tibetans in Switzerland, who are earning a good deal, often send money to His Holiness to help their fellow-refugees.

My dreams sometimes seem to give me true indications. Before we left Lhasa I dreamed, every now and again, that our home had changed from its usual condition into a poor, unlivable house. And many times, finding no money in my purse in India, I have remembered this dream. Also, when we were in China in 1954 I dreamed that the Jokhang was completely dark and that there was no image of the Lord Buddha on his seat. I wondered then; and now I think this may have been an indication that the Chinese Red Guards were going to destroy the Jokhang. Anyhow, I am trying hard not to be superstitious about my dreams, since all superstitions are bad in the light of Buddhism.

The news of the Red Guards' attack on our beloved Jokhang broke our hearts in pieces. Afterwards refugees brought the relic of Chenrezig to India and gave it to His Holiness, and at Dharamsala it was shown to the crowds who came to get its blessing.

When people die the next generation replaces them, but when a whole culture is destroyed it can never be replaced.

Tibet has always been quite separate from China in religion, culture and language. We have a right to be free and we are confident that we shall get our country back—maybe after many years. Meanwhile we feel that it is a scared duty to preserve our culture in exile. Lord Buddha's preaching of peace and love is cherished by the whole world and it is this great teaching that has given Tibet its culture. Tibet must be Tibet; when so many other peoples are getting back their devoured countries surely Tibet should be restord to the Tibetans.

In India we have built several Buddhist temples and our people are eager to contribute anything they can to preserve our culture and religion.

For years now I have been trying to remember, every moment of the day, that great teaching of the Lord Buddha which says 'Holy company brings desirelessness, desirelessness brings peace of mind, peace of mind brings freedom from illusion, freedom from illusion brings immediate liberation.' This is difficult to practise, yet one can find real happiness only by avoiding desire and hatred. Whenever I feel unhappy or worried I look into myself and find the root of my unhappiness hidden in a dark corner of selfishness. Milarepa has said that by pretending and deceiving we cheat and mislead ourselves, so I carefully watch my mind all the time. The practice of my religion is giving me more and more confidence in myself and I pray to Dolma to overcome all my weaknesses. Until our human weaknesses are overcome we have to be born again and again into suffering; only Enlightenment frees us from rebirth and to reach Nirvana we must try to improve our understanding in each lifetime.

I try constantly to avoid the sorrow of selfishness, but my love and longing for my own children is always there, as any mother's would be. I miss them when I get good food to eat, I miss them when I am given plenty to wear—and especially when I see the pale moon I miss them, for we all can see the moon, yet we cannot meet.

When we get back our own country, Tibet can never be the

same as before. The next generation will not be fooled by superstitions and delusions; they will be more knowledgeable, and by preserving our religion and culture at the present time we can make sure that in future the Truth will be practised by all Tibetans. Lord Buddha himself has said that whether we have great teachers or not the Truth is there — and no one can alter it, neither can anyone improve it. This Truth which the Lord Buddha preached is now being sought all over the world and when religions are compared the principle of Truth is seen to be the same in each one. All religions remind us to do good and by following our various religions we can help one another to gain happiness.

Epilogue

When I wrote my autobiography in 1970 I had no idea what was really going on in Tibet and had had no news of our children. My husband and I were totally preoccupied with the children in the Tibetan school and the children's homes in Mussoorie.

I drew inspiration from this opportunity to serve my country and delighted in taking care of the orphans, educating them as my own children. These destitute children became a substitute for my own and for almost twenty years I dedicated my life to them. Today there are twenty-seven homes belonging to the Tibetan Homes Foundation and over one thousand children at the school.

For twenty years we had had no news of our children. Then in 1979 we heard the voice of our grandson, Jigme Wangchuk, speaking on the radio from Lhasa, saying they were all alive and well. I realised how much I had been blessed. Shortly after this we learnt from Chinese Radio that Tibetan refugees were now allowed to visit their relatives in Tibet and return to their respective countries if they wished. Tibetans were also being allowed to travel to India. Although we could hardly believe the good news, we wrote to Jigme Wangchuk inviting him, his brother and two sisters – the children of Tseyang (or Betty La, as we call her) – to visit us in India. Some time later Jigme and his younger sister, Kunsang, arrived from Tibet. Both were now married, with children. Kunsang brought her younger son, Dorje Gyaltsen, and told us that our other two grandchildren were well but would only be allowed over once they themselves had returned. They stayed in India for nine months but, just before they left, we were saddened to hear that our eldest granddaughter, Nordon, had died in childbirth.

At the time we left Lhasa Jigme had been nine, Kunsang seven and Tenzin Norbu five. They had been looked after by our daughter Ngodup Wangmo (Peggy), although she had three sons of her own. Later, Nordon had been taken care of by Kate Shata, and Tenzin Norbu by Kasur Sondonla – both nieces of mine – who were also enduring hardship, together with their own children. Ngodup Wangmo found it hard to feed the children as all her belongings had been confiscated by the Chinese. Jigme and Kunsang returned with heavy hearts on hearing that their eldest sister, Nordon, had died before they could get back.

After that we began to write to our two daughters Ngodup Wangmo and Yangdol (Una), inviting them to visit us. They wrote back to say they would approach the Chinese authorities for the necessary permission but that it would take at least a year. We were very anxious and prayed hard for our wishes to be granted and later heard that the authorities would let them come.

At that time (1979), Ngodup Wangmo's husband, Tenzin Dhondup, was still in prison in Lhasa. He had been imprisoned in 1959 and released in 1961, when he earned his living by driving a horse and cart, taking stones from the quarries. He was helped by his eldest son, Tenzin Wangdu, who was twelve. They were made to live in a very dark, damp room. Before long, Tenzin Dhondup was imprisoned again – during the Cultural Revolution. A group of people had come to the house, beating drums and blowing horns. They threw the family's belongings all over the place and kicked and dragged Tenzin Dhondup away from Ngodup Wangmo and the children and put him in prison again, this time for thirteen years. None of the family were allowed to see him for several years although later, in the 1970s, the Chinese allowed his wife and children to visit once a month with food, until he was finally released on 18 December 1979. Ngodup Wangmo and the children were thrilled to have him home again but he had suffered so much in prison that he had lost the sight of one eye and almost all his teeth. He also suffered from asthma. Just after his release, the Chinese asked Tenzin Dhondup to join a cultural tour to China, and he accepted. While he was away Ngodup Wangmo was given permission to come to India with two of her sons, Tenzin Gyurme and Tenzin Namgyal. Tenzin Dhondup was also given permission to come with them, but their eldest son, Tenzin Wangdu, was not. After the death of Mao Tse-Tung and the end of the Gang of Four the Chinese themselves realized their cruelty to the Tibetans. The hardship that the Tibetans had endured was incredible. Ngodup Wangmo and the children, for example, lived on a very poor diet for many years during which time meat and butter were unobtainable for months. She often pretended she had eaten and gave the food to her sons instead.

Now they are so happy and enjoying their stay with us. Both Tenzin Dhondup's and Ngodup Wangmo health has improved. Their two sons Tenzin Gyurme and Tenzin Namgyal were taken to England by the late Miss Joyce Pearce of the Ockenden Venture. Tenzin Gyurme, who had worked so hard to keep them alive, always helping his mother, came to us quite illiterate. In England he was lucky enough to meet a Tibetan girl from Canada. Tsering Yangki, a lovely, well-educated girl, and they married and now live in Canada. Tenzin Namgyal, who came back to us, has learnt very good English in a short time and hopes to study further and be of service to his country. He was the only son to have gone to school, where he learnt Tibetan and Chinese.

It was another blessing to have Ngodup Wangmo's eldest son, Tenzin Wangdu, visit us in India this year (1985) with his wife and son, and a little girl was born to his wife shortly after they arrived. He had been a truck driver and had had no schooling at all since the age of twelve when he had to go with his father to drive the cart. He too is now determined to study Tibetan and English.

Our youngest daughter Yangdol also came to us from Tibet in 1980 with her daughter, Tsering Chodon, who was only three months old during the uprising of 1959 in Lhasa. Her husband, Kalsang Thubten, had to come to India with the Dalai Lama and Yangdol had been left behind with the small baby. She was driven out of her house by the Chinese and everything was confiscated except for a few old clothes and some food. She was made to live in a mud hut with one wall up against a public latrine. She became very poor and was forced to attend purge meetings at night and work on a construction site during the day without pay or food. She suffered greatly and by the time her daughter was seven or eight she could no longer feed her and had to leave her with a Chinese family as a babysitter. Tsering Chodon tells us that her mother relished the waste food she collected in a tin during the week and brought home to her at weekends. At the age of fourteen Tsering Chodon went back to live with her mother and together they worked as labourers on the construction site. They were so poor, without enough to eat or to wear, that Yangdol often had to send Tsering Chodon to borrow *tsampa* or money from people who were little better off than themselves. Tsering Chodon tells us that this was her hardest task – to go and borrow *tsampa* and money. In winter they had only a few old blankets and Tsering Chodon acted as her mother's hot water bottle at night.

Poor Yangdol had to work very hard, carrying mud and heavy stones on her back. She worked particularly hard during the building of the Lhasa river embankments and once, while carrying a heavy stone, she fell and fractured her leg. Tsering Chodon, who was working at the same place, hired a cart to take her mother to hospital, but they wouldn't admit her because there were no beds for the children of nobles, so Tsering Chodon had to take her mother home and beg and borrow food for her.

Yangdol gradually got well enough to work again and because she was known as a hard worker the construction site supervisor always chose her when there was heavy work to be done. Eventually, due to malnutrition and overwork, she got very ill again and was told that her intestines were drying up; she had no food and no medicine because she had no money to buy them with. Nodup Wangmo came as often as possible and tried to share her food but she was just as poor as Yangdol and her daughter. One of my nieces, Kate Shata, suggested Yangdol should take some Terramycin which Ngodup Wangmo was able to buy from the Nepalese traders. After taking it Yangdol made a seemingly miraculous recovery.

Eventually, Yangdol and her daughter got permission to come and visit us. They brought with them Shilok, my great-granddaughter, who lost her mother just as she was about to visit us. Shilok suffers from epilepsy but we have been able to place her in Welham's Girls' School in Dehra Dun and she has many kind friends who sponsor her education and give her love.

Yangdol's husband, Kalsang Thubten, is a mental patient in Seattle. He is a very nice man but constant worry has made him ill. He wants to remain in the United States, where Yangdol was able to join him in 1983. She is very happy there and has a permanent job in a hotel. Her daughter, Tsering Chodon, married before she came to India. She became pregnant and a son was born here in Dehra Dun. Her husband, Tsering Chophel, later came from Lhasa and joined her and they had another little daughter. Tsering Chodon was completely illiterate when she first arrived but she learnt very quickly and now speaks Tibetan and English quite well.

Tenzin Norbu, Tseyang's second son, also came from Tibet at the same time as Yangdol. He is a talented painter and carpenter and wants to continue his studies. Another little grandson of mine, Tseten Dorje, has arrived and we have put him in a school in Dharamsala in the Tibetan Children's Village. Altogether, our three daughters, four grandsons, one granddaughter and six great-grandchildren are with us. We are very grateful to the Indian Government for giving us asylum. Many of our friends helped us build a house in Rajpur and helped us get enough money to live on. Miss Virginia Judkins from England has given us a regular allowance since we retired in 1975. We are so grateful to all our friends who have supported us with their love and sympathy.

We are now looking after the Tibetan Old People's Home in Rajpur where we have fifty-two residents. Our work for them gives us great satisfaction and we are delighted to see all the old people happy and living in peace like ourselves, in a home away from home.

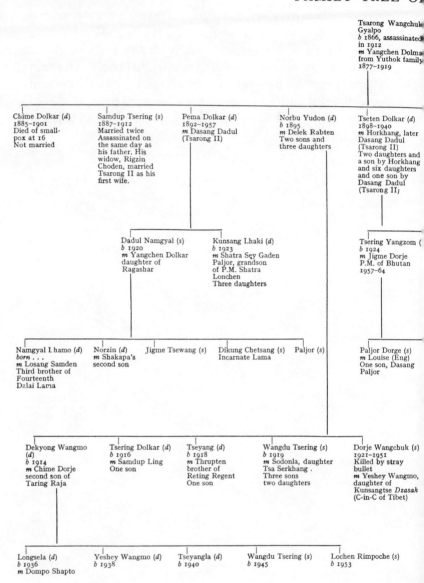

Tsarong Wangchuk
Gyalpo
b 1866, assassinated
in 1912
m Yangchen Dolma
from Yuthok family
1877–1919

Chime Dolkar (*d*)
1885–1901
Died of small-
pox at 16
Not married

Samdup Tsering (*s*)
1887–1912
Married twice
Assassinated on
the same day as
his father. His
widow, Rigzin
Choden, married
Tsarong II as his
first wife.

Pema Dolkar (*d*)
1892–1957
m Dasang Dadul
(Tsarong II)

Norbu Yudon (*d*)
b 1895
m Delek Rabten
Two sons and
three daughters

Tseten Dolkar (*d*)
1898–1940
m Horkhang, later
Dasang Dadul
(Tsarong II)
Two daughters and
a son by Horkhang
and six daughters
and one son by
Dasang Dadul
(Tsarong II)

Dadul Namgyal (*s*)
b 1920
m Yangchen Dolkar
daughter of
Ragashar

Kunsang Lhaki (*d*)
b 1923
m Shatra Sey Gaden
Paljor, grandson
of P.M. Shatra
Lonchen
Three daughters

Tsering Yangzom (
b 1924
m Jigme Dorje
P.M. of Bhutan
1957–64

Namgyal Lhamo (*d*)
born ...
m Losang Samden
Third brother of
Fourteenth
Dalai Lama

Norzin (*d*)
m Shakapa's
second son

Jigme Tsewang (*s*)

Dikung Chetsang (*s*)
Incarnate Lama

Paljor (*s*)

Paljor Dorge (*s*)
m Louise (Eng)
One son, Dasang
Paljor

Dekyong Wangmo
(*d*)
b 1914
m Chime Dorje
second son of
Taring Raja

Tsering Dolkar (*d*)
b 1916
m Samdup Ling
One son

Tseyang (*d*)
b 1918
m Thrupten
brother of
Reting Regent
One son

Wangdu Tsering (*s*)
b 1919
m Sodonla, daughter
Tsa Serkhang .
Three sons
two daughters

Dorje Wangchuk (*s*)
1921–1951
Killed by stray
bullet
m Yeshey Wangmo,
daughter of
Kunsangtse *Dzasak*
(C-in-C of Tibet)

Longsela (*d*)
b 1936
m Dompo Shapto

Yeshey Wangmo (*d*)
b 1938

Tseyangla (*d*)
b 1940

Wangdu Tsering (*s*)
b 1945

Lochen Rimpoche (*s*)
b 1953

TSARONG

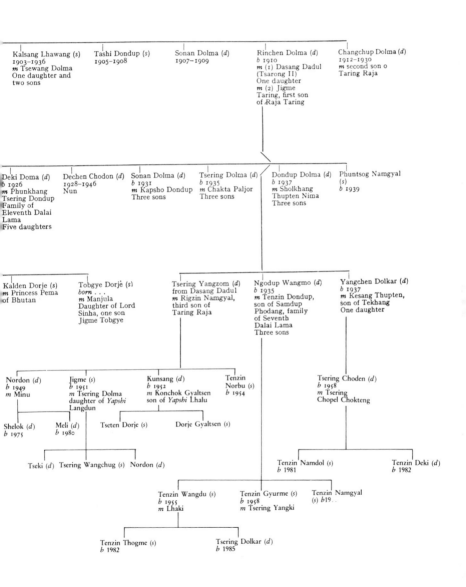

Kalsang Lhawang (s)
1903–1936
m Tsewang Dolma
One daughter and
two sons

Tashi Dondup (s)
1905–1908

Sonan Dolma (d)
1907–1909

Rinchen Dolma (d)
b 1910
m (1) Dasang Dadul
(Tsarong II)
One daughter
m (2) Jigme
Taring, first son
of Raja Taring

Changchup Dolma (d)
1912–1930
m second son o
Taring Raja

Deki Doma (d)
b 1926
m Phunkhang
Tsering Dondup
Family of
Eleventh Dalai
Lama
Five daughters

Dechen Chodon (d)
1928–1946
Nun

Sonan Dolma (d)
b 1931
m Kapsho Dondup
Three sons

Tsering Dolma (d)
b 1935
m Chakta Paljor
Three sons

Dondup Dolma (d)
b 1937
m Sholkhang
Thupten Nima
Three sons

Phuntsog Namgyal
(s)
b 1939

Kalden Dorje (s)
m Princess Pema
of Bhutan

Tobgye Dorje (s)
born . . .
m Manjula
Daughter of Lord
Sinha, one son
Jigme Tobgye

Tsering Yangzom (d)
from Dasang Dadul
m Rigzin Namgyal,
third son of
Taring Raja

Ngodup Wangmo (d)
b 1935
m Tenzin Dondup,
son of Samdup
Phodang, family
of Seventh
Dalai Lama
Three sons

Yangchen Dolkar (d)
b 1937
m Kesang Thupten,
son of Tekhang
One daughter

Nordon (d)
b 1949
m Minu

Jigme (s)
b 1951
m Tsering Dolma
daughter of Yapshi
Langdun

Kunsang (d)
b 1952
m Konchok Gyaltsen
son of Yapshi Lhalu

Tenzin
Norbu (s)
b 1954

Tsering Choden (d)
b 1958
m Tsering
Chopel Chokteng

Shelok (d)
b 1975

Meli (d)
b 1980

Tseten Dorje (s)

Dorje Gyaltsen (s)

Tseki (d)   Tsering Wangchug (s)   Nordon (d)

Tenzin Namdol (s)
b 1981

Tenzin Deki (d)
b 1982

Tenzin Wangdu (s)
b 1955
m Lhaki

Tenzin Gyurme (s)
b 1958
m Tsering Yangki

Tenzin Namgyal
(s) b19..

Tenzin Thogme (s)
b 1982

Tsering Dolkar (d)
b 1985

Index

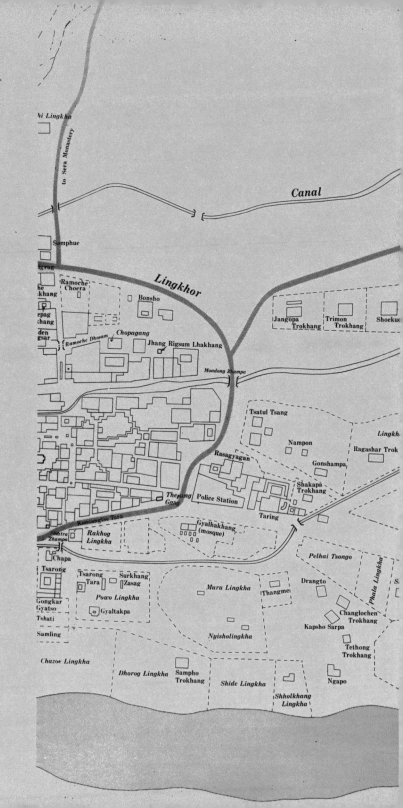

hi Lingkha

to Sera Monastery

Canal

Somphue

grug

Lingkhor

Ramoche
Choera

he
khang

Bonsho

epag
hang

Jangopa
Trokhang

Trimon
Trokhang

Shoekue

den
sar

Ramoche Dhosam

Chopagang

Jhang Rigsum Lhakhang

Mondong Zhampa

Tsatul Tsang

Lingkh

Nampon

Ragashar Trok

Rasagyagan

Gonshampa,

Shakapà
Trokhang

Thepung
Gose

Police Station

Taring

Kunsangtse Tara

Shatra
Zhampa

Rakhog
Lingkha

Gyalhakhang
(mosque)

Pelhai Tsongo

Chapa

Tsarong

Tsarong
Tara

Surkhang
Zasag

Muru Lingkha

Thangmei

Drangto

Phala Lingkha

S

Powo Lingkha

Changlochen
Trokhang

Gongkar
Gyatso

Gyaltakpa

Kapsho Sarpa

Tshati

Nyisholingkha

Tethong
Trokhang

Samling

Chazoe Lingkha

Dhorog Lingkha

Sampho
Trokhang

Shide Lingkha

Ngapo

Shholkhang
Lingkha

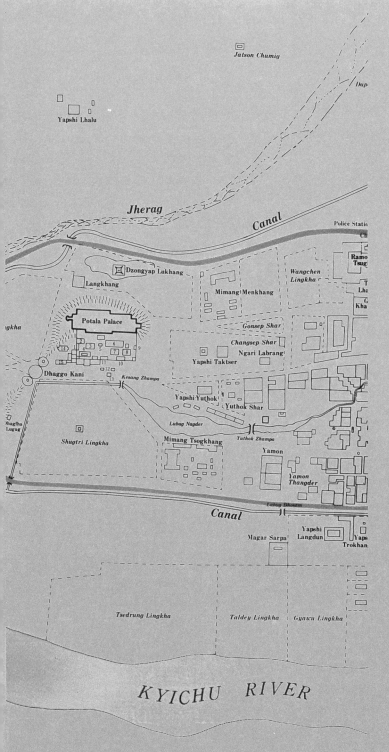

Jatson Chumig

Yapshi Lhalu

Jherag

Canal

Police Station

Dzongyap Lukhang

Langkhang

Wangchen
Lingkha

Mimang Menkhang

Ramo
Tsug

T
Lha

G
Kha

Potala Palace

Gonsep Shar

Changsep Shar

1
2   3   6
5   7   8
9

Ngari Labrang

Yapshi Taktser

Dhaggo Kani

11
12
3

10

Kesang Zhampa

Yapshi Yuthok

Yuthok Shar

Dhagtha
Lugug

Lubug Nagder

Shugtri Lingkha

Yuthok Zhampa

Mimang Tsogkhang

Yamon

Yamon
Thangder

Canal

Yapshi
Langdun

Yaps
Trokhan

Magar Sarpa

Tsedrung Lingkha

Taldey Lingkha

Gyawu Lingkha

KYICHU   RIVER

Map continued on back endpaper

Daughter of Tibet